PERGAMON INTERNATIONAL LIBRARY
of Science, Technology, Engineering and Social Studies

The 1000-volume original paperback library in aid of education,
industrial training and the enjoyment of leisure

Publisher: Robert Maxwell, M.C.

Psychological Research in the Classroom
(PGPS-108)

Pergamon Titles of Related Interest

Apter TROUBLED CHILDREN/TROUBLED SYSTEMS
Cartledge/Milburn TEACHING SOCIAL SKILLS TO CHILDREN:
Innovative Approaches
Conoley/Conoley SCHOOL CONSULTATION: A Guide to Practice
and Training
Liebert/Sprafkin/Davidson THE EARLY WINDOW: Effects of
Television on Children and Youth, Second Edition
Monjan/Gassner CRITICAL ISSUES IN COMPETENCY
BASED EDUCATION
O'Leary/O'Leary CLASSROOM MANAGEMENT: The Successful
Use of Behavior Modification, Second Edition

Related Journals*

CHILDREN AND YOUTH SERVICES REVIEW
EVALUATION IN EDUCATION
EVALUATION AND PROGRAM PLANNING
STUDIES IN EDUCATIONAL EVALUATION

*Free specimen copies available upon request.

Psychological Research in the Classroom
Issues for Educators and Researchers

Teresa M. Amabile
Margaret L. Stubbs
Brandeis University

PERGAMON PRESS
New York   Oxford   Toronto   Sydney   Paris   Frankfurt

Pergamon Press Offices:

U.S.A.   Pergamon Press Inc., Maxwell House, Fairview Park,
Elmsford, New York 10523, U.S.A.

U.K.   Pergamon Press Ltd., Headington Hill Hall,
Oxford OX3 0BW, England

CANADA   Pergamon Press Canada Ltd., Suite 104, 150 Consumers Road,
Willowdale, Ontario M2J 1P9, Canada

AUSTRALIA   Pergamon Press (Aust.) Pty. Ltd., P.O. Box 544,
Potts Point, NSW 2011, Australia

FRANCE   Pergamon Press SARL, 24 rue des Ecoles,
75240 Paris, Cedex 05, France

FEDERAL REPUBLIC   Pergamon Press GmbH, Hammerweg 6
OF GERMANY   6242 Kronberg/Taunus, Federal Republic of Germany

Copyright © 1982 Pergamon Press Inc.

Library of Congress Cataloging in Publication Data
Main entry under title:

Psychological research in the classroom.

(Pergamon general psychology series; 108)
Includes indexes.
1. Educational research--Addresses, essays, lectures.
2. Psychological research--Addresses, essays, lectures.
I. Amabile, Teresa. II. Stubbs, Margaret L. (Margaret Louisa),
1947-   . III. Series.
LB1028.P77 1982   370'.7'8   81-21114
ISBN 0-08-028042-0   AACR2
ISBN 0-08-028041-2 (pbk.)

Printed in the United States of America

To our parents,
Carmela and Charles Amabile
and
Louise and John Stubbs,
our first and best teachers

Contents

Preface

This book grew out of a friendly feud that the two of us began four years ago. Margaret Stubbs, having just completed ten years of classroom teaching, had come to graduate school hoping to gain the expertise she felt she needed to convince others of her views on education. Teresa Amabile, one year into her career as an assistant professor of psychology, had immersed herself in a program of research that she hoped would help her build a theory of creativity. We found each other because of our shared interest in education. Stubbs wanted to see if psychological theory supported her educational philosophy, and Amabile wanted to see if her ideas on creativity were valid in educational settings.

From the start, our collaboration was an uneasy one. We spoke different languages. Stubbs talked of her feeling that children's imaginary companions were important, while Amabile talked of the need for precise operational definitions of "imagination" and "creativity." Stubbs found it difficult to articulate the justification for her methods of fostering independence and creativity in children, but Amabile found it difficult to understand why anyone would be satisfied with anecdotes rather than looking to well-controlled laboratory experiments. Although we found each other intellectually stimulating and genuinely interested in the other's position, the frustration and impatience we sometimes felt during our first months of collaboration were barely concealed beneath a thin layer of tact.

The initial breakthrough came when Stubbs convinced Amabile that psychological researchers need to talk more with teachers, to learn from them, and to lend their expertise to solving teachers' problems. As a way of moving toward these goals, in the fall of 1979, we organized a small, one-day conference at Brandeis University on research in education. The participants came from richly varied backgrounds and orientations: classroom teachers who had spent years conducting research in their own classrooms; staff developers who worked to help teachers better investigate their methods and outcomes; critics of traditional academic research; school administrators responsible for judging the merit of research proposals; academicians from graduate schools of education; and psychologists who had conducted research in classrooms or were interested in doing so.

Our discussion that day touched on several topics of mutual concern: the attitudes of teachers and prinicipals toward the research enterprise; the attitudes of researchers toward the teachers and principals they had dealt with in trying to conduct their research in classroom settings; what researchers and educators could learn from each other; how they could better collaborate on deciding which research questions to pursue and on implementing well-designed evaluations of school programs; and how educators and researchers might work together to publicize their findings and encourage educational innovation. These discussions threatened, at times, to become a full-scale version of the private feud that the two of us had enjoyed for several months. Beyond the disagreements, however, we glimpsed some points of agreement, some feelings of sympathy between researchers and teachers, and some common goals.

In an effort to develop further the insights that were born that day, we tried to locate published discussions of the issues with which we'd been dealing. Nearly all of the volumes that we found on classroom research were collections of either theoretical research that happened to be conducted in the classroom or teacher-initiated research that failed to meet academically accepted standards of methodology. In no single source did we find teachers and researchers confronting and attempting to solve the problems that can separate them so widely.

This volume is designed to fill that void. It presents a wide variety of goals, concerns, and methods for several types of classroom research, including academic psychological research, traditional educational research, and non-academic teacher-initiated research. The teachers, administrators, and researchers who contributed to this volume explore the problems of conducting and using classroom research and possible solutions to those problems from diverse vantage points. There is much overlap in the views presented, but there is a great deal of essential disagreement as well. We have tried to preserve both the agreement and the dissent. In doing so, we hope we have made it possible for our readers—researchers and students of research, teachers, administrators, and students of education—to gain fresh insights into the conception, conduct, and use of psychological research in the classroom. Perhaps with the aid of those insights, the "feuds" now being carried on by researchers and educators will end as ours did, in an enlightening, exciting, and productive collaboration.

Acknowledgments

There are 16 contributors whose names appear on the chapters of this volume, but, in fact, hundreds of individuals contributed to the ideas expressed here or the manner of their expression. It is impossible to mention all of them, but we will try to single out those who were most generous with their time and support.

Several of the individual chapters were shaped considerably by assistance from a variety of sources. Bill DeJong and Mick Watson provided important conceptual and editorial assistance on Chapter 8. Molly Watt acknowledges Patricia Carini, with whom she did most of the classroom documentation reported in Chapter 10. Kathe Jervis and Adeline Naiman offered useful editorial comments on Chapter 11, and Claryce Evans thanks Norellen Stokley for stimulating her original interest in the classroom observations reported in that chapter. Roland Dwinell and Janet Berman were helped in their preparation of Chapter 12 by the insightful editing of Louise Thompson, Assistant Superintendent for Curriculum and Instruction in Brookline, Massachusetts. Ricky Carter acknowledges Jeanne Bamberger, Eleanor Duckworth, Edith Churchill, and Becky Corwin for their contributions to Chapter 13. Kim Marshall, a teacher and writer, assisted Roland Barth in preparing Chapter 14, with comments offered during the course of several conversations. Two individuals contributed to the work reported in Chapter 15 by Mary Ann Haley: Bob Lemaire and Julie Nann, by helping to initiate the project, providing access to notes and records about the project, and persevering throughout its development. Chris McVinney, author of Chapter 16, acknowledges Deborah Begner for her invaluable contribution to their partnership in building the Concord Children's Center. Finally, financial assistance for the research reported in Chapter 17 came from Research Grant HD-09613 to Susan Harter from the National Institutes of Health, U.S. Public Health Service. Susan Harter thanks several people for their contributions to that research: "I am particularly grateful to the teachers of Sagebrush Elementary School in the Cherry Creek School System of Denver, Colorado, who have been primarily responsible for much of the education of this particular researcher!"

Beyond these contributions to individual chapters, we must acknowledge those who offered much to the book as a whole. Many of the themes repeated through these pages were first raised (at least for us) during the Brandeis

Conference on Research in Education in September 1979. Indeed, Chapters 2 and 3 draw on discussions recorded during the conference. Although many of the participants in the conference appear as authors here, several were unable to contribute manuscripts to this volume. Nonetheless, we all owe an intellectual and spiritual debt to them; their collective wisdom was considerable. In addition, we appreciate the confidence placed in our endeavor by James Lackner, Chairman of the Brandeis University Psychology Department, and by the administrators of Brandeis University, who provided financial support for the conference. The administrator and secretaries of the Brandeis Psychology Department, Verna Regan, Judy Woodman, Marilyn Elliot, and Ingrid Edes, helped with their skillful preparation of portions of the manuscript.

Margaret Stubbs is grateful to her teachers, who made learning exciting for her, her students, who taught her much about teaching and learning, her practitioner-colleagues, whose special concern about children's learning strengthened her commitment to classroom teaching, and her husband, Richard H. Allen, who continues to help her temper her serious thinking with humor and relaxation.

Finally, Teresa Amabile expresses deep gratitude to her husband, Bill DeJong, and their year-old daughter, Christene Amabile DeJong. Not only did Bill originally suggest that this volume be created, he also lent his ruthless but unerring pen to editing much of the manuscript (including these acknowledgments!), acted as both coach and cheerleader when the task became discouraging, and pretended not to mind a rather long series of spouseless evenings. Christene provided no help whatsoever, but did stimulate some strenuous exercises in efficiency, and did inspire a renewed curiosity about how children learn in classrooms and in everyday life.

Psychological Research
in the Classroom
(PGPS-108)

Part I:
The Issues

Introduction to Part I

If researchers and educators are to overcome the philosophical and logistical problems that render psychological research in the classroom so difficult and of such limited practical utility, they must, obviously, begin to discuss these problems. The chapters in this section illustrate, however, that mere discussion is not enough. Certainly, an exchange of ideas and a clarification of positions can serve the function of enlightening both groups and leading them to a recognition of their common goals. Just as often, however, educators confronted with researchers' passionate insistence on experimental methodology and controlled observation experience nothing so much as dismay, and researchers brought to a realization of teachers' preference for their own methods of inquiry over the procedures of traditional research express frustration and chagrin. Still, it must be admitted, a discussion of the issues is the only place to make a start toward overcoming these difficulties.

In Chapter 1, Stubbs and Amabile present two brief scenarios of teachers and researchers, each in their own milieu, considering the same question about the behavior of children. These scenarios, in highlighting the approaches of both groups, serve to outline the major issues confronting classroom research. Chapters 2 (Amabile) and 3 (Stubbs) elaborate on these issues by presenting excerpts from actual conversations between researchers and educators. The themes emphasized in Chapter 2 concern the gap between these groups—a gap caused by philosophical disagreements on the formation and function of theory, methodological disagreements on the utility of experimental and nonexperimental techniques, and ethical disagreements on the acceptability of manipulation and deception. Chapter 3 illustrates teachers' reluctance to alter their individual beliefs about children and about teaching, even in the face of research evidence. They describe themselves as less interested in theoretical research than in "action" research that is directed at solving a particular problem in their classrooms. They explain that this preference is often motivated by the need to bolster their positions in political arguments. In Chapter 4, Rathbone, Amabile, and Watson present a fictional conversation between teachers and researchers that considers some problems of classroom research in even finer detail, including the utility and ethics of research and the logistical problems inherent in doing research in a classroom. Although Chapters 2, 3, and 4 focus primarily on difficulties and disagreements, each of them includes some hint of possible resolutions.

3

Chapter 1

Psychological Research in the Classroom: An Introduction to the Issues

Margaret L. Stubbs and Teresa M. Amabile

Two groups of professionals are involved in an inquiry into the nature of human behavior. Both groups are deeply committed to understanding cooperation and competition among boys and girls, yet their approaches to reaching that understanding could hardly be more different.

In the large, comfortable living room of an old Victorian house, several teachers are just beginning their weekly after-school seminar on children's thinking. As they take their coffee and settle, weary but attentive, into their seats, a young teacher begins to describe the competition she observes between the boys and girls in her class.

My seventh-graders have become obsessed with playing "Capture the Flag" lately. The way they choose teams and play the game, although ostensibly fair and fun-loving, involves a tremendous amount of competition. The girls find that the team leaders, invariably boys, choose them last so that they never get a chance to play. They complain about feeling excluded because they might not be good enough. And the competitiveness among the boys is even worse. The good players are arrogant; they don't want to play a game where, according to the rules suggested by the girls, you have to choose the bad players first and start with a handicap. Everyone takes the game very seriously and today, as we were discussing the problem, the feeling was very intense. Someone even cried—a girl, of course. What's happened to these kids? I watch the first-graders playing this game, and I'm struck by the vivid contrast. There, the kids seem most interested in how to play the game and how to make it more fun.

But another teacher describes competitiveness between boys and girls even in the first grade:

> I see the block area as something that can be very important, academically, for children this age. Yet, periodically some of the girls in my classes complain about not being able to work in the block area. I tell them it's open all the time—why don't they just go in? They answer that the boys won't let them, the boys get there first and don't want the girls to come in. The boys, on the other hand, complain that if the girls do come in they just leave right in the middle of playing. I tried again yesterday to encourage the girls to use the block area, and I think that what happened might provide a clue to the real problem. They went, but returned after a short time, saying, "The things we build aren't as good as the boys'. We don't know why, they just aren't." I realized then that I had failed in all my efforts to make block play a noncompetitive thing, and I think these kids were suffering because of it.

On the same afternoon, at a university not far away, a group of graduate students is gathering around a seminar table. They have just finished reading part of the psychological literature on cooperation and competition among children and, as they open their notebooks, the young professor begins to describe one of the definitive experiments in the area:

> One of the most important features of this experiment is its use of the time-lagged, reversal design. The ABA pattern was used in class 1, and the AAABA design was used in class 2, where A represents a week of baseline observations, and B represents the introduction of the experimental manipulation. In this way, it's possible to control for initial differences between the classes of pre-school children used in the study, and it's also possible to control for whatever sort of extraneous factors might have varied in that nursery school over the duration of the study. Can someone describe the procedure in more detail?

A graduate student paraphrases from her notes:

> The study was designed to see if teachers' expressing approval of cooperative cross-sex play—play between girls and boys—could increase the frequency of such play. The observers were eight undergraduates who recorded the behavior of children in the class during each half-hour free play period for each day during the study. They used a coding scheme involving three operational defini-tions: solitary play, when a child is more than three feet away from the other children; parallel play, when a child plays within three feet of another child but does not share the same play goals; and cooperative play, when children are playing in close proximity and have the same play goals. During the baseline periods, the teachers simply behaved as they normally do. During the experi-mental period, though, the teachers commented favorably on instances of coop-erative cross-sex play that they observed. They were trained to make one com-

ment every five minutes whenever they saw such play. That comment had to indicate approval, mention the names of the children involved, and indicate that they were doing something together, like, "I think the house that Patty and Joe just built is great." The comments had to be loud enough for the whole class to hear.

The professor concludes the description of the study with an explanation of its results:

Right. Let me spend a minute discussing the analyses, since you haven't yet covered this in your statistics class. They used two straightforward analyses of variance—between subjects, comparing the experimental period for each class with the baseline period for the other class; and repeated measures, comparing each class's baseline period with its own experimental period. They generally found significant differences. For example, for class 2, there was significantly more cross-sex cooperative play during the experimental period than during the control period; the F value, with 1 and 13 degrees of freedom, was 18.33, p less than .001. That means that there's only one chance out of a thousand that this difference between experimental and control periods occurred simply by chance and not because of the teacher's contingent praise. Of course, you should notice that during the final week when the teachers stopped praising kids for cross-sex cooperative play, instances of this kind of play dropped back down to the low baseline levels.

These scenarios suggest that, in many ways, teachers and psychological researchers are living in two different worlds. The teachers have hours of actual experience observing cooperation and competition between boys and girls whom they know well and about whom they care deeply. The researchers have virtually no such experience. They, on the other hand, have carefully articulated definitions of the concepts they are dealing with; they have what they consider to be a well-controlled observational method; and they have a set of sophisticated techniques at their disposal. The teachers, who have none of these, have instead a network of colleagues who bring their own rich store of anecdotes and observations to a consideration of common themes.

Clearly, though, both groups are talking about the same thing—cooperation, or the lack of it, between boys and girls. How might each group evaluate the inquiry being conducted by the other, if they were able to eavesdrop on the other's conversation? Most probably, the teachers would be struck by the apparent artificiality of the researchers' methods and observations. They would feel that, in contrast to their own observations, those of the researchers were too constrained by the presence of strangers in the classroom and by the somewhat arbitrary coding scheme to have any validity. As a result, they might doubt that the results, even if they are statistically significant, could suggest any practical applications in their own classrooms. Beyond this concern with artificiality, the teachers might feel indignation at the experimental manipulation of teachers and students, and confusion at the seemingly complicated statistical analyses.

Researchers, listening to the teachers' discussion, would probably dismiss their observations as a mere series of rambling anecdotes, protesting that this cannot be considered a legitimate method of inquiry. They might suggest that the teachers are biased observers who are too close to the situation to view it objectively and that, moreover, their observations are unreliable since they are made by single individuals. The researchers would probably note that the teachers seem to be more interested in adding to their store of anecdotes than in making generalizations about the phenomenon of cooperation. They might similarly object, if the teachers did try to make generalizations, to the inability of their methods to provide any valid, generalizable conclusions.

These, then, are the major issues that surface repeatedly throughout this volume. Both educators and researchers are intrigued by questions of human behavior but they disagree on the proper ways to answer those questions. Both are keenly interested in children, but teachers are more concerned with individual cases, while researchers are more interested in group trends. Both expect answers from research, but teachers want immediate results that they can apply in their classrooms, while researchers want long-term generalizations about human behavior.

Given these divergent goals, concerns, and methods of inquiry, it is not surprising that the conduct of psychological research in the classroom is often problematic. And it is not surprising that only a few classroom studies have inspired improvement in educational practice. Quite clearly, this is a pity, given the difficulty inherent in providing a high-quality educational environment and the ever-diminishing resources available for accomplishing this task. The contributions to this volume explore in detail the factors contributing to this dilemma, consider whether the gap between educators and researchers can or even should be bridged, and offer suggestions for bringing educators and researchers closer, both ideologically and practically. All are cognizant of the need for more effective classroom research. None believes there is a simple solution.

Chapter 2

Conversation I:
The Gap between Teachers and Researchers

Teresa M. Amabile

A conversation can often be the starting point for changing perspectives and reformulating old modes of thought. At a recent working meeting of several researchers, teachers, and others involved in the educational enterprise, a number of topics were discussed that bear on central themes in this book. In particular, these discussions served to illuminate reasons for the fundamental disagreements that often arise when educators and researchers attempt to work together, and possible resolutions to those disagreements. This chapter will present excerpts from some of the conversations that most clearly emphasized the major points of divergence, including the purpose and use of research, the choice of research methodologies, and the meaning of theory. In the next chapter, excerpts from conversations on the difficulty of applying research to educational practice will be presented.

The discussants whose comments appear in this chapter may be briefly described as follows:

• Teacher 1: an elementary-school teacher, educational researcher, and educational consultant;
• Principal 1: an elementary-school principal, formerly a teacher and education instructor;
• Education Instructor 1: a professor in a university teacher-training program, formerly a classroom teacher and principal;
• Teacher 2: a teacher in preschool and junior high school;
• Researcher 1: a social psychologist teaching in a university;
• Researcher 2: a developmental psychologist teaching in a university;

9

- Principal 2: an elementary–school principal, formerly a teacher;
- Educational Consultant 1: a staff developer, formerly a teacher;
- Teacher 3: an elementary-school teacher;
- Researcher 3: a developmental psychologist doing research in a graduate school of education;
- Teacher 4: a high-school teacher;
- Education Instructor 2: a professor in a university teacher-training program, formerly a high-school teacher;
- Educational Consultant 2: a critic of social-science methodology and educational assessment, formerly a physicist, working on a student-training program; and
- Teacher 5: a graduate student in psychology, formerly a classroom teacher.

THE PURPOSE AND USE OF RESEARCH

Although psychological researchers tacitly accept the premise that formal research is worthwhile and, indeed, may be the only way to answer most questions about human behavior definitively, many teachers seriously question this basic premise. They question the ultimate utility of traditional research, largely because of its paradigms.

Teacher 1: I'm doubtful about how much formal research can really tell us. Things that are known, for example, about how a child should work with materials for maximum memorization have mostly been developed in very limited one-to-one laboratory conditions. Those findings may not hold at all in the classroom, even if the researcher can reproduce them reliably in the lab or in small-group situations. The classroom has so many more variables. The fact that Thorndike says something is so, that he looked at a question for years and has all these studies to prove his conclusion, doesn't convince me that I can make it work in my classroom.

So I think part of our work as teachers is to find those particular research results that we think are relevant to our classrooms—maybe from studies that were done in classrooms similar to ours. Certainly, teachers do make use of research. But they probably don't make use of it in the way the original researchers would have suggested. The way that Piagetian ideas are being introduced into education and used by teachers probably makes developmental psychologists very upset and angry. But that stuff is filtering in in some way, partly because teachers think they've found something that can be useful.

Even when they accept the potential validity of the research enterprise, teachers may feel that research is primarily useful as a weapon in battles they must fight with administrations, school committees, parents, or federal agencies, as a means of convincing others that their position is correct. Researchers, on the other hand, might object to a seemingly selective attention to research findings, and an apparent neglect of the objective advancement of knowledge.

Teacher 1: It seems that there are a couple of different ways in which research can be conceived of and used. The first is research that feeds into political decision making at whatever level, whether it's the individual classroom or the nation or anything in between. Then there's research looking for general findings to advance knowledge about education. That's probably what most so-called researchers are interested in—questions like, what kind of motivation works better over the long run.

Principal 1: Does anybody know of a situation where a difficult educational or political decision had to be made in school, and research data was used to inform that decision? I can't think of one. I'm not aware of one situation in which such a decision was made on any other than very pragmatic or political grounds—like, we've only got two buildings, and we've only got X number of bucks, so this is how big the classes are going to be. I can't imagine my school committee saying, "Well, you know, Shmuchgavitch and Yaxen investigated this question, and their chi square showed. . . ."

Education Instructor 1: Well, I can't think of an instance where a given piece of research was solely responsible for the final decision. But I think that if a school system, for example, was thinking about going into team teaching, the school board might be responsive to five hot-shots from the local university coming in and giving testimonial evidence.

Teacher 2: No, I don't believe that communities would pay much attention, even if there were convincing studies. For example, in my community, we're considering whether a middle-school system is better than a K-8 arrangement. But, even in my upper-middle-class community, it's not being considered because some researchers suggested one or the other as the best way to organize. The only reason it's coming up is an economic one. That's the only time anybody moves to do anything, when it's economically beneficial.

Education Instructor 1: Or politically. You know, I wonder if anybody has examined how the post office makes decisions about moving the mail. We know that it doesn't work very well, we know that the postman on his route probably has lots of practical experience that would be helpful to the planners, we know that there are traditions about transportation patterns and communication. But we also know that there are a lot of people who want their cronies in the post office—patronage, and so on. It's so messy because of the politics. You're never going to get the pure truth out there, even if you set up all the universities in the country to look at the post office. And I don't think it's going to happen in the schools either.

Researcher 1: Why this assumption that every decision a teacher might want to make must have political implications? I don't think that's necessarily true. Obviously, things like the grouping of grades depend on economics and politics. But aren't there a lot of decisions that teachers have to make in classrooms, decisions that could simply be better informed, without having implications outside of the purely educational?

Principal 1: I really don't think so. I'd say that there's very little leeway for teachers to make any significant decisions in classrooms without political implications. Even on a very small scale—if a teacher decides to structure her classroom differently, there's going to be an administrative response, there's going to be a response from other teachers, from the parents. Maybe there wouldn't be much fall-out over a teacher deciding to use white instead of yellow chalk. But even there you could get involved in politics—a parent says, "Gee, I have a special-needs kid with a visual handicap, and he sees better with yellow." I think there really is that political dimension to every significant decision.

Teachers, necessarily concerned with concrete and specific problems that they encounter every day in their classrooms, are, understandably, often more interested in action research on those problems than in formal research on rather esoteric or general issues.

Researcher 2: Often, you have these specific problems that the teacher sees. That can be the best place to start—with the person who's really curious about something and isn't quite sure of the answer yet. But to translate that into good research, scientific research, whether using the physics model or whatever model, takes some doing. Because, for example, you don't really want to answer the question, "Should this bookcase be moved over there, will the kids read more if it's over there?" Answers to very specific questions like that just can't be generally useful. That's why I think we need researchers and educators talking to each other, to do good principle-oriented research. But we do have to start with the educators' questions.

Principal 2: I don't agree that's the way to approach it, at least it's not the only way. I *do* think that one approach is to take that one question by that one teacher, even if it doesn't apply to anybody else. Find out whether we should move this bookcase over there. Then go next door and find out if the boys should be forced to sit next to the girls—which can be a real question. Get some tiny little pieces that don't add up to theory and don't add up to anything, but serve real purposes for real individual people. I think that after a time we would begin to see some patterns that ought to give us a clue.

Educational Consultant 1: Something that strikes me is that, with researchers, there is an attempt from the start to make a generalization and to derive a principle prematurely. This kind of thinking masks individual effects among children in a class. Most research questions could be asked starting at a much lower level, trying to build up a body of research to see if it's even *possible* to draw generalizations. What I'm trying to say is that the initial question is often framed with *too much* precision and without consideration of the context of things. It would be better to start with research that looks at very small pieces— for example, identifying things that are effective at this grade level or that grade level. The problem with most research is that the researchers are trying to immediately derive general principles they can apply nationwide.

Education Instructor 1: It occurs to me that there's an awful lot of *something* going on, on a small scale, that wouldn't normally be dignified by the term "research," but is nonetheless very important. It's the record keeping and the documentation that's done, for whatever purpose—whether it's teaching the kids to document for themselves what they're doing, or justifying some new curriculum. When I was teaching I often found myself looking to my records of the past, documenting something that had been successful so that I could draw a parallel with something in the present. I could say, look, I don't know why I've got these troubles in this situation, but let me show you what we did last year. We took these measures and drew up these charts. . . .

There's a lot of record keeping and documentation and reporting to parents, self-evaluation by teachers and evaluations of kids. . . . all of those things go on in all schools, and in the better schools they're done better. This can all be very useful. But I don't think teachers talk much about this, and I don't think principals spend a whole lot of time encouraging teachers to come up with new ways to report and document. If we were doing a much better job at that level, we might be able to raise the quality of this "small-scale" research.

Teacher 3: And there's a related issue. It's pretty rare, right at the local level, for all the people teaching one grade—say, all 12 third-grade teachers—to get together frequently in a forum where they can share their observations and intuitions. There could be lots of small-scale research going on in any one classroom that could well be generalized to the other classes. Never mind the grand research projects that are done on a thousand classes throughout the country—I don't know where you even begin with that. But we could have a tremendous resource right at the local level, with informal research going on by local teachers for themselves. This possibility shouldn't be ignored, but it doesn't happen very much.

Researcher 3: I support the idea of small-scale research, but I think it has to be open-minded. I don't think it works to start out with something you intend to just use as ammunition in convincing someone of your position. I'm not sure that anybody learns anything from research if they go in expecting to find nothing but what they already believe.

Teacher 4: I have an analogy for research that might be helpful. A teacher who, at the start of the school year, has hundreds of observations, intuitions, and questions, is like someone who starts out with a messy garage full of stuff.

Research can provide the shelves for organizing, categorizing, seeing, and using that stuff. Good teachers will try on their own to build some shelves before the garage is full, by informal research. Then they find that their shelves aren't adequate, that they can't put everything on the shelves, and they look to new people—maybe to researchers—to provide new structure for them. But often the researchers try to give us "heavy" research, on esoteric topics. What we feel we need is action research.

On our research evaluation committee, we find that the proposals that come from academic researchers tend to be "generalizable" general topics. The stuff that originates inside the school system is more attuned specifically to a particular thing going on in a particular class, school, or discipline.

The academic research can give us structure—shelves—but small projects oriented to immediate action are important, too.

Educational Consultant 1: A structure, properly formulated, will help us see things on the garage floor that we didn't know were there. But we can't formulate a structure properly if we don't first of all rummage around in the junk and see what's there. The best researchers are those who, prior to starting work on their theories, spend a lot of time rummaging around in the phenomenon. That's a very powerful way to inform theory formation.

One issue that perplexes many researchers is the apparent lack of interest in research among teachers, the seeming disregard for research questions and answers. There are, however, a number of forces impinging upon teachers' daily lives that might help to explain such instances.

Education Instructor 2: Somebody suggested that there are a lot of teachers out there who are just brimming with questions about their classrooms, questions for researchers to help them answer. I'm not sure that's true. I'm reminded of some work that Philip Jackson did about 11 years ago. He did some research on teachers and found, among other things, that they were remarkably uninterested in research, that they were intuitive rather than rational in their approach to the classroom, that they were opinionated rather than open-minded about teaching. But rather than derogating teachers for this, he suggested a quite reasonable explanation. He said that, because the classroom is such a complex phenomenon and because the teacher has so much to cope with, by and large the best teachers do not concern themselves with research and, when confronted with it, brush it aside. So while teachers' lack of enthusiasm for research may in part be attributed to politicians and the public, it may be something inherent in the classroom that causes much of the difficulty.

METHODOLOGY

Perhaps the most fundamental disagreements between teachers and researchers who attempt to work together arise over issues of methodology. In many cases, researchers' main concerns lie with the internal validity of a study—the level of certainty with which one can draw conclusions about behavior in the experimental setting. Teachers' main concerns, by contrast, often lie instead with the ethics of the research and the extent to which it appears to have been conducted under natural, generalizable conditions. Thus, teachers often object strenuously to research that uses any kind of deception (by commission or omission) or any kind of experimental manipulation.

Teacher 1: I believe that research must be conducted with complete openness and mutuality. This applies to teachers as well as student-subjects. Research designs that manipulate student or teacher behaviors and then watch the result should be banned from the classroom. An example is the famous study in the late 60s of "Pygmalion in the Classroom." Teachers were deliberately fed misinformation about students, and then researchers looked at the effects on student achievement. The results were trumpeted around the world that teachers were such-and-such, and they affect kids in such-and-such ways.

This has done immeasurable harm to researchers working in schools. I don't think there's any teacher who doesn't know about that result, and I would bet that most researchers who work on anything that seems similar will find that teachers are suspicious: "What's your theory, what's your real motive, what are you trying to find out about us?" This is a very difficult thing for researchers to overcome at this point. In addition, I suspect the results of that research. I've wondered whether the published version reports the *real* purpose of the research, or if the real research is the effect of public reaction to this kind of information about teachers. . . .

I'll sum it up very bluntly by saying that lies cannot produce truth. That's a very powerful principle governing any research, including research with kids. The purposes and methods of any educational research should be explained to the students as clearly as possible.

Futhermore, although research which involves manipulating student behaviors is more generally acceptable to schools than research which involves manipulating teacher behaviors, it's not acceptable to me. Neither students *nor* teachers should be manipulated in any way. I know that I would not participate in any experiment that required me to behave differently from another teacher, and prohibited me from changing my behavior during the course of the experiment if I felt I had learned something.

When they consider the basic paradigms used by traditional research, teachers might also object to the very notion of doing experiments with humans, on the grounds that humans are prohibitively complex.

Educational Consultant 2: I keep hearing the word "research" and the phrase "experimental research" being used more or less interchangeably by researchers. I have difficulty with that. There are some sciences that clearly don't do experiments; astronomy doesn't. They do a lot of careful observations and create a set of theoretical constructs that seem to evolve in the process of looking at the data. But, fundamentally, astronomy works with unmanipulated data. The data are brought in and classified and constructs built on this.

It is my view that we deceive ourselves into thinking we can do experiments with people. I think that, when you talk about doing experimental research, you make the implicit assumption that you can do the same thing over again, and that the second time will differ in no important way from the first time. There is really no reason to believe that any human interaction is the same in all important ways the second time as the first time. So I'm questioning whether there really is such a thing as experimental research with humans.

Researcher 1: I have a couple of comments to make. First of all, it's true that humans are constantly changing in human interaction. You cannot ever exactly repeat any situation in human interaction. You can never exactly repeat any situation anywhere, even in the physical sciences. In that sense, it's not. . . .

Educational Consultant 2: No, no, wait. . . . I really need to add something. In the theoretical construct that says, I'm going to do an experiment on this collection of 100 million electrons and then I'll do another on another collection of 100 million, I am willing to state that the first collection of 100 million electrons is no different in any important respect from the second collection. Now, to the extent that you're willing to state that the first experimental subject is no different in any important respect from the second experimental subject, then I'm willing to grant your assertion that research on human subjects can use that model of research. If not, I won't.

Researcher 1: I'm talking about careful observation in controlled situations— that's really what an experiment is. When we talk about doing an experiment with people, all we need in the simplest case is to look at two groups of people who were randomly divided. We're not assuming that they're interchangeable as people—certainly not. We're just assuming that the important ways in which they differ, and there are important ways, cancel out in the two groups. We assume that what we're looking at will not be importantly influenced by initial differences between the groups. Then we set up conditions differently for the two groups, and observe what happens.

Educational Consultant 2: Absolutely, but it's built on the assumption that all the situationally relevant variables are essentially the same in both groups.

Researcher 1: If you have enough people in each group and they're randomly assigned, you can make that assumption.

Educational Consultant 2: That's where I differ. I don't think you can ever have enough people to satisfy my criteria of the relevant variables being controlled. I don't think it's statistically possible. I believe that there are other research paradigms that should be used with humans, rather than an imitation of what's done in physics.

One educator, in suggesting an alternative to traditional formal research, proposes that the researcher attempt to deal with a classroom phenomenon at all levels simultaneously, or at least sequentially:

Educational Consultant 1: To me, an essential element of good research is the seamless flow of activities, from one to the other, across an entire range: from research in cognitive development, to "seat of the pants" classroom observation, to curriculum development, to working with parents and teachers to get some sense of the values in the community, to trying to understand the politics of change in a school system, to trying to understand the climate of public discussion around that issue.

It sounds chaotic, because it sounds like you're trying to address the whole world in all its complexity at once. I confess, it does not have the nice reductionist features of traditional science, of saying, "Let me solve this piece of the problem first because it's largely decoupled from the rest." We're saying that the system is complex. It is generically complex. To try and deal with it by artificially carving off a piece is doing it a disservice.

Another alternative that many teachers find attractive is the extensive use of anecdotal evidence. While researchers object that such evidence is of limited utility because humans are such biased observers and so poor at discerning patterns correctly, teachers suggest that it is far more meaningful to them than more formal methods.

Researcher 1: Many of the teachers here have mentioned "storytelling" as a method of research. I'd be interested in exploring the issue of what can be gained from storytelling. Do you see it more as a way of elaborating things people already feel they know, or really as a way of discovering something new and changing ideas?

Principal 1: What it's done for me is to reduce loneliness. I can remember reading *Summerhill* on the train when I was an undergraduate going into graduate training in education. I can remember sitting on that train and crying because I suddenly felt, "My God! I'm not totally insane; here is a guy who's more insane than I am—somebody who really sees things as I see them." Often, for me, books and stories like that have been almost life-saving. They have given me courage, and a little support. I realize I am not alone. That's one thing storytelling can do.

Researcher 2: What you're talking about is case-study research, or anecdotes well told. I don't think there's anything wrong with that. But does that methodology have to be diametrically opposed to traditional research methodology? Can you even have one without the other?

Teacher 1: Well, it depends on who the audience is. In the work I do on training kids in computer programming, we do a lot of rather technical task analysis. But when I talk to the teacher about the work, or to a parent, I tell stories about some of the kids. That's really meaningful to people, and they can say, "Ah, I see why that was useful," or "I see the advantage in this." I don't think other kinds of presentations are nearly as useful in general, although they would be useful to someone who wanted to do a formal analysis.

Researcher 1: I'm trying to understand your distinction between methodologies. Observing kids, doing very careful observation, is one methodology. Another methodology is randomly assigning children to different groups, giving them different kinds of experiences, let's say, and then looking at outcomes. You can take a result from a study like that and describe it to people by means of anecdotes. You can extract a general principle and communicate it by telling a story about particular children in these groups. But the result is based on a very different kind of methodology, not on storytelling.

Teacher 5: I see the storytelling that some of us have done in teachers' seminars as being a kind of research in itself. One person relates an incident from the classroom and it calls up another incident in someone else's mind. By the end of the session, not only do I have half a dozen ideas I'd like to think about, but I've got stories to help me remember them. That's an important part of storytelling for me; it gives me control over ideas, and allows me to keep them and use them in my own classroom. But it is very different from formal research.

THEORY

In considering the uses of research, researchers see themselves as builders of theory in a slow, tentative, but clearly cumulative process. Teachers, too, see themselves as theory builders—but the methods of theory building and the uses of theory may be very different.

Researcher 2: I think researchers and teachers might mean different things by the word "theory." When I think of theory, I don't necessarily mean a great unified theory, such as Piaget's. I mean an underlying conception of what's happening in a given situation. That conception will guide my predictions. Take, for example, children's unsupervised play—something that teachers are concerned with. That concern is the initial step. But then I formulate some guiding conception, go in to observe, and try to draw some conclusions. I see how well those fit the original theory and, maybe, modify it.

Teacher 1: There's a clear difference here between teachers and researchers. Teachers have all their anecdotes and want to see what kind of pattern emerges from them. Researchers want to have their theory, their pattern, figured out before they even look. They're not willing to even look at something unless there's some kind of pattern. I think that's wrong.

Researcher 1: I think the difference is in the kinds of data that you're using to build the theory. In both cases, the theory is built on data. It's just very different kinds of data. The teachers are talking about informal, observational, anecdotal kinds of data, and the researchers are talking about data from experimental studies or formal observations that are planned out in advance. The informal anecdotes aren't planned in advance in that the "dependent variables" often aren't even specified. The observers see whatever strikes them.

The major distinction lies in the level of certainty you can have about your conclusions. If you build a theory on anecdote, you probably have the feeling that you can apply your generalization to a lot of different situations. But you can't be very certain about that generalization. Certainly, you'd have a hard time convincing scientists that you've got decent generalizations. On the other hand, using traditional research methods, you can develop a theory that might not deal with a lot of complex variables, but the generalization would have a higher level of certainty.

SOME IDEAS FOR CLOSING THE GAP

There are no ready cures for the maladies that often plague collaborative efforts between academic researchers and teachers. One possible step toward bridging the gaps that exist might be made by the use of intermediaries—teachers with a special expertise in research, or researchers with a special understanding of the perspectives and needs of teachers.

Teacher 3: I keep coming back to the idea that what we really need are translators, people who can tell teachers about research in terms we can understand, people who'll tell us what we need to know, but not more than that. Certainly, large, complex studies need to go on, but I'm not interested in all the details—I couldn't handle them, if I were.

Teachers have to get into that classroom every day and fill a thousand roles. We need someone to build a bridge to research for us, someone who has a familiarity with research, and theory, and teaching, someone who can help us observe our own situations better and formulate our questions better, and can sometimes provide us with answers to those questions: What are my problems? What does research say about this? What's going wrong in this situation?

Educational Consultant 1: I think the translator would be useful not only for the teachers but also for the researchers, in a way that might protect the researchers. In a way, I'm sorry that researchers feel they have to apologize to educators. If we had translators, there would be a buffer for them. They could do their research, they could take their time, they could work on what appealed to them and what struck them as important. Translators would be the link between the teachers and researchers. They could carry the teachers' concerns to the researchers and vice versa.

Teacher 3: Yes. Teachers can't afford to get bogged down in all the details of the research. We need someone who can communicate our concerns to researchers, and can come back and help us translate research findings into practice in a sensible way.

Finally, one educator makes a modest but encouraging proposal: that researchers, rather than trying to change teachers who believe in the value of their informal research, acknowledge its potential importance, and that, at the same time, teachers, although they may see no immediate benefits from formal research, make the leap of faith that research results might have long-range utility, and grant academic researchers the freedom to continue their pursuits.

Principal 1: A lot of our discussion has had an adversarial quality to it—the researchers with their formal models of research, the teachers with their informal models, neither trusting the other. I'd like to offer a kind of compromise. It's beginning to seem to me that different sorts of research in different settings or for different purposes should have very different models. This may sound rather conventional, but I find myself thinking about a sort of peaceful coexistence between the two kinds of research. On the one hand, the teachers could do their own research, with their friends, helping each other to inform their practice by looking at things that are really important to them, day to day, and discussing their observations.

At the same time, in a different corner of the building, we would have researchers doing their formal sort of research, but without teacher involvement. We'd be civil to them, and they'd be pleasant to us, by giving us some volunteeer time or something for our library. But they wouldn't bother us very much and we wouldn't bother them very much. We could have the attitude, I know this research isn't going to do me any good, but if my daughter becomes a teacher someday, maybe what this guy is working on will inform her practice, as Piaget has informed mine.

Chapter 3

Conversation II: Issues in the Application of Research Results

Margaret L. Stubbs

In the previous chapter, teachers and researchers discussed a number of issues separating them. In this chapter, these discussants address the problem of applying research results in an educational setting. When talking to researchers about their perceptions of teaching and research, their own needs as teachers, and which of these needs researchers might be able to meet, the teachers participating in the present conversation focused on two ways in which they would like to use research. They mentioned, first, needing ammunition to affect the direction of educational policy, and second, wanting information both to guide them in changing their general classroom practices and to help them in planning for individual children whose learning styles and needs represent exceptions to their generalized notions of how children learn.

Listed in the order in which their comments appear, the participants in this conversation are:

- *Teacher 1*: a graduate student in psychology, formerly a classroom teacher;
- *Teacher 2*: a language-arts specialist in an elementary school;
- *Principal 1*: an elementary-school principal, formerly a teacher and education instructor;
- *Researcher 1*: a social psychologist, teaching in a university;
- *Researcher 2*: a developmental psychologist, teaching in a university;
- *Educational Consultant 1*: a critic of social-science methodology and educational assessment, formerly a physicist, working on a student-training program;

- *Teacher 3*: an elementary-school teacher, educational researcher, and educational consultant;
- *Researcher 3*: a developmental psychologist, doing research in a graduate school of education;
- *Principal 2*: an elementary-school principal, formerly a teacher;
- *Educational Consultant 2*: a staff developer, formerly a teacher;
- *Teacher 4*: a high-school teacher;
- *Teacher 5*: a graduate student in psychology, formerly a resource teacher; and
- *Educational Consultant 3*: an administrator in a large public school system; liaison for that system to a graduate school of education.

RESEARCH AS POLITICAL AMMUNITION

Some teachers feel a sense of frustration when their opinions are relegated by others to the category of "mere" intuition. They are perplexed and dismayed when they are not taken seriously by those who make policy decisions.

Teacher 1: When I was a teacher, I found myself confronting a curious paradox. I found that, frequently, parents and administrators expected me to be an expert. When I began teaching, I was told which was to be my classroom, given a supply of pencils, a set of 30 math textbooks, and, with no other directions or advice from my principal, expected to begin work competently within a few weeks. But when I put in my orders for additional math or reading materials and art supplies, I found that the expertise upon which those decisions were based was not taken for granted. I quickly learned that my opinions about optimum class size, or the need for tangible as opposed to abstract math materials, or my preference for multiaged groupings as opposed to single-aged groupings of students, were just opinions, personal opinions that carried no weight by themselves and did not command the attention of my superiors. I remember feeling many times that if only I could reinforce my opinions with examples from research, or link myself up in some way with someone who held the same opinions that I did but had been recognized publicly as an expert, then my positions might become more credible. There wasn't enough time, especially in my early years of teaching, to develop articulate arguments to support certain pieces of my practice. I really had no idea of how to track down the work of researchers who might have been investigating the topics that I needed information about. The most important thing for me was to teach, to refine my methods. Articulating and justifying my practice for others took a back seat, given the demands of my classroom.

Alternatively, other teachers find it exasperating to be asked for their opinions, as Teacher 2 explained:

Teacher 2: When we *are* asked for opinions it often seems to happen in response to some sort of crisis, and dealing with the crisis consumes the energy needed to articulate our opinions effectively. Last summer it became apparent that roofing repairs for two elementary schools in my town would not be completed on schedule, and as a result, the two schools would have to relocate in another town building for an indefinite period of time in the fall. Over 600 people were required to function in an outdated school facility which in its day was an adequate educational setting for considerably fewer students and teachers. After about a month or so had gone by, a rumor started circulating in the community. If the two schools could function so well in the old facility, did the community really need to have both schools repaired? The question overwhelmed us. We were exhausted from efforts beyond the call of duty already expended in the creation of what we felt was a successful, if crowded, educational setting in a temporary location. Our principals urged us to talk to the parents about the crowding problems. Exasperated, we panicked. How were we going to find the time to argue about the long-term effects of crowding, let alone describe all we had done to make the situation bearable, when we had all we could do just to keep our heads above water day to day? It would have been nice to have an ally to turn to, someone who had access to and could get us copies of the right studies, so that we could pass them along to people in the community. We didn't really have the time or energy to argue effectively that, of course, both schools were needed.

In their remarks, both of these teachers refer to their own knowledge of the situation in which they work. The first complains that her knowledge is regarded by others as mere opinion. Both mention that it is often too difficult to articulate what they know. Both acknowledge that research results are more convincing than teachers' opinions and both wish that they had a researcher in their corner to give them information and credibility. How might these teachers have reached the particular conclusions that researchers "out there" had answers to their questions and that they could use research findings as ammunition in their arguments? Teacher 1 recalls:

Teacher 1: When I stop to think about it, I first learned about research in elementary school. My classmates and I were often required to do "research" projects. When this happened, the most sophisticated of us who liked to read went to the library, withdrew as many books as we could about the topic of interest, read these, copied various paragraphs verbatim, and finally arranged these in some order to produce the required research report. But most students consulted only one source, the encyclopedia, and copied what was there.

Regardless of how many sources we consulted, our conception of research at this stage, and throughout most of our grammar– and secondary–school education, was that it involved reading what other people had said about a topic and proving that we had done the reading by writing a report of it. As we became older, we were encouraged to recast this material in our own words. The idea of venturing one's own opinion about the information was not introduced until much later, and the notion of evaluating how the sources quoted had obtained the information in the first place was introduced only briefly in some college classes.

Curiously, at the same time that we were beginning to do research reports in school, we were introduced to the scientific method of research. We dutifully memorized the outline of the procedure and the definitions of its four basic components: observation, making hypotheses, experimentation, and generalization. It was made clear to us that primarily scientists used this method to get information.

But it would not be the method that we as students would most often use to get information. We learned then, perhaps not directly, but nonetheless emphatically, that the real investigators, the experts, were set apart from us in a number of special ways, and that our only access to scientific and other factual material was through reading what they had to say.

Like Teacher 1, many people still maintain the view that research is the special province of groups of experts who carry out their investigations in special settings removed from the din of everyday life. They reason that particularly when we are unsure about or unfamiliar with a subject, we assume that some group of experts has investigated it impartially and has some definitive information about it. In order to become more knowledgeable about something, we need to consult the experts about what they know. Even in areas with which we have some familiarity, we often look to outside experts for advice. We may think of ourselves as good parents or teachers, but because we are participants in those activities, we wouldn't presume to generalize for others on the basis of our own experience, except perhaps over coffee with friends, when we might be likely to engage in friendly persuasion. The assumption is that research experts have looked at the topic of parenting or teaching more broadly and from a greater distance than have the rest of us. As a result, many people think of researchers as the collectors and keepers of more "trustworthy" and reliable information, information that is supposedly untainted by personal bias or the result of idiosyncratic influences.

What is perhaps not so obvious to most people is that teachers in their classrooms, as well as other practitioners in other settings, also make use of the scientific method. They observe, guess about what happened or what would have happened if something were a little different, and sometimes even construct and carry out tests to see if they're right. But, unlike researchers, they don't use a mathematical model to evaluate the conclusions they reach. They don't label their own hypothesis testing "research" or give it the same kind of status that "research" is awarded in the culture at large, nor do they tend to generalize from it or tell other teachers to do what they did. In a sense, then, in order to operate successfully in the classroom, teachers necessarily *do* do research. Nevertheless, most teachers wouldn't include "research" within their job descriptions.

In addition to the notion of teaching as exclusive of research activities, all teachers receive the clear message of powerlessness from the culture at large (Davis, 1981). Explicit statements made in the media and warnings given to teachers during their training and in their work setting emphasize supervision, externally imposed curricula, and accountability. Given this state of affairs, few teachers would be likely to place their own expertise on the same level with that of academic social-science researchers whose expertise has traditionally been recognized by the public.

Consequently, some teachers feel the need to try to bolster their own opinions by seeking out research results that support their point of view or criticize that of their adversaries. Unfortunately, when they do so, they are likely to become discouraged. One teacher who had attempted to consult the traditional research literature on a topic in which he was interested described the extraordinary gulf that he found between the traditional research and his own work in the field. He reported that he couldn't understand most of the articles that came his way. It wasn't that he considered himself intellectually inferior to academic researchers; rather, he felt that the research reports to which he had access, like a majority of journal articles, consisted of convoluted prose and specialized terminology which takes far too much time to decode into meaningful material.

Even if one is able to achieve the translation that teachers believe is nearly always required in order to make sense of "scientific" reports, one may find that research flies in the face of practice. A principal describing this dilemma commented:

Principal 1: Something which is of deep interest to teachers, and something which has been researched quite extensively, is class size. I don't think I've met a teacher who said it doesn't make a difference. Every teacher I've met said class size really makes a difference, and although I'm not steeped in research on class size, I don't know of any studies that say anything else but that class size makes *no* difference to school achievement. It seems a very simple topic; it seems a topic that current research methods, whatever one may say about them, might throw light on, and yet they don't seem to. I'd like to know why. . . . I know of only one study which suggests that if you go from a class of 28 to a class of 22 something sort of better happens. Please correct me, since I'm not steeped in this literature, but everything else that I know says it doesn't matter whether you have 20 or 35 students in a single class. And yet this flies in the face of reality, doesn't it? I think most of us as teachers would say it makes a hell of a lot of difference . . . not just to the teacher and the number of headaches she may succumb to if class size increases, but also to the children and what they get if there are 20 rather than 30 students in a classroom.

When research presents conclusions that contradict those that teachers draw from their experience in the classroom, it may be, in part, because teachers and researchers, though interested in the same general topic, may define that topic differently and may use different measuring tools to gather information about it.

Researcher 1: If researchers are looking solely at one tiny bit of achievement information, in research on class size, they might be using a test that people don't generally agree on. Obviously there are lots of things that teachers have in mind when they say that class size matters, that it does make a difference. But what teachers have in mind might not even overlap with what the researchers are looking at.

Researcher 2: This is a validity problem. I think that, before a project is carried out, researchers and educators need to agree on what results, in the best of circumstances, would convince anyone to do anything differently about the topic of interest. In this case, it boils down to the question of what would convince you to make a decision about class size one way or another. Before anyone puts all the time and effort into a study, perhaps all involved need to address together the issue of whether or not there is anything that can be learned which would cause people to change their behaviors. Maybe we should establish validity *before* doing the study, rather than coming up with the experiment first and then wondering about how or even if the results are going to be used later.

RESEARCH AS A GUIDE TO PRACTICE

Unfortunately, both teachers and researchers are often pessimistic about the application of research results in the classroom. Like Researcher 2, many wonder whether or not research results will be used at all, whether as ammunition to influence others' opinions, or as information to guide the classroom practice of individual teachers.

Educational Consultant 1: I think there is very little evidence to support the assumption that there are unambiguous research findings in any domain that in fact will inform practice. Take this question of class size or any other question about which researchers purport to find an answer to; do we have any reason to believe that if an answer were to be found and even universally agreed upon, that, in fact, it would inform practice? I have some suspicions as to why research findings don't affect teachers' practices. I think it stems, in part, from the fact that too much of what happens in any interaction between schools and the larger community is adversarial in character. A receptive understanding of what happens in schools and what problems occur there doesn't exist on the part of the community. Failing that understanding, I think the community has no predisposition to accept ideas or recommendations that say, "Yes. practice will change." Ultimately, power, budgetary power and political power, resides within the community; and nothing changes unless the community authorizes it to change.

Researcher 1: Isn't it conceivable that, on an individual level, a teacher might have a nontrivial question that could only be answered by a methodology involving manipulation? Say a teacher who's interested in the different effects of same-sex or opposite-sex groupings. That's an important kind of cause-and-effect question which could be answered by certain kinds of experiments.

Unfortunately, many teachers, like Teacher 3, do not trust cause-and-effect research or its findings:

Teacher 3: As a teacher, if I have reading groups in my classroom, I have them grouped according to what I feel will best serve the kids' reading needs as I see them at that moment. I know there are many variables that affect what is going to happen to those kids' reading. A manipulative methodology can't possibly capture them all. I look upon the process of a person's growth as a very long-term developmental experience which includes a personal relationship between the teacher and each child in the classroom. When I change my strategies with kids, I try to adapt to what I perceive as the needs of different kids and of different groups of kids. I do not experiment on the kids in a cause-and-effect kind of way. I don't start out by deciding that I'm going to find out if sex grouping makes a difference to reading. I'm not interested in someone coming in and saying, "Now, for the next two months, we're going to put two boys and two girls in each group." I'm not willing to do that as a teacher. I *am* willing to have someone come and observe my groups to look at the interaction between the boys and the girls. But I want to be able to conduct and to change and adjust my reading groups as I see best meeting the overall needs of me and my kids.

Researcher 3: Are you willing to study differences in the ways that teachers do things?

Teacher 3: After observing in my classroom, someone could go to the next class and say, gee, they do things differently, and, after visiting say 1,000 classrooms, she might be able to say, gee, in classrooms where the groups were all boys and all girls, the reading achievement seems to have been higher, in these 1,000 classes. But even that wouldn't change what I did. I'd still be grouping my own way.

Researcher 1: I would put less faith in an informal observational study on 1,000 classes than I would in a well-done experimental study on two classrooms. I think it's much too extreme to reject the kind of traditional research that researchers conduct. Certainly, teachers need to be able to make informal observations well and quickly and use the observations to help them make moment-to-moment decisions. That's fine if all they want is simple identification. But there are lots of other things they have to do besides identification and description. If they want to know *why* kids are behaving the way they are, *why* some things work and others don't, informal observation (even if it's careful) won't be good enough. It's because people are bad observers, biased observers, apt to miss events or patterns, or to report them incorrectly. We can't make decisions about these important questions by simply looking informally. That's where experimental research and formal observational research are important.

Educational Consultant 2: I wonder, though, about how useful it really is to try to generalize at all. One teacher, for instance, found it advantageous to increase her class size because she felt that she needed more diversity in her classroom. She felt that with more children in the class, her students would relate to each other better. She was convinced that more students contributed to a better classroom atmosphere and she guessed that, had outcome achievement measures been taken that year, the scores would have been high. But in the class next door to her, it was advantageous to reduce the class size because that teacher had some special needs children in the class who had not been formally diagnosed by the courts as such but who were very active and had needs that demanded more time. A generalization which claims to hold in all cases is useless to teachers. What is important is that they be able to consider each class and each child in the class on an individual basis before making decisions.

Researcher 2: But do you really want to limit investigation to the individual case? That kind of investigation isn't going to help anyone else except that individual teacher. It seems to me that one would want to find a way of applying the individual case to some kind of principle that can be used over the years or in other classrooms.

Researcher 1: I think that it would help if psychologists looked to people who know about schools and people who know about teaching for researchable questions. What was said before was that the effect of class size depends on the students involved. If one adds a certain group of academically skilled students to a class of predominantly special-needs students, and the addition provides diversity, then adding those kids might help. Obviously, adding another sort of student might not help. It depends on the teacher as well. Those kinds of things are the independent variables. Teachers know that those kinds of things can mediate or influence the effect of class size. But researchers won't know what those things actually are unless they know something about schools. I think that given this information, as researchers, we can try to frame large studies that *will* be useful. They'll be very complex, and they'll be difficult to do, but I think they'll be the only ones that can give us any generalizable answers.

Educational Consultant 2: I still think that if research starts at the level of pushing to get an answer that can be used nationwide, then many of the smaller contextual points will be masked; the resulting answers will be lousy and consequently inapplicable.

Teacher 3: I agree. I think it's foolhardy to imagine that there are general findings which can be published, read by all teachers, and then applied in a straightforward way with predictable results. Teachers read things derived from research all the time, and sometimes they say, "Ah, hah! That makes sense to me; I think I'll try that!" But it's not because the findings were scientific. It's because the findings fit a particular problem they've been working on, provide a different perspective on the problem, and fit with their intuitions. Magazines, even the popular teachers' magazines, are full of information from studies, or from things other teachers have done, and so on. Sometimes the suggestions work, and sometimes they don't.

As for research, I feel that I could get any answer to any question that I wanted from some researcher. Since I've been involved more in research, my experience is that it is in fact possible to set up a study to get any results that would be useful to me. I think that if the study didn't turn out the way I wanted, then I could just quietly bury it and do another one which would do a little better.

Teacher 4: That brings up another dilemma. We need to be somewhat objective about using research for any purpose. When research is used as a tool to support anyone's vested interest, then the researcher has been had.

An additional problem embedded within Teacher 3's particular stance toward research is that without a means of evaluating the soundness of various research projects, teachers often believe that one study is as good or as bad as the next. Perhaps more familiarity with the general strategies and details of research design would permit teachers to consider the usefulness of each study individually, rather than categorically accepting or rejecting the validity of *all* studies.

Given the long list of obstacles mentioned thus far in this conversation that could thwart the application of research results in the classroom, one might think that teachers would be discouraged from trying to get answers to their questions from researchers. On the contrary. One discussant asked a group of teachers what kinds of things they would like to know if they had a group of researchers at their beck and call. He reported that the teachers, when asked, could generate interesting questions, and that, as he analyzed them, their questions fell into four general categories:

Teacher 5: First, teachers wanted information about current themes or fads in education. Some of them, for instance, wanted information about how to incorporate special-needs students into regular classrooms. Others were interested in the identification of gifted children, and with reference to this, asked about the effects of labeling certain children "gifted," and the effects of tracking on all children. Other teachers wanted information about heterogeneous and homogeneous groupings. Was it possible, they wanted to know, to be specific about when either might make a difference? Is one kind of grouping more effective for certain aged children or for teaching certain kinds of academic subjects? They wanted to know if there was any evidence for the detrimental effects of standardized testing on children. They expressed a lot of concern about the validity of such tests and wondered about the extent to which they failed to measure certain abilities or were inaccurate.

Second, teachers wanted researchers to work with them to develop specific curriculum materials or instructional techniques. While expressing this need, teachers referred to the pressure stemming from the public's cries for accountability. Several mentioned that they'd like to find the least time-consuming method of keeping track of what students do in the classroom. Even a review of the different ways that others have kept track of children's activities in the classroom would be helpful. Teachers were also interested in becoming better observers of their own students and in learning ways to become more attuned to children's different learning styles. They mentioned that they'd like some better diagnostic materials which would help them get a fuller and deeper picture of the children which would include information about their social and emotional as well as cognitive developmental levels.

Third, teachers would like to request direct feedback from researchers about what was happening in their individual classrooms. One teacher, for instance, was concerned about the times she did or didn't follow through on something that she had initiated. She wanted to know what impact her directions had on her students. Another teacher was interested in having someone characterize the kind of authority that she held in her classroom. She sensed a split between her philosophical beliefs and her actual classroom practice with regard to this issue and she wanted information about whether or not the split evidenced itself in the classroom.

Finally, teachers were interested in finding out about topics of general interest that are not necessarily tied to current trends in education: the measurement of developmental stages, what enhances a student's ability to work independently, the effects of peer pressure, how best to respond to students' inattention, the effects of informal classrooms.

While this list is by no means complete, it does suggest that teachers are looking for information about a variety of topics. These teachers were asked specifically what questions they would address to researchers. But not all school people believe that researchers have the answers to their questions.

Principal 1: At the moment, I'm feeling that as teachers, we don't need researchers in the classic sense. It seems to me that as teachers, what we need is training in how to answer our own questions. The only level of certainty that makes any difference to us is an incredibly rough and ready level. As teachers doing our own research, we need a pair of binoculars, like birdwatchers. With our binoculars, we look very quickly, and can say, "It's a blue jay; it isn't a kingfisher. I know that; I don't have to look that up in the book." That's very different from the biologist who puts a feather from a blue jay which has been fed a certain diet under an incredibly sensitive microscope. The biologists makes very fine adjustments, and realizes that yes, a calcium diet of a certain level does make a difference to the feather. As teachers, I don't think we're one bit interested in that kind of precision. I don't think it helps us; I think it's a plain waste of time. Teachers can't justify anything at the .05 level of certainty. We aren't interested in that. We need to be able to answer our own questions well enough so that we become better at our jobs, and to do that, we don't need university professors. We need a friend who will help us, talk with us about our questions, ask tough questions of us, and come and sit in our classes—not to do a Flanders interaction analysis, but to say, "Gee, Fred can't stand more than ten minutes of doing any one thing, can he?" "Oh, I hadn't noticed that."

Rather than wanting to be partners in designing traditional psychological research in the classroom, these teachers would urge researchers to suspend their usual orientation to research so that they can help teachers in investigations of the teachers' own choosing and design.

Teacher 1: We need something in between traditional university research and what is thought of as teachers' trial-and-error speculations, perhaps a researcher whose role is to facilitate teachers' understanding of the questions they're asking, someone who could provide background information or give advice about how others have answered such questions in the past so that teachers could gain a broader perspective about how they might conduct their own investigations.

One educator commented on the kinds of researchable questions being discussed. In her view no one was addressing the really difficult issues, and she wondered why.

Educational Consultant 3: What about questions about behavior toward various ethnic groups and minority groups, males and females, or who gets suspended, or categorized as "special needs?" Why isn't anyone studying the books being thrown, the bombshells, the fights that are interfering with any possibility of teaching kids to read and write? What about these nasty issues?

Principal 2: Here's a nasty problem for someone to research. There are a number of children in my school who have been diagnosed as hyperactive and are being given the drug Ritalin, which is supposed to calm them down. I would be happy to have any information about how such a diagnosis is made, what the short- and long-term effects of this drug are on children, and most of all, whether or not the drug is doing what it's supposed to be doing. Often the physicians who prescribe the medication advise the parents of these children not to tell school personnel when the treatment begins. Apparently, the doctors don't want the teachers' expectations for a child to change and thus perhaps influence the child's behavior. Consequently, we're left in the dark, and are forced to evaluate the child's classroom behavior without the benefit of having all of the information that we should have in order to make such a judgment responsibly. I have very mixed feelings about treating behavior problems with drugs. I would welcome research on the topic. What kind of study could be done? Would you have to give Ritalin to some kids and not to others?

Researcher 2: One could observe those children who are already taking the drug over a long period of time.

Educational Consultant 1: It's very important to distinguish between someone coming in and observing present drug-use practice in the schools as opposed to someone coming in and manipulating drug use in the school. The two are entirely different.

Researcher 2: In the observational study, the researcher doesn't have complete control, but you can never be sure that you have complete control in any study. At least if you observe those who are already taking the drug, you know that you have a sample consisting of children whom physicians have already diagnosed and separated from the rest of the population. There's still the problem of confounding variables though, because some of these children may be worse off because they are more hyperactive than others in the sample to begin with.

Researcher 3: But you've also got other physicians with other kids.

Researcher 2: I guess you could try to involve other school systems, include other physicians, some of whom would prescribe Ritalin, some of whom would not.

Researcher 3: Would there be any objections to this research? If someone wanting to do such a study came to a school, would anyone object?

Educational Consultant 3: The school system might not even let you in the door because they might not want to admit that such behavior problems exist. Even if the school committee approved it, you'd have to go to each parent and ask permission. You could not go into my school tomorrow and ask to see the records indicating how many kids are taking Ritalin. All of that information is confidential.

Educational Consultant 1: If you wanted to look at my kid's records, and that violated her privacy, I'd sue the hell out of you.

Teacher 4: You also have to ask each student over a certain age if he wants to participate in the study before you include him as a subject.

Researcher 2: Researchers don't want to be unethical in any sense, but unfortunately, what happens is that because we know that we're going to have fights over methodology and logistical problems just getting the study under way, we sometimes sidestep some of the nasty issues. I'll give you two more examples. Recently, in our department, there was an undergraduate student who was very interested in the effects of divorce on kids and whether kids really did feel guilty about bringing on a divorce. The department rejected the project because the question was so touchy. Instead, we asked her to do a retrospective study requiring adults to look back at their own past experiences. This revised study was mediocre compared to what she could have done, but there was too much involved in her first design. In another case, one of my colleagues wanted to do research on altruism or helping behavior. School systems rejected his study because they felt it was inappropriate for him to set up situations where he could actually observe when kids would be either helpful or selfish. When it was rejected, he gave up and did something trivial. I don't know how to get around these stumbling blocks that prevent our doing more meaningful studies.

Educational Consultant 3: My feeling is that researchers worry too much about getting their studies approved. They jump over the hard part, which is simply raising the tough issues. I'm interested in researchers articulating the hard questions even if they can't get consent to go ahead and try to find some answers. At least they could raise their voices out there, point out to the public what problems are affecting schools and kids in large proportions, and support those who are arguing for large amounts of money to be funneled into solving those problems. It's too easy to become trapped by what we believe we cannot change, and to think only in terms of what is possible or permissible. You know that if you ask some of those ugly questions, that there'll be a lot of problems and that you probably won't get another grant. What I'm proposing is that, collectively, researchers could raise some of the significant issues affecting the educational and developmental processes without trying to raise money to study those processes at the same time. We need added voices.

SUMMARY AND CONCLUSIONS

The teachers and educational consultants participating in this discussion indicated a need for support from academic researchers. All would advocate some kind of collaboration with researchers in the design of research intended to improve education. But the specifications of such collaboration are less easily determined. As this conversation reveals, in our culture, the educators of children and adolescents are caught in a bind. They are not granted the status of experts on child development, cognitive development, or any other processes associated with the educational endeavor. Having failed to achieve the public's respect for what they do know about children's learning in classrooms, many teachers accept without question the notion that their knowledge base, convincing as it may be on an individual level, is grounded on speculation rather than certainty.

When educational practitioners find others disregarding their opinions and advice, they sometimes find it necessary to turn to the culturally recognized authorities on human behavior, the academic researchers, who, they hope, will substantiate some of their own views and lend them credibility in their efforts to affect educational policy at the larger level.

Unfortunately, this referral system only serves to maintain the status quo. The educational practitioner who passively cites information collected by researchers retains her inferior status, while the researcher to whom she has turned is recognized as the expert whose opinion is valued by those in the position of making decisions about educational policy.

The educational practitioners taking part in this conversation are clearly interested in collecting additional information about various aspects of their work, not only with the goal of influencing large-scale educational policy, but also with the intention of improving their own decision making in their classrooms. Their desire for more information is thwarted by the fact that practitioners often regard the research literature as inaccessible, either because they have little time to locate academic journals, or because when they do collect scientific reports on a topic, the reports are often too technical or too poorly written to be of use. Even when practitioners are able to translate the research reports into comprehensible prose, they often discover that the research findings fail to substantiate conclusions they've drawn from their own experience. Consequently, practitioners find themselves in the awkward position of having to reject or argue against recognized authorities. These practitioners seem to agree that if research is to inform educational practice on either the large-scale policy level or within individual classrooms, research results must be accessible to them; that is, they must be both easy to locate and easy to read and understand. There is simply not enough time for practitioners to labor over technical jargon.

Some of the educators commenting in this conversation reject the notion that traditional academic research is at all useful to them. They are suspicious of experimental manipulation, particularly in the study of human beings, and of premature generalization. They do not wish to become bogged down in the quagmire of researchers' attempts to ensure adequate control of extraneous variables. Instead, these practitioners advocate a shift away from using the traditional scientific method as a background for research design. They want researchers to support their efforts to conduct their own investigations as they try to establish their own particular type of credibility.

From the comments included in this conversation, it may be concluded that primary among the factors that affect the application of research results in an educational setting are teachers' perceptions of their own work and of research. Unless these are articulated and understood by both teachers and researchers, it is doubtful that research results will significantly improve educational practice.

Reference

Davis, C. Teacher-initiated research seminar: A short report. In Evans, C., Stubbs, M., Duckworth, E., & Davis, C. *Teacher-initiated research: Professional development for teachers and a method for designing research based on practice.* Final report for NIE project number 0-0219, 1981.

Chapter 4

A Visit to the Teachers' Lounge: A Dialogue on School Research

Charles H. Rathbone, Teresa M. Amabile, and Malcolm W. Watson

It was gorgeous the day I visited the college lab school—the first really nice day in some time, and the children were taking full advantage of it in the play-yard. Yet the director scurried out, advising the teachers to bring the kids in early because the psych students were expected at 10:30 to do their testing. Later, the director showed me with pride the triple interlocking schedule she had devised: schedule number one was of children tested (to guarantee that no child served as subject more than two times per week), number two noted times for testing, and number three specified place ("under the front stairs," I recall, could accommodate one child at a time while "front lobby" had room for two). From my perspective, this was more *laboratory* than *school*; research needs had clearly overridden educational functions.

The observer in this scenario displays a resentment toward psychological research that seems to be common among teachers. Often, teachers are suspicious of and even hostile toward researchers, sometimes without even voicing these sentiments except among themselves. Researchers, on the other hand, seldom take the time to discuss the basic issues of research with teachers, and are often insensitive to the problems their presence causes. Here we present a discussion that might take place if researchers were to visit a teachers' lounge with the aim of addressing these issues. Rathbone, formerly a classroom teacher and presently a professor of education, raises questions and objections that he has heard in his experience with teachers. In addition, he presents several negative examples of researchers working in classrooms. Amabile and Watson, as researchers in social and developmental psychology, respond to those questions, objections, and examples.

THE UTILITY OF RESEARCH

Issue 1

In dealing with kids, context is all. During your brief stay with us in the school, the odds are good that you'll overlook or misunderstand the existing context, and the result will either be that you will inadvertently do something to alter that context (leaving us to straighten things out later) or fail to take its influence into account (and thus invalidate your conclusions).

Response 1

First, we have no intention of altering the context of your classroom without your full knowledge and willing cooperation, and we try to ensure that such alteration will not take place inadvertently. Second, as to understanding the context of the school: that's really what most research is all about—context and its effect. Of course it is difficult to take all context variables into account when you do research in the "real world." The only way to eliminate this problem is to do nothing but highly controlled lab research, or to have teachers involved in a massive project under a long-term commitment. Since neither of these alternatives is very attractive to you, we can only observe context as carefully as we can, building into our studies your perspectives on how context affects our procedures and observations.

Issue 2

The record of the college lab school—in terms of producing first-class research—is dismal. Why should we expect anything better to come of your use of our school when you have been so ineffective with your own?

Response 2

College lab schools represent only one small part of psychological research applied to education. They are not the typical setting for our research. Even so, the record is not that dismal. For example, Kagan, Kearsley, and Zelazo (1978) did a massive study in a laboratory day-care center and obtained some rather definitive results on day-care centers. (They found, among other things, that day care does no harm to developmental sequencing or the rate of development in young children.) Besides, what do you consider dismal? It's very easy to expect too much from research. This is a difficult business: look how long it took astronomers to figure out the center of the solar system. Children, teachers, and classrooms are infinitely more complex than that, and so are the results.

Issue 3

It takes too damned long to profit from research! If you come in to look at my class or my kids in October, I want some practical suggestions that I can implement in January—not some article stating tentative findings (and no implications for practice) three years hence.

Response 3

You should realize that we often need a rather long period of time to analyze our data adequately and draw conclusions from it. Moreover, we feel that we must be cautious in drawing implications for practice on the basis of any one study; such caution takes time and care. Ideally, research is conducted so the results *will* be generalizable. If we do a study in October, the results might well be applicable to your class next year or five years from now. The major question is whether you, as a teacher involved in research, will value the contributions that we can make to teachers in general or must we always pay you back directly for the use of your class?

Issue 4

Theory is useless unless it palpably improves practice.

Response 4

What you say is partially true; improving practice is one goal of research. But your comment is shortsighted. We need to build up a store of knowledge—in the form of theories, if you will—before recommendations for practice can have any merit. Without theory, we have nothing but a collection of unorganized facts that will have little or no impact on education. The theory is the organization that leads to real understanding; we need that understanding in order to make sensible improvements.

Issue 5

What you are doing is insignificant.

Response 5

No, it's not. Building a science—an organized body of knowledge—is hard work and takes time, but it is not insignificant. Psychology has successfully increased our understanding of many areas, such as learning processes, motivation, and cognitive development. Science in general (and psychology in particular) has radically modified our world and has the potential to modify educational practices even further. It is unfair to belittle us for any lack of success our enterprise has suffered if you don't acknowledge the contributions that have already been made, and if you are unwilling to offer us help in future research.

Issue 6

The only credible research on children is longitudinal. Your short-term, dissertation-length study can't hope to tell us anything reliable about kids.

Response 6

Your statement is only true if we are looking at change in *individual* children (for example, the gifted children in Terman's [Terman and Oden, 1947] famous 25-year study). There are, however, many other issues and questions related to children and to development. Each problem may require slightly different research methodology and, indeed, most questions can be answered through the use of cross-sectional designs.

Issue 7

Since there's no way of holding all the variables constant, anything that you investigators purport to discover is suspect in our eyes.

Response 7

It's always true, in any science (as it is in any evaluations you try to make of your teaching success), that there's no way of holding all the variables constant. That's why we need to use sound techniques of methodological design and statistical analysis. At least then we can make some reasonable inferences about what causes what (or what goes with what), rather than simply basing conclusions on informal observation.

Issue 8

Despite all our behavioral objectives and "scope and sequence" charts, we acknowledge, deep down, that some of our hopes for children cannot be specified in advance, and although we can write out justifications for certain activities, there exist important outcomes for which we can hardly find the words. If you could help us articulate these goals, fine, but if your efforts instead accentuate the already specifiable and thus legitimize our neglect of the ineffable, you are doing us no great service.

Response 8

This is why we need to collaborate with you—so we can understand these things, so we can do some of our research on questions *you* want answers to. In addition, we would suggest that many of the things you consider "already specifiable" have not been adequately studied, but simply assumed.

Issue 9

We have been fooled by your statements of certainty. We're drawn to them, repelled by them, seduced by them, suspicious of them. We realize you're under a good deal of pressure to produce demonstrable proof ($p < .05$) and we crave the sort of certainty such results promise, but we know in our heart of hearts that life and children aren't ever that consistent or predictable.

Response 9

Good researchers know that their results only provide probability judgments, not perfect consistency or predictability. More extensive training in the rationale for good research methods could help you to understand what to expect from research. *Some* degree of certainty is the best research can do for us; nevertheless, *some* knowledge and predictability are better than none, and more predictability is better than less. That is what research can provide.

VALUES, MOTIVES, AND ETHICS

Issue 10

When the chips are down, an investigator's primary obligation is to his data. Since this is so, and since parents aren't on the scene, it is up to the schools and to classroom teachers to safeguard the children from harm. We cannot assume, for example, that children will be competent to assert their own rights of privacy. To afford satisfactory protection would require our constant and vigilant monitoring and, frankly, we already feel understaffed.

Response 10

We disagree. When the chips are down, we feel that our primary obligation is to the children—as is yours. We would argue that most contemporary researchers have a very keen sense of the ethics of research, and are particularly sensitive to these issues when children are involved. In fact, all researchers must now have their proposals approved by ethics committees at their respective institutions, so there's a double system of protection. Almost everywhere, these committees are very stringent and cautious. Ultimately, our concerns about the children are no different from yours.

Issue 11

Although we know that school can't and shouldn't be value-free, we recognize our obligation to scrutinize the environment for all values—implicit and explicit—that are taught and modeled. We realize the special pressures researchers are under to maintain their neutrality (and thus keep their data clean); at the same time, we worry that there are some issues about which professed neutrality threatens to teach indifference, or worse. For example, a child might easily misinterpret the behavior of an adult who continued to take notes as a fight broke out, instead of intervening.

Response 11

Although it is important that we not let our values and prejudices contaminate our data, application of the scientific method does not necessitate an unfeeling, robotlike indifference to people. Researchers do have very human needs and concerns; we have a real interest in children, and we can't imagine a way in which children could learn indifference from us. You can expect from us what you'd expect from any person visiting your school—reasonable, normal, and natural adult behavior.

Issue 12

You college people really have two agendas: the first is to do research, and the other is to train your students in the business of doing research. The risk that something will go wrong escalates sharply when inexperienced trainees are put into direct contact with children.

Response 12

You are right about our two agendas. But your criticism that some research assistants are "inexperienced trainees" reminds us of the dictum, "Don't go near the water until you have learned how to swim." Everybody has to start somewhere in working with children at school; you yourself started as a student teacher. We do take responsibility for the people who work with us; we try to train and supervise them adequately. Moreover, we think it's important for you to take some time to meet with them beforehand. If they are not acceptable to you, we can find someone else.

Issue 13

We worry that you gossip about us and suspect that you disdain our work. Since you are really coming in to evaluate our performance, we're preparing to bar the gates!

Response 13

We are *not* interested in evaluating your performance as teachers. We do not want to study individuals, but general techniques, or curricula, or settings; any scientific work is designed to be generalizable to whole situations, or groups, or approaches, beyond any specific person or technique. Indeed, much of our research doesn't involve observing the teacher at all. The fact that you misunderstand our goal suggests that we should spend a lot more time discussing our research with you.

Issue 14

What you are doing is potentially dangerous.

Response 14

In almost all cases, you are wrong. None of the researchers of our acquaintance has done anything dangerous to children. Indeed, virtually nothing that psychological researchers do to people—children and adults—is outside of the regular, day-to-day experience of those people.

PRACTICAL AND POLITICAL PROBLEMS

Issue 15

Can't you see how busy we are? In the past decade, our curriculum has proliferated to the point where every objective is carefully specified and every activity scheduled in advance. Unless you find a way to influence our budget, our principal, or our year-end test, we simply can't find time for your project.

Response 15

Although it seems terribly mundane, this is probably the single largest obstacle we have found to research in classroom settings. Teachers and administrators feel they cannot afford the time or the effort to plan around research projects. In short, they often feel that they simply can't be bothered. We do understand how busy you are; many of us have the same sorts of hectic schedules. While we realize that disruptions of any kind can be difficult, we'd argue against the view that any change in the day-to-day program must be detrimental to the business of the school. We hope we can convince you that it's worthwhile to accommodate our project if we do our best to accommodate your schedule.

Issue 16

You college people are notoriously unreliable. You don't even follow the same calendar as ours! Just when the children begin to get used to research people being around, you disappear.

Response 16

We think it's important, for your peace of mind and ours, to work out schedules as far in advance as possible. Just as you have no control over your academic calendar, we have no control over ours. We can only try to make our presence comfortable for the children, choose the most reliable people we can to work on our research with us, and plan our work with you well ahead of time.

Issue 17

Where were the colleges when we were in trouble? Have the universities, in fact, been fair-weather friends, deserting the schools when we've been threatened? Did you speak out forcefully about Proposition-Thirteen-type budget cuts? Did you work to influence P.L. 94-142 legislation to our advantage? Were you with us on recent changes in the state certification requirements? What sort of relationship can we expect in the future? We will be much more likely to let you work in our classrooms if we can realistically expect your support in these other, more public areas.

Response 17

Many of us are relatively unaware of the political problems schools face. If we become real collaborators, if we can develop more personal relationships with you, that awareness and concern might come more easily. In fact, in many cases, our research itself might be used to help you win some arguments. Although you cannot expect that we will always agree with you politically, you should realize that most of us have a real interest in preserving the quality of the schools.

Issue 18

If things do get political on account of your research, and an angry parent turns up at a board meeting, the school is inevitably left holding the bag. Although we can share student time with you, we cannot ever share our ongoing responsibility for the children entrusted to us. We're bound to get nailed for your mistake.

Response 18

Ultimately, the responsibility for the children is yours. But remember that there are risks in nearly everything you do—bringing volunteer aides into the classroom, for example. We can only hope you'll believe that the benefits from becoming professionally involved with us will outweigh the potential liabilities. Naturally we will try to minimize any risks but, if a parent becomes upset, we're more than willing to help you hold the bag.

Issue 19

Worth*while* is worth *money*! If the colleges consider student-teacher placement worth a free course credit, why not the placement of a research team? Such a gesture might convince some of our skeptics that this isn't just another rip-off.

Response 19

We definitely should try to do something for teachers, in reciprocation for their help. If our university administrations approve, we might be able to offer course credit; or, alternatively, we might be able to find college students who can help you as volunteer aides.

SOME NEGATIVE EXPERIENCES

Example 1

One teacher I know allowed a college researcher into her class to ascertain the pronoun acquisition of her three-year-olds. While it had been clear that the investigator intended to use little dolls as props, she had neglected to mention that they would be arranged as a nuclear family. Unfortunately, it was this arrangement that proved so disconcerting to one little girl; she had been trying to clarify her feelings about the fact that, unlike her classmates, she didn't have a daddy. With the added pressure of a stranger's questions, she was soon in tears, and the investigator had no notion why.

Comment 1

This is an unfortunate instance, and there are several points to be made. First, the researcher should have been sensitive to the child, and should have been able to deal gently with her as soon as she became upset. It is not clear whether this was the case or not. Second, the researcher should have discussed the procedure with the teacher in detail before the study started, so that the teacher could have averted such potential problems. Did the teacher miss an opportunity to alleviate the problem? Finally, though, it must be recognized that what the researcher did was not outside the ordinary experience of that child. Surely, very frequently, other people mention daddies, and other situations (such as television) lead her to think about nuclear families. The researcher should not be reviled for this. The researcher might have begun, "Some families have just a mommy, some have just a daddy, and some have both. This doll family has both." This, along with a previous awareness on the part of the teacher, should have alleviated any problem with the procedure.

Example 2

I once witnessed a questionnaire being administered orally to a three-year-old. The research was intended to discover the child's thoughts about the process of government, but in so doing the investigator was actually using the words "government" and "process" with the child. Predictably, she was getting nowhere; the level of abstraction was wholly inappropriate to the age of the subject. I wondered what she thought these nonresponses meant. I also wondered whether the child was mature enough not to be intimidated; a four-year-old might say, "That's stupid," while a three-year-old might conclude, "I'm stupid."

Comment 2

That sounds like a really dumb researcher. Again, the researcher should have discussed the procedure beforehand with the teacher, in detail. Also, the researcher should have done some pilot testing of the procedure with one or two children of that age to see if it was workable.

Example 3

My friend went to a strict Montessori school to ask if he could do research on imitation in their mixed-age setting. He was interested in determining when and how younger children might imitate the behavior of older children. He was told, in effect, "Yes, they do; Maria Montessori has written about the phenomenon. You should go read what Montessori wrote and not bother researching an issue that has already been settled. You may *not* do your research here."

Comment 3

That seems to us to be a terribly closed-minded and unscientific attitude. Throughout the history of science, people have made pronouncements on the basis of intuition or informal observation or poor experimentation that have subsequently been found to be full of holes. Of course, if a school says "no," there's not much we can do.

Example 4

Two difficulties arose when a college team came into a school district to develop an instrument to measure "classroom climate." First, the control-group teachers, who *weren't* trained to improve their climate, began expressing apprehension and later anger; and second, a third-grader confessed conflict between two quite honorable ideals: personal loyalty to her teacher, and honesty. When a certain questionnaire was administered, the child was asked to rate her teacher in various areas. She wanted to be loyal, yet didn't want to answer untruthfully. She complained to her parents, and the situation became rather messy because she was the daughter of a prominent judge and her mother made a public issue over the episode. The superintendent tells me that the district now has a new set of policies regarding testing, especially those instruments that deal with affect.

Comment 4

We think that two precautions should have been taken here, and these probably would have averted the crisis. First, the researcher should have made the intents and methods of the research team known to teachers and parents beforehand. Both should always have veto power—teachers for their classes, and parents for their individual children. Second, once a child had agreed to work with an experimenter (and children should always be asked), it should have been made very clear that she did not have to do anything she didn't want to do, or answer any questions that she would rather not. These precautions are written into the guidelines used by most university ethics committees to evaluate and approve research projects.

RESEARCHERS' SUMMARY

It seems to us that many teachers do not have a clear understanding of the enterprise of psychological research. First, they misunderstand the motivation for the research. Most of it is undertaken not to evaluate them or their children personally, but to arrive at some general conclusions about human thought, behavior, and development. At the same time that they are carrying out their observations or their hypothesis testing, researchers are not, typically, dispassionate and unfeeling machines; on the contrary, they are often interested in children and teachers, and in what goes on in the schools. Second, there seems to be a basic misunderstanding of experimental design and statistical analysis and the conclusions that can be drawn from research. No researcher sets out with the expectation that absolute certainty will be obtained, and no consumer of research (including the educator) should expect such certainty. Typically, experimental designs in which different groups are randomly assigned to different treatments can afford greater certainty about causality than observational methods, but no method can result in findings that a teacher can immediately apply to practice with complete confidence in the outcome. That is and has always been a fact of life in science. Knowledge is accumulated only gradually, and theories can be built only through a painstaking and time-consuming process involving many studies. This does not mean, however, that researchers have nothing to say to teachers about practice. Even one well-conducted study can sometimes provide teachers with important insights and suggestions about practice. Third, some teachers seem to feel that researchers have no regard for ethical issues in research. On the contrary, most contemporary investigators are quite sensitive to protecting the rights and well-being of children and teachers.

Many of these problems appear to stem from an underlying fear and suspicion of researchers on the part of teachers. Teachers seem to be alarmed by the notion that experimental procedures involve the "manipulation" of children; manipulation has understandably negative connotations of unnecessary and possibly harmful control. In almost all studies, however, "manipulations" involve nothing more than the systematic use of the kinds of procedures and experiences that normally occur unsystematically in the child's everyday life. Indeed, in this sense, teachers are constantly introducing untested manipulations into their classrooms. Also, teachers appear to harbor the basic belief that psychological researchers are not doing something of value. As we noted above, it is necessary to take a long view of the scientific enterprise in order to see the enduring value of any individual study. In addition, though, each researcher can and should attempt to make each project an enjoyable, educational, and rewarding experience for the particular children and teachers involved.

Researchers are partly to blame for any lack of understanding on the part of teachers. Seldom in the past have academic researchers taken the time to discuss issues of hypothesis generation, experimental design, statistical analysis, or even ethical consideration with teachers. This is surely a situation that can be remedied. The remedy, however, will require a genuine desire and commitment on the part of teachers to make the effort required to learn about these issues.

Finally, it is certainly true that researchers have not been sufficiently sensitive to the practical and political problems that teachers face. Most researchers have no experience in elementary or secondary schools beyond their own dimly recalled school years, and few have concerned themselves as adults with the educational and noneducational issues that teachers constantly face. It seems possible, though, that with improved communication and collaboration between researcher and educator, such sensitivity might be developed.

TEACHERS' SUMMARY

Despite sincerest assurances and most plausible explanations from the researchers, certain concerns linger. Some come straight from anxiety; others are more substantive. They hover over the teachers' lounge and will not be simply wished away.

Horror stories abound in schools, of course, and they inevitably feed teachers' worst anxieties. And when anxiety's high, it doesn't take much to keep it there: a single foul-up endures in the imagination as well as in the memory. Conversely, it requires innumerable illustrations of productive or even simply benign collaboration to assuage the concerns of those whose guard is now up.

Dialogue will help, especially if on a long-term, one-to-one basis—where the same research personnel work in the same schools year after year. Only then will trust levels rise and anxiety levels fall. Interpersonal ease, however, is insufficient; teachers must be brought in, not just as informed, friendly observers of classroom research, but as true colleagues in the total enterprise. To accomplish this will require some very fundamental alterations of role and attitude—on both sides.

The present situation involves an essentially unequal partnership: the senior partner informs the junior partner of decisions already made and solicits cooperation in their implementation. No wonder the subordinate feels resentful, suspicious, oppressed, envious, petulant, or depressed!

Only when teachers make decisions about what problems should be addressed, only when they understand the statistical procedures employed, only when they are satisfied with the relevance of the questions being asked and comfortable with the motivation for publicizing results, only then will they perceive themselves as operating from strength and from a position of equality with the college-based researchers.

Even for the relaxed, confident, unself-conscious teacher, however, some doubts remain—doubts about the fundamental significance of school-based research as it is currently conducted. All too often, the results of this research have appeared trivial from the perspective of the teacher, and this is a charge not so easily dismissed. Theory building and hypothesis testing do proceed methodically, cautiously, and incrementally, and, unless one is thoroughly immersed in the business, it is often very difficult to perceive long-term progress. Similarly, it is often hard to grasp the relationship of parts and whole—between, say, the exciting concept of creativity and some essentially pedestrian subtest on ideational fluency being administered to a second-grader.

What is needed, then, is a new sort of relationship, one that enables the teacher to share in all decisions made about research conducted in schools. Increased knowledge will undoubtedly bring down to a realistic level the rampant anxiety and mistrust now prevalent; increased teacher responsibility may well produce both goals and methods that seem more appropriate from the perspective of the practitioner. All of this will require tolerance and patience on the part of the researchers who, of course, know more about research methodology. Researchers must also acknowledge a willingness and a need to learn what some teachers already know about life in classrooms, effective strategies for teaching and learning, differences among learning groups, and the like. With a combination of forbearance, humility, and openness from the researchers and a little more courage, trust, and effort to learn on the part of the teachers, research in schools should improve immeasurably.

REFERENCES

Kagan, J., Kearsley, R. B., & Zelazo, P. R. *Infancy: Its place in human development.* Cambridge, Mass.: Harvard University Press, 1978.

Terman, L. M., & Oden, M. H. *The gifted child grows up: Twenty-five years follow-up of a superior group.* Stanford, Calif.: Stanford University Press, 1947.

Part II:
What Research Can Offer

Introduction to Part II

Before attempts are made to improve attitudes toward classroom research and to raise the quality of that research for both theory building and application, it is important to confront the question of whether research really does have something to offer to education. The chapters in this section argue that it clearly does. In Chapter 5, Amabile focuses on the potential contributions of social psychology. She suggests that social psychologists' interests in classroom research might exist because schools simply provide a good subject pool for basic research, or because the classroom presents a particularly interesting setting for the study of social behavior, or because the researcher has an active concern for educational environments and practices. Given the nature of social psychology, these researchers can offer teachers not only basic information on a number of relevant issues, but also a rich array of methodological techniques for answering teachers' questions.

In Chapter 6, Watson, after suggesting that developmental psychologists and educators share many of the same goals, explores some of the reasons for the difficulty they often have in working together: differential emphases on theory building and improving practice, differential concerns with inference versus description, and differential weightings given to logistical problems. This chapter concludes by outlining some of the ways in which developmental psychology, although its impact on education has been surprisingly limited in the past, might contribute substantially to educational practice.

Traditional educational research on teaching methods and curricula, while quite distinct from basic psychological research, has actually accomplished a great deal in its own realm. This point is made emphatically by Saphier in Chapter 7, when he suggests that a vast store of usable knowledge on teaching and classroom behavior has been gained through educational research. Saphier proposes that there are two major problems with this research: it is disorganized, and educators do not read the research reports; he proposes some remedies for these problems.

Finally, Chapter 8 (Amabile) considers the role of various research methodologies in the advancement of both psychological and educational inquiry. This chapter presents a guide to fundamental methodological issues for teachers and for researchers who want to educate teachers about these issues. It also points to special methodological considerations that distinguish classroom research from research in other settings.

Chapter 5

Social Psychologists
in the Classroom

Teresa M. Amabile

Research conducted in classrooms can be roughly classified into three broad categories: nonexperimental or informal observational research, usually carried out by teachers themselves; educational research, experimentation on teaching methods or curricula, usually carried out by academicians from graduate schools of education; and psychological research, experimentation on all aspects of human behavior, usually carried out by academicians from university psychology departments. Many teachers have no familiarity whatsoever with research, and some know only the informal observational variety. Of those who are familiar with research, however, most think exclusively in terms of educational research—work that is specifically designed to test or build theories of instruction.

Although developmental psychologists have always conducted much of their basic research in schools, as other psychologists become increasingly more interested in applied research or in doing theoretical work in field settings, educators are more likely to be approached by academicians whose interests might at first seem quite foreign to them. I will attempt here to do what researchers should probably do more frequently for teachers who have little familiarity with traditional experimental psychology—explain what psychologists (at least social psychologists) are really up to. Although I will focus on the interests, purposes, outcomes, and limitations of social psychology, much of what I say will apply to psychology in its other specializations as well. In concentrating on social psychology, I will argue that many of the questions that teachers have about their classrooms and their students could be answered with the aid of social-psychological methods, and that many of the questions that social psychologists formulate about human behavior could be studied quite successfully in school settings.

Although of limited utility, an informal definition can be offered: social psychology is the study of the ways in which social experiences influence an individual's thoughts, motives, and behavior. Social experiences are very broadly defined and include all types of contact with other human beings. In many ways, however, this definition does not include everything that social psychologists study. For example, they not only study the ways that one person's behavior—say, a parent's or a teacher's—can influence a child's self-concept; they also study the ways that the child's personality can influence his or her behavior toward other people. Indeed, social psychologists even examine the effect of the inanimate environment—temperature, noise, physical objects—on attention, affect, and social behavior. So, most broadly, social psychology should simply be defined as whatever social psychologists study. If it has anything to do with the external environment, with people affecting or being affected by people, you can find a social psychologist who is interested in studying it.

Traditionally, most social–psychological research has been experimental, but some is observational. Whatever the method, nearly all of the research has been motivated by theoretical interests. Recently, though, social psychologists have begun to talk about—and carry out—evaluation research. In conducting evaluation research, investigators use both experimentation and observation, as appropriate, to assess the effects of various interventions, programs, or settings: Do token-economy programs in mental hospitals improve patients' self-concepts? Are crimewatch programs effective in reducing residents' level of fear? What cognitive and social effects do "open" classrooms have, as compared to traditional classrooms? Evaluation research is usually research designed to assess the impact of a specific real-world program, often at the request of the people initiating or funding the program.

THE SOCIAL PSYCHOLOGIST'S INTEREST IN SCHOOLS

Often, when teachers and principals are approached by social psychologists (and other psychologists) who want to do research, they wonder whether the researcher's expressed interest in education is genuine. Does this person really want to find out how children learn, or how they behave, or how they feel in various situations, in order to advance knowledge and make teachers' judgments a little more informed? Or does he think he has found a large untapped subject pool, a group of subjects he can use to help him turn out a quick publication? Does he really think that, ultimately, his results will be worthwhile to teachers? Sometimes, of course, the answer to these questions is "yes," and sometimes "no." It depends a great deal on the researcher and the project. In trying to sort out the reasons for social psychologists' interest in doing research in the schools, it might be helpful to describe the context in which social psychologists are trained and in which they work.

Most social psychologists are trained to be theoreticians as well as empirical researchers but in most graduate programs, theoretically oriented experimentation is clearly valued over purely empirical work. The more a social psychology journal is devoted to theory, the more highly it is regarded in the field. And, of course, the more publications an individual has in the better journals, the more chance that individual has of receiving promotions in the academic tenure track. Also, although social psychology has now been essentially cut off from federal funding, the agencies that had funded most social psychology grants—the National Institute of Mental Health and the National Science Foundation—usually gave the highest priority to proposals that were firmly grounded in theory.

This emphasis on theory has produced a crisis of sorts in social psychology, a crisis that has been much discussed during the past decade. Social psychologists have begun to examine the progress of theory making in their field, and more often than not, have found it wanting. There are those (for example, Gergen, 1973) who argue that it will never be possible to build theories in social psychology in the way that theories are built in physics; they suggest that social-psychological knowledge is historically bound, that generalizations which hold in one place and time do not necessarily hold in another. There are others (such as Schlenker, 1974) who argue that there *are* invariant laws of social behavior, and that these laws may be discovered by taking into account all the variants of time and place. Most social psychologists have taken a cautiously optimistic position, agreeing with Schneider (1976), who said:

> There are some who feel that scientific social psychology is neither scientific nor useful for generating knowledge. It is asserted that social psychology has no laws of the form found in physics and no unqualified generalizations which hold up reasonably well across various situations. . . . I think it fair to say that such generalizations are few. Social-psychological knowledge is not as advanced as that of physics. The field is younger by a few hundred years, and my assumption is that social psychologists are trying to explain phenomena which are more complex than those studied by physical scientists. [Pp. 540–541]

The message, which many social psychologists appear to accept, is that comprehensive and enduring theories of social behavior are not possible at present. Given that more and more social psychologists are finding less and less satisfaction with purely theoretical pursuits, many are turning to research that, while it may be useful in theory building, is more directly concerned with solving practical problems on human interaction. Increasingly, journal editors and granting agencies are recognizing the importance of applied social research. In this way, then, the interests of many social-psychological researchers in education *is* genuine; they are no longer single-mindedly striving for a unified theory of human social behavior but are instead trying to contribute to the body of knowledge about social behavior while finding solutions to real-world problems. The classroom presents a setting rich with questions about the impact people have on one another. Educators need to know the answers to those questions and social psychologists, with their training in conceptualization, methodology, and analysis, are well equipped to help them find the answers.

WHAT DOES THE SOCIAL PSYCHOLOGIST HAVE TO OFFER?

Teachers may—justifiably—wonder what a social psychologist has to offer beyond an ability to conceptualize problems, design studies, and analyze data. What do social psychologists *know* about the kinds of social forces that operate in classrooms and faculty lounges and school-board meetings, forces that influence student learning and teacher self-confidence and educational policy decisions? What insights do social psychologists have to offer?

First, it must be said that, given the limited training most teachers have in research methodology, the technical contribution that researchers can make is far from trivial. Nonetheless, it should be acknowledged that the direct experience that most social psychologists have with classrooms is limited to college teaching and, in the distant past, their own childhood experiences in elementary and high school. For the most part, they do not have a clear notion of what teachers' and students' major day-to-day concerns are. What they do know about, however, are general patterns of human social behavior—social behavior that appears just as surely in the school as it appears in the laboratory or the factory or the home.

There is a wide range of topics that social psychologists have developed research methods for and have, in many cases, amassed a rather large body of information on; moreover, each area is directly relevant to questions that could arise in classroom settings: (1) Motivation. How does the behavior of teachers, parents, and peers influence a child's eagerness to learn on his own? (2) Social relationships. What does friendship mean to young children? How do they form friendships? (3) Self-perception and self-concept. How do success and failure influence children's self-concepts? What teacher responses can make a difference? (4) Environmental psychology. How does the arrangement of furniture in a classroom affect social interaction and feelings of comfort? What about the effects of noise, or extremes in temperature? (5) Group processes; (6) Conformity and independence; (7) Aggression; (8) Cooperation and competition; and (9) Attitudes and attitude change.

My own research has looked at the effects of various social factors on creativity. I have found, in essence, that if people expect that what they are doing will be evaluated, and if that evaluation is made salient to them, they will often be less creative in doing it, when compared with people who do not expect evaluation. Although this research is grounded in some social-psychological theories of motivation, and although most of the research has studied adults, it is an area that obviously could be fruitfully applied to classroom situations. In fact, the original idea for the research grew out of my own experiences as an elementary-school student and, more recently, as an elementary-school teacher. I feel that other educators would share my interest in this question, and that many social psychologists and educators could find a number of such questions of mutual interest.

SOME EXAMPLES

To date, a substantial segment of mainstream social-psychological research has been conducted in school settings. Some of this research has been excellent, and has found its way into the very best social-psychology journals. It is safe to say, however, that almost none of it has found its way into the practice of educators, or even into their consciousness. I think there are some clearly identifiable reasons for this state of affairs, and some steps that can be taken to correct the problem. In order to illustrate this, I will briefly describe three social-psychological studies that were done in school settings.

All of these studies were grounded in social-psychological theory. The first two were attempts to demonstrate the "overjustification effect": if a person who is initially interested in some activity is made to perform that activity in order to gain some extrinsic goal, that person's interest in that activity will decline in subsequent situations where the extrinsic goal is no longer present. This is called the "overjustification" hypothesis because it deals with a situation in which a person's behavior is overjustified: her own intrinsic interest would have been enough to justify engaging in the activity, but then an additional, unnecessary, and salient extrinsic goal is introduced. Self-perception theory (Bem, 1972) predicts that if the extrinsic goal is salient enough, that person will come to see herself as motivated by that goal so that later, when the goal is no longer present, she will show much less intrinsic interest in the activity.

One of the earliest tests of this hypothesis was done with children in a university nursery school (Lepper, Greene, & Nisbett, 1973). The researchers placed a set of magic markers on a separate table in the classroom and, by observing from behind a one-way mirror over a period of several days, were able to identify those children who showed the most intrinsic interest in playing with the markers. Those children were chosen for the study and were randomly assigned to one of two basic experimental conditions. (There was a third condition, included for theoretical reasons, which will not be discussed here.) In the "reward" condition, the experimenter escorted the child to a separate room and offered him or her a "Good Player Award" for drawing with magic markers for a few minutes. All of the children eagerly agreed and, after drawing for about five minutes, they were given the award. Children in the "no reward" group were also asked to draw with the markers, but no reward was offered. Again, all eagerly agreed. Two weeks later, when the children were again unobtrusively observed in their classroom, it was found that the children in the "reward" condition showed significantly less interest in the magic markers than did the children in the "no reward" condition. Not only did this study provide support for the overjustification hypothesis, but it suggested that the use of "token-economy" systems of reinforcement in classrooms may, under some circumstances, be detrimental to intrinsic interest.

Since their original study was not a direct test for this latter implication, these researchers set out to do such a test in a public school setting (Greene, Sternberg, & Lepper, 1976). They chose a school that already had an elaborate system of rewards for performance of math activities and worked within that system to assign students randomly to one of several experimental conditions. As in the original study, they had baseline measures of each child's interest in the various math activities as well as follow-up measures of interest after the reward system was withdrawn. Although the results of this study were considerably more complicated than those of the lab study (as was the situation in which it was conducted), for the most part they do confirm the overjustification hypothesis as applied to a token economy in the classroom: subsequently, children showed lowered intrinsic interest for those activities they had been systematically rewarded for working with.

The study by Greene, Sternberg, and Lepper relied on a great deal of teacher involvement and support. My third example, a pair of studies by Miller, Brickman, and Bolen (1975), required even more teacher involvement (which the researchers say was willingly and enthusiastically given). These studies pitted two theories against one another in their prescriptions for modifying behavior: attitude-change theory, which suggests that persuasion is the way to change behavior, and attribution theory, which suggests that people will change their behavior if they can be made to see themselves differently. In the first study, the researchers attempted to modify fifth-graders' littering behavior by having the teacher either use persuasion (lecturing them on the dangers of pollution and sloppiness, putting up "Don't Litter" signs, and so on) or attribution (telling them they are ecology-minded, putting up a sign saying, "We Are Anderson's Litter-Conscious Class," and so on). In a posttest, the attribution classroom was significantly neater than the persuasion classroom or a control classroom. In the second study, the researchers attempted to determine whether the math achievement of second-graders would be affected in the same way. Teachers either used persuasion ("You should be a good arithmetic student," "You should work harder at arithmetic") or attribution ("You are a very good arithmetic student," "You really work hard in arithmetic"). Again, it was found that attribution was superior to persuasion in helping children to increase their math scores.

These studies could, conceivably, be of great interest and practical importance to educators. They might provide insights into how teachers can preserve children's intrinsic interest in learning, and how they can help children improve both social and academic behaviors. But I would guess that these studies, and many others like them, have had virtually no impact on how teachers think and what teachers do. A large part of the problem is that they were all published in the *Journal of Personality and Social Psychology*, the leading journal in social psychology, but one that almost no nonsocial psychologists read. This is common in social psychology—publishing in such an outlet is well rewarded by academia—but the situation is, I believe, changing. As the field itself gradually becomes more receptive to applied-research problems, individual researchers become more alert to the responsibility they have to bring their ideas and findings to the attention of the people who might profit from them most.

I would argue, then, that the purposes of most psychological researchers who work in classroom settings would be quite acceptable and even exciting to most educators—if the educators only knew what those purposes were. Misunderstandings and suspicions abound because, to a large extent, researchers have simply not let teachers really know what they are up to. Certainly, few teachers have been trained in experimental methodology, and many are ignorant of the specific goals of social psychology. As I have tried to demonstrate here, however, it is quite possible to provide straightforward explanations of the research endeavor and to generate examples of researcher-educator collaborations that were fruitful for both sides. Researchers must, as a group, begin to recognize the misunderstandings that exist and take the relatively straightforward steps necessary to correct them. The result will almost certainly be better-informed practitioners and higher-quality educational research.

REFERENCES

Bem, D. Self-perception theory. In Berkowitz, L. (Ed.), *Advances in Experimental Social Psychology*, Vol. 6. New York: Academic Press, 1972.

Gergen, K. Social psychology as history. *Journal of Personality and Social Psychology*, 1973, **26**, 309-320.

Greene, D., Sternberg, B., & Lepper, M. Overjustification in a token economy. *Journal of Personality and Social Psychology*, 1976, **34**, 1219-1234.

Lepper, M., Greene, D., & Nisbett, R. Undermining children's intrinsic interest with extrinsic rewards: A test of the overjustification hypothesis. *Journal of Personality and Social Psychology*, 1973, **28**, 129-137.

Miller, R., Brickman, P., & Bolen, D. Attribution versus persuasion as a means for modifying behavior. *Journal of Personality and Social Psychology*, 1975, **31**, 430-441.

Schlenker, B. Social psychology and science. *Journal of Personality and Social Psychology*, 1974, **29**, 1-15.

Schneider, D. *Social Psychology*. Reading, Mass.: Addison-Wesley, 1976.

Chapter 6

Developmental Psychologists in the Classroom

Malcolm W. Watson

A developmental psychologist whom I know once attended a workshop for psychologists and preschool educators. The psychologists were to give the educators information gleaned from research that would be useful in enhancing day-care and preschool practices. As became apparent, the information did not seem particularly useful to the educators. Rather, it was trivial and irrelevant and seemed to skirt the central questions and issues raised by the educators. One preschool director asked the psychologists what information they had available on cooperative, parent-run day-care centers versus noncooperative centers. This question, like others, made the psychologists look like fools with their lack of information. One psychologist said that this question would be an interesting one to study to compare the effects on children of the two types of centers. The educator who had asked the question then admitted that, in fact, some researchers had approached her center to study just that issue but that she had decided not to let them use her center in the study.

This incident illustrates some central problems that often block efficient and successful educational research. Developmental psychologists and educators have many common goals and values: most important, learning more about development and successful educational techniques and helping children develop and learn. But they seem to differ in other important ways: their research objectives, research methods, and decisions on when and how to use children as subjects. As in the above case of the educator who wanted information that psychologists could not provide, educators may see psychologists as interested in trivial issues, knowledge for its own sake, and intellectual games rather than in knowledge which is applicable to current educational problems. On the other hand, it often seems to developmental psychologists that educators are themselves interested in trivial issues in their narrow-minded approach to specific problems rather than in underlying developmental principles, and that, as in the case of the educator at the workshop, they want to obtain information without contributing the facilities and means of ever obtaining it.

These differences between developmental psychologists and educators are somewhat baffling. Perhaps each group is simply suspicious of the other. As teachers may see it, psychologists know theory but do not know real children or what it is like to be a part of the daily world of classroom teaching. As psychologists may see it, educators know the practical aspects of teaching and dealing with children but cannot see the forest for the trees. These suspicions may be part of the problem but why do they exist? They seem to be symptoms of problems rather than explanations. Both groups need to analyze further the various problems and differences between them and then formulate ways to reconcile these differences.

DIFFERENCES IN THE GOALS OF RESEARCH

To say that developmental psychologists are interested in basic research and educators are interested in applied research may seem oversimplified but does indeed cut close to the core difference between the goals of each group. I would argue, however, that the differences in interest in basic or applied research are not the most serious hindrances to cooperation between psychologists and teachers. The differing values placed on theory building may be. But first we should discuss basic versus applied research.

Applied research can be defined as research that has the solution to a specific, real-life problem as its main objective (e.g., the evaluation of the effectiveness of a teaching technique or of an educational policy). It involves using the results directly and immediately, whereas basic research involves the objective of obtaining results that are meant merely to lead to a better understanding and to formulating and testing theories. If the results of basic research are ever put into practice, the application usually comes after some time lag. The difference applies to the motivations for a particular research study or the subsequent use to which the study is put more than to the research procedure itself, however. Although this difference relates to goals of research, it alone does not differentiate between basic and applied. In either case, applied, real-life problems may initiate scientific curiosity, and results may be applied to solve an immediate problem.

The contrast between the theory building of basic research and applied research may be seen as a difference of primarily induction being used by psychologists versus primarily deduction being used by educators. In theory building, the psychologist induces general principles from a set of specific phenomena. In applied research, the educator deduces specific predictions from general principles. Yet Lerner (1976) and others have argued that basic, theory-oriented research is primarily deductive rather than inductive. They say that a purely inductive approach, in which the researcher starts with facts and looks for more facts to build eventually a theory, carries the risk that, in starting without a theory, the end result may be a mere collection of disorganized facts rather than well-organized principles. According to Lerner, since most successful basic research (as I am arguing developmental psychologists prefer) involves hypothesis testing based on testable theories, it must be considered deductive rather than inductive. As noted above, however, applied research is also deductive. So the use of deduction does not differentiate basic from applied research, since both types of research seem to involve deductive reasoning.

The use of inductive reasoning may still differentiate between basic and applied researchers. Cattell (1966) has argued that all scientists should be engaged in developing theories (i.e., inductive reasoning). According to Cattell, the entire scientific process involves a cycle of inductive reasoning, hypothesis formation, and deductive hypothesis testing that is continually repeated. So a major question is: does applied research follow the same cycle as basic research?

Basic research is first theory building and then theory testing; applied research can be theory testing or theory application (which is a form of theory testing). Therefore, the main difference seems to be a matter of sequencing in the research cycle. Research, to the extent that it is applied, occurs after the basic theory building (and inductive reasoning) has already taken place. This difference between basic and applied research may be minor indeed. Basic research may be quite applicable or lead to applied research, and applied research may certainly be scientific and theory oriented and lead to basic research. My main point is that the differences (in sequencing) between basic and applied research need not be stumbling blocks to more cooperation between psychologists and educators. There is another difference, however, that may be more serious.

Both basic and applied research are different from a mere technological approach in which research is conducted without the goal of using or building on underlying theory. Some educators and applied researchers seem to believe that a concern with theory reduces or destroys the educational usefulness of the research. For example, Egan (1979), in spite of being a theorist, argued that developmental research generally has failed to lead to worthwhile educational applications *because* developmental psychologists are interested in discovering general laws as ends in themselves. He believed that to apply the findings to practical situations required a technician who would not be biased by the underlying theory. Yet such a technological view of research is limited in its generality in large part because it is not based in theory.

McCandless (1967) attempted to delineate various dimensions of developmental research, one of which is an atheoretical-theoretical dimension. Atheoretical research is primarily designed to answer immediate problems or simply to satisfy curiosity. This type of research often leads to a dead end of simply supplying facts that fit into no organization and are useless because the investigator has developed no framework or connections to make them generalizable. For example, research on the specific seating arrangements and timing of activities that are most conducive to successful learning will be useless to all but the teacher involved in the study and the particular classroom unless the research is based on general principles and theory. A theoretical framework allows the investigator to transcend the specific setting of the study and apply the results to other settings not identical to the original and thus engage in the scientific enterprise rather than merely in technical problem solving.

Theoretical research is primarily designed to explain causal relations and integrate facts into general principles (i.e., to build a theory if none exists), as well as to generate testable hypotheses and new facts. Studies of classroom seating and activities, for example, may be based on principles of attention, reinforcement, motivation, and developmental differences, and, thus, the results of the study could be used to support or modify the original principles and generate deductions for other situations. Theoretical research leads to questions of why things happen rather than simply what happens in a given situation. The "why" questions and answers seem to be more easily generalized across time, setting, and people involved, than the "what" questions and answers.

In conclusion, although the major difference in research goals between developmental psychologists and educators seems to be differing preferences for basic and applied research, this difference need not block reconciliation. Basic and applied research refer to different parts of the research cycle and reflect intended use of results rather than actual research methods. Whether in basic or applied research, underlying theory is essential to true scientific inquiry. Any researcher who disregards theoretical foundations and principles (i.e., theory building and hypothesis testing) may answer some specific question but may not be able to contribute any generalizable knowledge, even when using adequate methodology. This lack of generality would apply to educational applications as well as to other areas of research.

Some examples from my research may illustrate these arguments. In one set of studies, the early pretend play of infants and young preschoolers was assessed to determine how children develop the ability to use symbolization. We found a developmental sequence of symbolic transformations (or substitutions) that children could perform on objects of play (Jackowitz & Watson, 1980; Watson & Fischer, 1977). The predicted sequence was based on theoretical principles of changes in cognitive skills as children developed.

Although this research was basic with no direct application to education, it led to subsequent research on play and had implications for understanding the development of art and language in preschool children.

One of the subsequent studies was an applied-research experiment on the assessment of the effects of role-play training in a preschool day-care center. I compared the differences between training children to role-play in groups and training children in motor-coordination games. The dependent measures were the effects training conditions had on the children's subsequent skills in perspective taking, cooperation, imagination, role concepts, and adjustment in the day-care center. The purpose of this example is not to report results but to note that the study had as an aim applications to early educational curricula related to the value of role playing and training in imagination and the respective values of group and solitary training. The findings were not intended, however, to be limited to the specific curriculum that was used in the study. Although this experiment was an applied-research project, it was based on developmental theory regarding play and the functions of imagination (e.g., Rosen, 1974; Singer, 1973; Watson & Fischer, 1977). In addition to providing guidance for training programs, the results were intended to be used to reassess some aspects of the original developmental theory. Thus, this research, while applied, was theory oriented.

Both of these research areas seem to me to have value in increasing understanding of the development of pretending, imagination, and symbolization, as well as eventual applications to early education. And yet, some educators might argue that the studies of early pretending were not valuable in terms of educational application and that the study of role-play training was of lesser importance than other possible studies of specific teaching programs, for example of early reading or arithmetic abilities. Although their assessments may be correct, it is not because a particular study was applied and another was not. Educators and psychologists may ask, "In the long run, is it more important to gain information about the development of symbolization or about the effectiveness of a specific early reading program?" For me, the answer does not depend on whether the study is basic or applied but on which study can best advance theoretical and general educational principles.

One final point. A major problem that remains unresolved is that in most basic research there is a relatively long latency between finding results and their applications to the classroom. The delay is due in part to the length of time it takes to complete and analyze the results of a study, to get the results published, and to translate the results into specific teaching procedures and administrative practices for educators. Psychologists often cannot provide results that will be directly applicable to those students and teachers who are involved in a given study. Some educators cannot accept a delay in applicability, which sometimes takes a number of years, if it comes at all. There is no clear resolution of this problem except possibly a compromise in the goals of each group, i.e., that the psychologists plan more "quick" research that will be directly applicable to the teachers, and that the teachers cooperate in more research that will not benefit them directly.

DIFFERENCES IN THE METHODS OF RESEARCH

In addition to the dimension of atheoretical versus theoretical research discussed above, McCandless (1967) delineated other dimensions of developmental research which also may be used to separate developmental psychologists from educators. On one dimension, research can be either normative (i.e., descriptive and concerned with means and frequencies) or explanatory (i.e., concerned with determining causal relations). On a second dimension, research can be either naturalistic (i.e., carried out under real-life conditions) or manipulative (i.e., carried out in a controlled, laboratorylike setting where variables are manipulated).

Many psychologists view normative, naturalistic research methods as being second rate because of the sacrifices these methods require. In normative research, the basic questions concerning causal relations are virtually impossible to answer because controlled comparisons of possible causes are not carried out. Research carried out in naturalistic settings, such as a classroom, usually involves an inability to carry out all intended manipulations and comparisons or to use the most precise dependent measures available. Thus, even in a school, a psychologist is likely to prefer testing children in an isolated room for greater control of extraneous variables. In other words, psychologists may try to simulate the laboratory in naturalistic settings to be able to conduct explanatory, manipulative experiments.

On the other hand, teachers, when they do get involved in research projects, tend to be suspicious of explanatory, manipulative research methods. These methods, based as they are on a laboratory model, seem to sacrifice impact, face validity, and generalization to real-life situations for the sake of control and precision.

In debating the value of these two methodological approaches, teachers may stress the similarity of the experimental context to the actual problem context as the best way to generalize the findings to real-life applications, whereas psychologists may stress the control of variables and precision of measurement as the best way to generalize the findings to real-life applications.

Although McCandless (1967) implied that normative, naturalistic research is more or less of one piece, as is explanatory, manipulative research, this isn't necessarily the case. Researchers in both groups use all combinations of methods. Nevertheless, developmental psychologists could benefit by thinking more in terms of the descriptive value of nonmanipulative observations and the generalizability that comes from research in naturalistic settings (and indeed this is the trend in developmental psychology). Educators could be more open to research in laboratories as also generalizable and to the importance of better control and manipulation even in classroom settings.

In conclusion, to argue the merits of normative, naturalistic versus explanatory, manipulative research seems fruitless. Both have their place, and, in fact, the differentiations may not even be realistic. Research can be both naturalistic and manipulative, for example, and such research methods could meet the goals of either psychologists or educators.

DIFFERENCES IN VALUE SYSTEMS CONCERNING LOGISTICS AND ETHICS

As with the two previous areas of difference, for the sake of comparison, a discussion of this area requires some generalizations to be made even though psychologists and educators do not fall neatly into a dichotomy. In the domain of logistics, developmental psychologists seem to attach a different value to particular logistical problems than do educators. For most psychologists, the time that a child must be absent from regular classroom activities and the inconvenience to teachers are minor prices to pay for successful completion of an experiment. After all, the benefit could likely be general, applicable knowledge that can be provided later to the teacher. Few psychologists would be worried that occasional breaks in the school schedule or occasional absences would in any significant way decrease learning or school adjustment, and, therefore, this problem seems of minor consequence to them.

Nevertheless, this is no minor problem for most educators. The rigidity and concern of some teachers and principals concerning class schedules and students' absences from specific assignments has several explanations. First, some teachers may actually think that occasional breaks or absences are detrimental to learning in some significant and permanent way, but this reason is unlikely in most cases. Second, teachers are usually under pressure from parents and administrators, some of whom seem to be overly concerned that teachers waste no time with such outside activities as research. Because of the various political and special interest group pressures on the educational system, an extreme awareness of specific educational goals and disallowed activities seems to pervade many schools. This concern is in part the result of pressure to maintain achievement scores that have a habit of continually decreasing. Research doesn't maintain scores or teach basics; therefore, educators don't waste time with it. Third, teachers, in preparing schedules, may become too attached or committed to their plans. In addition, they usually develop an attachment to their students and feel protective of their charges and their territory. They do not demonstrate a simple unwillingness to cooperate or a laziness in adjusting to changes so much as a reaction to disruptions in a well-organized, controllable day, as we all at times react to disruptions in our plans. This reaction may be especially prevalent when psychologists demonstrate little sympathy for the teacher's tight scheduling demands and little understanding of the daily challenges and routines of the classroom.

Whatever the reason, though, teachers' concern with logistics can prove to be a major stumbling block for researchers. In the role-play training study mentioned previously, the amount of training, the number of children in each condition, and the dependent measures used were all less than ideal. These compromises resulted partially from the demands and fears expressed by parents and teachers that the study would disrupt the normal schedule and activities of the day-care center. As a result, the interventions had less impact than could have been possible, and several tests of the effects had to be neglected.

In the domain of ethics, contrary to some views, neither group seems to be more or less concerned with the ethics of research projects. From my experience, it seems that few psychologists, as well as few educators, would even consider performing studies that would be risky or dangerous to children, either physically, psychologically, or educationally. Neither psychologists nor educators, in most cases, place the collection of data above the rights of the children involved in a program.

Most developmental psychologists have no need even to consider deception as part of their research procedures. Nevertheless, some educators seem to think that psychologists are generally deceptive in their research and that any intervention invades the privacy and rights of the students and teachers. In fact, some educators are not as rigorous as the psychologists performing the research in maintaining confidentiality and rights of privacy. In some cases, the teachers expect to be given information on the individual children used as subjects and sometimes misuse or overgeneralize results in ways that the psychologists try to avoid. Although psychologists should provide information that benefits individual children, both psychologists and educators should be cautious in using information for purposes other than those specified when the parents and children agree to participate in the research.

A COMMENT ON THE PROBLEMS

These three problem areas contain some differences between developmental psychologists and educators that have inhibited them from cooperating more fully in developmental and educational research. In the three areas of differences discussed, two major problems seem to be especially bothersome: latency time from results found in basic research to any educational application and the problem for educators of finding enough time in the classroom schedule to allow researchers to carry out adequate comparisons and well-designed experiments. These two problems present real hindrances to successful, cooperative research. Nevertheless, this discussion should indicate that the other difficulties are not insurmountable and are often at a core level quite minor. In fact, it seems that most of the differences in research goals, methods, and values placed on logistics and ethics are more apparent than real. Of course, this conclusion assumes that both groups actually recognize a value in research, that both groups believe that developmental psychology *does* have something to offer to educational practice.

CONTRIBUTIONS OF DEVELOPMENTAL PSYCHOLOGY

Since there appear to be a few major differences between developmental psychologists and teachers, along with many minor differences, it might be appropriate to ask why we should bother trying to overcome them. Can developmental psychology in the classroom lead to educational improvements, or is it more trouble than it's worth? I would suggest that it is worth the trouble and that developmental psychology has already made important contributions to education.

Abraham Lincoln once said, "If we could first know *where* we are, and *whither* we are tending, we could better judge *what* to do, and *how* to do it" (Sandburg, 1954, pp. 232–233). Although Lincoln was not referring to the interface of education and developmental psychology, his statement provides an excellent summary of why developmental research is important to educators. The major value of a developmental approach is its influence on teachers' thinking in terms of developmental processes and sequences. How can educators or psychologists make decisions concerning any intervention or training (i.e., "*what* to do and *how* to do it") unless they know where a person is in a developmental sequence, what the end point is likely to be, and what processes brought the person from his or her origins to the present position? By understanding developmental processes and developmental sequences, educators can decide when a person is developing normally, what training would strengthen development, or, conversely, what intervention might be used to change the direction of development. Most important, developmental research can provide information as to which educational procedures will take advantage of a person's current psychological processes and level of understanding rather than fight against them.

Developmental research has produced important educational conclusions in the areas of cognitive development (e.g., Bruner, 1973; Moshman, 1979), the development of arithmetic skills (e.g., Ginsburg, 1977), learning and memory (Bransford, 1979), reading skills (e.g., Williams, 1979), social cognition and perspective taking (e.g., Hollos, 1975; Shantz, 1975), competence motivation (e.g., Harter, 1978), peer relations and moral development (e.g., Hartup, 1976; Rest, Davison, & Robbins, 1978), child psychopathology and diagnosis (e.g., Blau, 1979; Schwarz, 1979), and effects of divorce on children (e.g., Hetherington, 1979). Of course, this list is far from exhaustive, but two specific examples from the general area of cognitive development may demonstrate the potential usefulness of developmental research.

Several recent studies have investigated children's development of metaphor use and understanding (e.g., Gardner, Kircher, Winner, & Perkins, 1975). Before this research was carried out, metaphoric understanding had been regarded as being either totally present or totally absent. It is most likely, however, that children gradually develop through a logical sequence— that understanding is not all or nothing. In addition, children may show differences in the development and processes of their spontaneous production, their comprehension, and their awareness of metaphors. This differing awareness would differentially facilitate children's intentional use and analysis of metaphors in reading literature and in writing.

In one study, Winner, McCarthy, Kleinman, and Gardner (1979) assessed the early precursors of later metaphors. They found that preschool children first used enactive metaphors, in which one object is substituted for another object in symbolic play and is then renamed. In a second and somewhat more sophisticated way, children used perceptual metaphors, in which one object is renamed based on its perceptual similarities to some other object. These early forms of metaphors are quite frequent in preschoolers, even though metaphor use declines in school-aged children.

In another study, Winner, Rosenstiel, and Gardner (1976) assessed a sequence of steps of metaphor understanding in 6-to-14-year-olds. Children were asked to explain several metaphoric sentences (e.g., "The smell of my mother's perfume was bright sunshine"). At young ages, some children gave only inappropriate or incomplete metaphoric explanations. Also at the youngest ages of six and seven years, children usually explained metaphors according to one of two stages in the developmental sequence—either magical, in which a magical world is invented to make the double meanings appropriate (e.g., "Her perfume was made out of rays from the sun"), or metonymic, in which the two ideas are rearranged and related through contiguity (e.g., "When she was standing in the sunshine, she was wearing perfume"). At older ages, children were able to use more advanced but nevertheless primitive metaphoric explanations (e.g., "Her perfume was a yellow color like that of the sun"), and, at the oldest ages, children could use genuine metaphoric explanations (e.g., "Her perfume had a wonderful smell"). Winner et al. also found that metaphors involving a cross-sensory reference (e.g., a *hard* sound) were easier to interpret than metaphors involving a psychological-to-physical reference (e.g., *hard* man). Spontaneous metaphoric production occurred first, then metaphoric comprehension, and finally the ability to explain the rationale of metaphors.

These studies provide knowledge concerning the orderly development of metaphoric understanding. If teachers were familiar with the sequence and its logic, they could base their teaching of writing, poetry, and literature appreciation on the ability level of their particular students and, in addition, use the sequence to develop exercises that would take advantage of children's early use of metaphoric precursors both to encourage school-aged children's use of metaphors and to help children develop through the sequence.

In a second area of cognitive development, investigators have begun to study the development of metacognition—a person's ability to monitor her own cognitive processes, her knowledge and experiences, and her strategies and goals (e.g., Flavell, 1979; Markman, 1977). This research demonstrates that some children are simply not aware of when they understand something, what strategies they use to solve a problem or memorize something, or what approach they should take in a given situation to maximize learning and problem solving. For example, young children who are asked to memorize a set of items usually cannot accurately say when they are ready to be tested, whereas older elementary school children can. It is not surprising that these abilities are correlated with age and various aspects of cognitive development. Flavell (1979) has begun to develop a model to study the components of metacognitive skills and to map out a sequence of development. For example, the first level of a child's awareness seems to be only that he or she understands something or not. Next, the child can monitor when a lack of understanding is likely to occur and what the signals are. As children develop further, they seem better able to monitor the accuracy of their feelings and to predict how they will know something given that they follow a particular course of preparation.

If I were a teacher, I would be expectantly awaiting further results in this area. It is directly related to teachers' choices of study techniques for children at different ages, for teaching children to study and memorize information, and for diagnosing children's learning difficulties. Perhaps more systematic training of metacognitive skills will be possible when we know the processes and sequences of normal development of these skills.

SUGGESTIONS

These two examples seem to me to demonstrate the applied utility of developmental research, and yet these results, like so many others, may be difficult to translate into practice. The reasons may be due in large part to the problems and differences discussed in this article.

Developmental psychologists and educators could resolve most of their differences through a series of actions that usually are not carried out in present-day research. First, psychologists need to gain more first-hand experience in educational settings before carrying out research, and educators need to learn more about research methodology. Perhaps these activities could be incorporated into the educational requirements for both disciplines. Second, an educator who is considering a particular project should become better informed of a given developmental psychologist's research goals and concerns, and vice-versa, and the two people should discuss the rationale for these goals and concerns. Third, they should strive to combine research that develops theory and investigates developmental processes with programs for specific applications, rather than considering them as separate areas. Fourth, they should be honest and realistic about the final compromises in logistics and the effects these compromises will have on the results.

These actions indicate that the best thing that could happen would be for developmental psychologists and educators to collaborate in research studies, with both contributing to the questions, designs, and decisions, rather than educators merely allowing psychologists to carry out the psychologists' studies and then expecting some pay-off in usable results. These actions would take time and slow down the course of a given research project, but this sacrifice seems to be a worthwhile price to pay for more contented research consumers and more long-lasting results.

REFERENCES

Blau, T. H. Diagnosis of disturbed children. *American Psychologist,* 1979, **34,** 969–972.
Bransford, J. D. *Human cognition: Learning, understanding and remembering.* Belmont, Calif.: Wadsworth, 1979.
Bruner, J. S. *Beyond the information given: Studies in the psychology of knowing.* New York: Norton, 1973.
Cattell, R. B. Psychological theory and scientific method. In Cattell, R. B. (Ed.), *Handbook of multivariate experimental psychology.* Chicago: Rand McNally, 1966.
Egan, K. *Educational development.* New York: Oxford University Press, 1979.
Flavell, J. H. Metacognition and cognitive monitoring: A new area of cognitive-developmental inquiry. *American Psychologist,* 1979, **34,** 906–911.
Gardner, H., Kircher, M., Winner, E., & Perkins, D. Children's metaphoric productions and preferences. *Journal of Child Language,* 1975, **2,** 125–141.
Ginsburg, H. *Children's arithmetic: The learning process.* New York: Van Nostrand, 1977.
Harter, S. Effectance motivation reconsidered: Toward a developmental model. *Human Development,* 1978, **21,** 34–64.
Hartup, W. W. Peer interaction and the behavioral development of the individual child. In Schopler, E. & Reichler, R. J. (Eds.), *Child development, deviations, and treatment.* New York: Plenum, 1976.
Hetherington, E. M. Divorce: A child's perspective. *American Psychologist,* 1979, **34,** 851–858.

Hollos, M. Logical operations and role-taking abilities in two cultures: Norway and Hungary. *Child Development,* 1975, **46,** 638–649.

Jackowitz, E. R., & Watson, M. W. The development of object transformations in early pretend play. *Developmental Psychology,* 1980, **16,** 543–549.

Lerner, R. M. *Concepts and theories of human development.* Reading, Mass.: Addison-Wesley, 1976.

Markman, E. M. Realizing that you don't understand: A preliminary investigation. *Child Development,* 1977, **48,** 986–992.

McCandless, B. R. *Children: Behavior and development,* 2nd ed. New York: Holt, Rinehart & Winston, 1967.

Moshman, D. Development of formal hypothesis-testing ability. *Developmental Psychology,* 1979, **15,** 104–112.

Rest, J. R., Davison, M. L., & Robbins, S. Age trends in judging moral issues: A review of cross-cultural, longitudinal, and sequential studies of the Defining Issues Test. *Child Development,* 1978, **49,** 263–279.

Rosen, C. E. The effects of sociodramatic play on problem-solving behavior among culturally disadvantaged preschool children. *Child Development,* 1974, **45,** 920–927.

Sandburg, C. *Abraham Lincoln: The prairie years, 1809–1861.* New York: Dell, 1954.

Schwarz, J. C. Childhood origins of psychopathology. *American Psychologist,* 1979, **34,** 879–885.

Shantz, C. U. The development of social cognition. In Hetherington, E. M. (Ed.), *Review of child development research,* Vol. 5. Chicago: University of Chicago Press, 1975.

Singer, J. L. *The child's world of make-believe: Experimental studies of imaginative play.* New York: Academic Press, 1973.

Watson, M. W., & Fischer, K. W. A developmental sequence of agent use in late infancy. *Child Development,* 1977, **48,** 828–836.

Williams, J. Reading instruction today. *American Psychologist,* 1979, **34,** 917–922.

Winner, E., McCarthy, M., Kleinman, S., & Gardner, H. First metaphors. In Wolf, D. (Ed.), *New directions for child development: Early symbolization.* San Francisco: Jossey-Bass, 1979.

Winner, E., Rosenstiel, A., & Gardner, H. The development of metaphoric understanding. *Developmental Psychology,* 1976, **12,** 289–297.

Chapter 7

The Knowledge Base
on Teaching: It's Here, Now!

Jonathan Saphier

The foundation of a knowledge base about teaching is here, now, all around us, scattered in bits and pieces like a 1,000-piece jigsaw puzzle, complete but waiting to be assembled. And the amazing thing is that neither teachers nor researchers realize it. This is a pity, for it leaves the researchers feeling inadequate and the teachers feeling both contemptuous of research and lonely in their quest for professional growth.

Researchers fail to see that over a period of 30 years they have created a comprehensive set of categories for conceptualizing what teaching is—if they could step back and see the forest for the trees. They erroneously believe that their inability to come up with consistent correlations between teacher behaviors and student achievement signals failure.

Teachers, for their part, fail to see that the culture of their profession walls them off from professional talk with each other (as well as from researchers) about what is important and effective in teaching. And thus they also fail to see themselves as reservoirs of knowledge and potential contributors to the knowledge base about teaching. They erroneously believe that research has little to offer them, and so they do not read it.

Happily, I see both these distressing situations beginning to dissolve into an age of clarity and collaboration for teachers and researchers. To back up that rosy prediction I would like to support my opening claim that we have a knowledge base about teaching—that it's here, now, and then go on to the specific obstacles both teachers and researchers must overcome so they can use it, communicate about it, and add to it. But first some background.

THE HISTORY

The Study of Teaching: Poised on a Golden Age[1]

[N]either the observation of master teachers nor that of large numbers of effective teachers . . . has led to findings that are either substantial or sufficient for understanding teaching as a process. [Stolurow, 1965, p. 226]

The findings from large numbers of studies consistently showed no relation between ratings of teacher effectiveness and measures of pupil growth. It is only reasonable that this dismal literature has led many people in education to assume that effective teaching is not identifiable. [Soar, 1973, p. 208]

It appears that teachers do not, by and large, remain in a stable ordering on measures of teacher effectiveness. If . . . the independent variables typically looked at are often unstable, and the measures of teacher effectiveness also show instability, the possibility of correlating teacher behavior with student achievement to determine effective teaching behavior is quite limited. In fact, unless we reconceptualize much of what we do in this research, our research will be ludicrous! [Berliner, 1977, p. 158]

[T]he results were so disturbing in their implications that we are presenting them here and now, not so much as answers as to emphasize how urgently answers are needed. . . . [the results are] startling in the mixed and negative support they offer for our best ideas about how an effective teacher behaves. [Coker, Medley, & Soar, 1980, p. 132]

Does this sound like the verge of a golden age?

These statements on teaching from eminent members of the community of researchers reflect their feelings of futility, impotence, and failure. They look at their own field and wince. Variables are labeled "trivial," "inconsequential"; research methodology labeled "95% . . . invalid" (Scriven, 1977). Those who can muster cautious optimism (like Rosenshine and Furst [1973], who preside benevolently over the annual "slaughter of the literature"), always accompany their optimism with the three-great-problems-of-the-research-to-date, or the 95-suggestions-for-improving-the-research-to-come. While the three-problems and the 95-suggestions sections of these articles are excellent, there is a positive side to this history that seems to have escaped notice.

We are not in blind alleys; the direction of previous research has not been futile. We are following an evolutionary process of inquiry that has grown in normal and healthy stages through an "adolescence," as it were; without that normal evolutionary growth we would not stand as we do today on the verge of serious theory formation, a new period in the short (since approximately 1950) history of research on teaching. We are poised on the edge of a decade when research on teaching can for the first time attempt to validate new informed theories of teaching that could not be constructed without the useful work that has gone before. In what follows, the literature since 1950 will be recast to show in steps how it has developed the concepts and the methodological tools to begin to transfer practical knowledge to classroom teachers.

RECASTING THE LITERATURE

Since 1950, when trait ratings of "effective" teachers began to be replaced by observational studies, we have learned much about what teaching is. In order to see that, we have to step back and understand the relation of various research traditions to each other. The chart in Figure 7.1 outlines their development.

In the 1960s, trait research responded to the trend toward classroom observation and began using live observation to produce its ratings on such global teacher variables as "clarity," "enthusiasm," and "variability," and to relate these ratings to pupil achievement. A few researchers attempted to validate these global variables by studying specific teacher behaviors at the same time so that they might tell us what, say, "clarity" means behaviorally (Hiller, Fisher, & Kaess, 1969). Studies that looked at countable and specific teacher behaviors became known as "low-inference" studies: you didn't have to do a lot of inferring to count how many times a teacher asked a factual recall question, or how often students called out in class, for example. Studies that looked at qualities like "clarity" or "cooperative classroom climate" became known as "high-inference" studies: you had to do a great deal of inferring from whatever it was you were seeing to come up with your "9" on a 10-point scale for Ms. Jones on "clarity."

In this period a variety of useful concepts were formed for describing aspects of classroom reality and used in descriptive field studies as more and more observational instruments were developed and tested. These studies sought to classify ongoing classroom phenomena into mutually exclusive categories. The researchers, who were not thinking about theory, were trying to develop reliable ways to capture selected aspects of teaching so that these aspects might be studied. These efforts were quite successful: reliable instruments were developed that were descriptive of classroom climate, classroom management, classroom social systems, forms of instruction, the logic and linguistics of classroom discourse, and the epistemological content of classroom learning activities.[2]

Research of the 1960s has been much criticized for not seeking correlations between teacher behaviors and student-outcome measures, and for

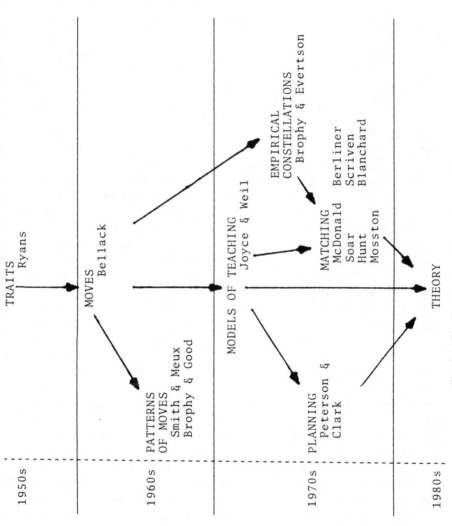

Fig. 7.1. The development of research on teaching.

obtaining inconsistent results in those instances when it did. This criticism was premature. The accomplishments of this period were: (1) to begin identifying elements of "teaching" at various levels of abstraction by observation at various levels of inference, and to rework and refine these categorical concepts with clearer and more meaningful definitions; and (2) to collect data about these elements with better and better technology. Of course, outcome correlations were erratic because the variables were not yet sufficiently refined, and more importantly, the *matching* considerations under which elements operated had not yet been addressed. By matching, I mean that researchers were not yet focusing on the *appropriateness* of teacher behaviors for different students and contexts.

Over this period we saw investigation of the "move"[3] (Bellack et al., 1966), the "episode"[4] (Smith & Meux, 1962), and the "venture"[5] (Smith, Meux, Coombs, Nuthall, & Precians, 1967). Teacher-pupil interactions were conceived as increasingly complex cycles of various lengths. From studying moves and clusters of moves we witnessed the landmark development of Joyce and Weil's (1972) work studying patterns of instruction they called "models of teaching." A model of teaching is a blueprint for a *kind* of lesson that approaches learning in a distinctive way, perhaps in a way that also develops inductive thinking (Taba's [1967] model), or personal creativity (Gordon's [1961] synectics), or logical thinking (Bruner, Goodnow, & Austin's [1957] concept attainment). With the development of models of teaching and the accompanying observational technology, we took a large step closer to theory. We could now look at a sample of teaching to see if a model was in operation and identify which one. If the teaching could not be associated with a model, then a certain nonrationality or at least nonintentionality might be attributed to it. This random versus nonrandom dichotomy gave us a powerful discriminator.

If, for example, we observe two teachers who have been trained to use Taba's (1967) inductive model to help students learn about Hemingway the man, both times we will see students (1) enumerate data about Hemingway; (2) group the data; (3) label their groups; (4) highlight distinctive features of each group; (5) compare and contrast the groups; (6) make inferences about Hemingway, and on through three other phases of the model. We will see this every time. That is what a model of teaching does for us; the events and teacher-student interactions are predictable because they are designed to attain a particular *kind* of learning.

If we observe two teachers using "discussion" to help students learn about Hemingway, we don't know what's going to happen. The two lessons may be radically different—both perhaps good, but different in unpredictable ways.

In addition to an observation technology, "models" gave us a concept traceable to specific or low-inference moves but referenced to high-inference and abstract elements of teaching like goals and objectives. It thus formed an intellectual bridge between the world of moves and the world of curriculum thought and gave us the opening for uniting ways of thinking about high-, middle-, and low-inference elements of what might comprise teaching.

At this point, around 1970, what we had was a 20-year history of researchers casting around for meaningful elements of teaching and developing increasingly complex concepts to capture aspects of that phenomenon's reality. The concepts themselves, while diverse and rich in possibilities, remained unintegrated in any unified scheme.

Relatively unaffected by the insights gained by Joyce and his associates (1972), researchers in the 1970s began to do very complex studies using multiple instruments at more than one level of inference simultaneously. They studied constellations of promising or appealing variables all at once and looked for correlations with student-gain scores. A landmark process-product study by Jere Brophy and Carolyn Evertson (1976) at the University of Texas created multiple data bases through both high- and low-inference instruments and introduced pupil differences as a variable in the research design. Thus for the first time we had a major observational study that correlated pupil outcomes with teacher behaviors which were matched to particular groups (not individuals) of students.

Brophy and Evertson found that many behaviors "related positively to effectiveness [with high S.E.S. students but were] unrelated or negatively related in the other group [low S.E.S. students]" (Brophy & Evertson, 1976, p. 173). And a number of behaviors seemed effective for both groups. The authors concluded, "teaching in general and good teaching in particular is not simply a matter of using a few crucial techniques regularly. Instead it is a matter of mastering and orchestrating a large number of principles and *using them as appropriate to specific situations*" (p. 126). Let's call that "matching" the teaching to the context. This is exactly the finding of McDonald et al. (1975) in the important "Beginning Teacher Evaluation Study" from Educational Testing Service. Their findings allowed for differential patterns of teacher effectiveness not only by grade (grade 2 versus grade 5) but also by content (math versus reading).

Now we had studies investigating wide-ranging empirical constellations of teaching variables, and we had recognition that these variables could be expected to have differential effects on different students under different conditions. The work left to be done prior to theory building is on the variables and the concepts of matching, both still in rather unrefined states (though promising work has been done by Soar [1977] and Hunt [1971; Hunt & Sullivan, 1974]). The variables need to be pulled together into some rational construct that accounts for all aspects (or at least as many aspects as we can conceive) of teaching as an entity, that include high-, middle-, and low-inference variables, and that can relate them to an operational model (see Saphier & Gower, 1980).

So where does this leave us? We are in a straight developmental, evolutionary track toward formation of a theory of teaching. The following things have been accomplished:
• A large number of variables, rich in possibilities, have been conceptualized at various levels of abstraction to account for important aspects of teaching.
• Reliable observational technology has been developed to classify, count, or detect the presence of these variables at various levels of inference.
• The importance of matching teaching to pupil characteristics and other context variables for valid process-product research on teaching has been addressed, at least in beginning stages.

What remains to be done? The incredibly wide variety of variables needs to be laid out in a model that can hypothesize their relations to each other and to teaching's outcomes. The important parameters of matching need to be conceptualized, tested, and then incorporated into the model to make a real theory of teaching.

Granted that is a lot of work—perhaps decades, perhaps lifetimes. Granted we are still in relatively early, possibly primitive stages of development. But we are on the right road; we should take pleasure in the rapid, orderly, and progressive development of the field of classroom research in just under 30 years.

CURRENT RESEARCH

Now let me change the tone a bit. Despite the great progress of the past 30 years, there are still some formidable confusions abounding in the research one sees today. Let me advance the notion that in effective teaching, matching is the name of the game; that is, what's effective will depend on doing what's appropriate for different individuals, groups, and curricula. Unfortunately the bulk of research fails to realize this, and so, much of it continues to look for correlations between isolated out-of-context teacher behaviors and improved student outcomes. Realizing all this explains the disquieting findings of Coker, Medley, and Soar (1980). These researchers studied 25 competencies commonly thought to relate to teacher effectiveness and observed a large number of teachers across all grades for two years. They found "few clear patterns . . . half had no significant relationship to either measure of student development, or did for students in some grades but not in others. . . . For many competencies the effects actually seemed to be negative" (p. 132).

Well, of course they got inconsistent and even negative correlations! What else could they expect? Any study of a teacher behavior in isolation from its context is probably going to be meaningless. Take teacher use of praise and rewards, for example: contextual conditions that could make that behavior effective or ineffective are:

1. The rewards are not things the students really want; they don't particularly care for stars and stickers. Or the rewards *are* things the students want; they love to be allowed to draw with the teacher's magic markers.
2. The students sense the teacher's praise is not genuine; it's always vague and delivered saccharinely. Or the students think she means it and the praise is usually a specification of what the student has done and why it's good.
3. They don't like the teacher. Or they *do* like the teacher.

Similar polar pairs of contextual factors could be offered to explain the effectiveness or ineffectiveness of any one of the behaviors cited in the Coker et al. study for a given teacher in a particular class. That is why, as Berliner says, "unless we reconceptualize much of what we do, our research will be ludicrous" (1977, p. 158).

In addition to this switch from studying isolated variables to studying matching, researchers have a great deal of catching up to do with school people on matters of practical significance. This is particularly evident in research on classroom management where admittedly sound research findings produce ungalvanic, "so what else is new" reactions from practitioners. For example, we are not greatly surprised or inspired to learn that a kindergarten teacher makes announcements and gives whole class directions from the same spot in the room and has a particular body posture for doing so—a combination her students have learned to respond to with attention (Shultz & Florio, 1979). We would greatly like to know, though, which kind of resistant student is a good candidate for behavior modification strategies as opposed to William Glasser's reality therapy or Rudolf Dreikur's logical consequences or any of the other major strategies of discipline (see Saphier & Gower, 1980). To my knowledge, no researchers have addressed that one.

Jargon and overcomplicated syntax in the reports of research findings are an old complaint, but deserve another replay here. It's a problem that doesn't seem to be improving. Unless research findings are put in more accessible language for teachers, not much application can be hoped for. Fortunately we have magazines, like *Learning*, these days that occasionally highlight important research findings and explicate them in plain language (see article on "Wait Time," Pierson, 1980). But these appear all too infrequently (and the one just cited appeared eight years after the research first came out).

The fact is that there is an assumption abroad, shared by teachers and indeed by many in the research field as well, that we have no real knowledge base about teaching. Nothing could be farther from the truth.

THE TREASURE TROVE

Yes, Virginia, there is a knowledge base about teaching! But it's not what you think. It's not a set of prescriptions, a list of behaviors known to produce effective learning (though there are a few of these). Nor could it or will it ever be! The knowledge base tells us there are certain things all teachers have to do, regardless of age group, grade, or subject. It tells us the situations or *missions* that all teachers have to deal with in one way or another. It tells us further what our *options* are for dealing with each area of teaching, and it tells us finally that *matching is the name of the game.* In some cases it even gives us good guidelines for how to go about the matching. Missions, options, and matching: let's unpack that a bit.

Teachers make decisions and act to deal with at least each of the following areas:

- gain and maintain students' *attention* to task;
- keep the *momentum* of events moving without wasted time;
- communicate appropriate *expectations;*
- *discipline* disruptive students;
- build *personal relationships;*
- set up *procedural routines*;
- use established *principles of learning*;
- practice *clarity* behaviors in explaining, reexplaining, or probing, for students' understanding;
- arrange use of *space*;
- manage and organize *time*;
- plan *learning experiences* for students;
- use *models of teaching;*
- create social, political, personal, and moral realities beyond prescribed curricula;
- choose *objectives;*
- *evaluate* student learning;
- *organize* curricular learning experiences for continuity, sequence, and integration.[6]

There are lots of ways to deal with each situation: 40+ ways to gain and maintain attention, for example (Saphier & Gower, 1980), five distinct kinds of objectives (Saphier & Gower, 1980), 20+ models of teaching (Joyce & Weil, 1980). If there are many ways to deal with each of the above jobs, then skillful teaching involves continually broadening one's repertoire in each of the areas and picking from it appropriately to match given students, groups, or curricula. The knowledge base about teaching to which I have referred is the *available repertoire of moves and patterns of action in each of the above areas, available for anyone to learn, to refine, and to do skillfully.* And, thanks to a history of thinking and of research, we know what they are. This knowledge base is made potent by applying its second component, matching, once one has developed a repertoire from which to choose.

Let's take a simple management situation: dealing with intrusions. A teacher instructing a small group has an interruption from a student who's stuck on an item in a workbook. The student comes up for help. There are several options the teacher may take, bearing in mind the need to keep the momentum of the group going and also not to cause the student who needs help unnecessary waiting time. The teacher can: (1) wave the student off; (2) wave the student in but have him wait for an appropriate moment to get help; (3) redirect the student to another student for help; or (4) teach students not to intrude to begin with when instructional groups are going on. The common feature of all these options is that momentum of the group and of Jimmy is not broken, or interrupted minimally. That is what's important. No one of the four is inherently better teaching, but you can surely imagine conditions where different ones would be appropriate. If Jimmy won't have the confidence or social skills to approach Mark, or is liable to get sidetracked on the way over, option 2 will be better than option 3. If Jimmy is overly dependent on the teacher who is trying to get him to rely more on himself, option 1 may be best, especially if the teacher believes he *can* do it himself.

In sum, handling intrusions is something teachers have to deal with. They should do it in a way that preserves students' momentum with their work (Kounin, 1970). There are lots of ways for doing that, but in any given situation with particular individuals, one particular way will be a best match depending on the student. Finding it is skillful teaching.

Some further examples from the knowledge base include the following: From the ancient (since the 1800s, anyway, and Ebbinghaus) tradition of learning-theory laboratory research, we have over 20 principles of learning directly applicable to classroom practice and, astonishingly, only a few are commonly seen in classrooms. Madeline Hunter and her colleagues have done a beautiful job of capturing these principles in programmed books for teachers (Hunter, 1969; 1971). Here are a few examples.

When a student answers a question incorrectly ("What's the formula for the area of a circle?" "2 *pi r*"), the teacher should supply the question for which that's the right answer ("That would be right if I'd asked you for the circumference"). Then the teacher should deliver prompts ("Do you remember how there's an exponent in the area formula?" Then hold the student accountable ("*Pi r*^{2}." "That's right. I'm going to check you on that at homeroom this afternoon and I'll bet you remember it!"). Three straightforward steps: supply the question for which the answer is right, deliver prompts, and hold accountable.[7]

Another principle of learning: student practice of new skills should be in short bursts, should be grouped in the smallest units that retain meaning, and should be frequent (Bugelski, 1971). This means that for learning new math facts, for example, drills should be short (2–5 minutes rather than 20) and frequent (twice a day not twice a week), and that only a few facts should be introduced at a time, mixed in with previously learned ones but drilled with more repetition than the previously learned ones. Furthermore, for the specific item of math facts, practice doesn't advance learning unless tied to speed; the drills must be timed at some point and speed increased up to a criterion to be effective.

This cluster of principles on practice has been repeatedly established and is as unshakable as anything we have in psychological research. Yet in thousands of classrooms over the nation we see absolute violations of these principles daily as students plod through workbooks in math for 20-minute periods or longer with no timed or controlled drills.

Mary Budd Rowe (1972) tells us about "wait time." If you have the patience to wait three seconds—endure three seconds of silence instead of the average 1.5—when a student doesn't answer a question right away, if you can hold off redirecting it to another student or supplying the answer yourself for that extra 1.5 seconds, achievement goes up. You're stimulating students to think.

There's also excellent material in the scholarly journals (which are written, it seems, mainly for researchers talking to each other). *Review of Educational Research* (*RER*) and the *American Educational Research Journal* are two important ones. A recent *RER,* for example, had two good articles on cooperative learning and its effects on students (Sharan, 1980; Slavin, 1980). Following a review of research in the field, Slavin (1980) concludes: "The effects of the techniques on the group cohesiveness variables, such as mutual concern and race relations, are unquestionably positive." Johnson (1981), citing his own review of the literature (Johnson et al., 1981) across 122 studies concludes that "cooperation is considerably more effective than interpersonal competition and individualistic efforts in promoting achievement and productivity. The students in the 50th percentile in the cooperative condition perform at approximately the same level as students in the 80th percentile in the competitive and individualistic conditions."

These are very strong claims and, one would think, of great interest to teachers. The articles containing them do not leave one wondering how to do cooperative learning either. They provide nice summaries of the practical steps and details of carrying out several forms of cooperative learning and give additional references for more detailed study.

Let's take a look at models of teaching. Research has shown that no one model is superior to another (Nuthall & Snook, 1973) for producing student gain on standarized tests. But that, of course, is because the different models are aimed at things standardized tests don't measure. We believe that Taba's (1967) model of teaching does increase the ability of students to think inductively, that Ausubel's advance organizer model (1963) is effective at teaching students to assimilate hierarchical information logically (Lawton, 1977), that Oliver and Shaver's (1966) jurisprudential model teaches advocacy and evidencing, and on and on through the 20+ models.

We could use more research to prove that the *kind* of thinking the model intends is actually developed by learning through the model. We do have sound research validating the ability of clinical instruments to identify how faithfully a model is being implemented (Gower, 1974; McKibbin, 1974; O'Donnell, 1974; Rude, 1973; Wald, 1972; Weil, 1974). And we have reliable training systems for teaching them to teachers (Joyce & Weil, 1980). Quite a cohesive and convincing body of research! And lo and behold, we hardly ever see the models in operation in schools, recitation and direct instruction instead dominating the scene as if the models do not exist. Of all the riches in the knowledge base, this material on models and the material on principles of learning are most clearly and most extensively developed, and most accessible to teachers. And they have been around in these accessible forms for over a decade. Why have most teachers not read this material? Why do most not even know it exists? It is time we looked at teachers and the culture of the school to fathom why this treasure trove remains substantially unused.

WHY DON'T TEACHERS TALK ABOUT TEACHING?

I am a teacher and for 17 years I have encountered colleagues in teachers' rooms, planning sessions, team meetings, faculty meetings, committees, and various social occasions, and done so in many different districts in three states. In recent years, as a consultant, I've been to over 50 schools, K–12, not just peeking in the door but hanging around long enough to know it's very unusual to hear teachers talk about teaching. And I'm beginning to understand why.

It's not that teachers aren't serious about what they do; they are—intensely so. It's not that they don't talk about students; they do—all the time. It's not that they don't struggle to be professional; they do—to the point of frequent burn-out. It's that they usually face their most serious problems alone, and when they do talk to each other about professional matters, it is usually about one of the following: scheduling; ordering; personnel policies; materials; union matters; placement; school organization; parents; kids; testing and record keeping; curriculum. To be sure, these are not trivial matters, but they are not about teaching. I arranged them in order as they approach teaching. Talk about teaching might sound like this:

". . . and that 12th-grade group really seems to respond to enlisting[8] and alerting[9] moves if you stick with them long enough; they need a lot of energy from you. . . ."

"Any of you using jurisprudential or group investigation designs for your units this month? Well, really I was wondering which one, if either, you thought might be appropriate for the Civil War material with the juniors?"

"What about cooperation? . . . Any of you been able to do anything with them in cooperative committees yet?"

"Hey, I need an idea. Whenever I turn to the board they inch up that front lab table a nudge. They're playing a game with me, pushing me just so far and then backing off. It's really very annoying."

This talk has certain distinctive characteristics, characteristics that set it apart from the above list that starts with "scheduling." First, it is about interactive teaching. Second, it both solicits ideas from others about nuts-and-bolts teaching issues and gives ideas. Third, it uses certain terms that come from an assumed shared technical vocabulary of the field ("enlisting," "alerting," "jurisprudential," "group investigation"). The teacher-talk one hears in lounges and offices is conspicuously lacking in all three, and the same goes for more formal settings.

It's not like that in other fields. Businessmen talk about management skills all the time. Doctors, athletes, electricians—many, many fields are full of informal talk and professional activities that focus on the skills of their practice. A skills approach looks at what one says and does when face to face with a difficult patient, a zone defense, a new house to wire. Skills are things that professionals have and practice and adapt. They come from behavioral repertoires from which practitioners choose, depending on the demands of the moment. Problems are solved by team efforts or input from colleagues and consultants. Practitioners have a common background in certain standard action techniques—the diagnostic sequence of a neurological exam, the football team's playbook, the trained dexterity of the electrician with needle-nosed pliers. Teachers don't have this in common—or at least they act as if they don't. The reasons I offer below may both explain the situation and suggest things to do about it.

Structural Isolation

Some of the blocks to professional teacher-talk are structural. Teachers work in separate rooms, separate spaces, with separate groups of students. They do not know what other teachers are doing. Once every two years, maybe, a teacher visits another school and says, "I wish I did that more often." Time schedules keep teachers apart except for some lunch periods and faculty meetings where agendas of current business supersede any possible talk about teaching. The few brief minutes shared in teachers' rooms during the day, grabbed as islands of respite, focus on socialization, as they probably need to. So, structurally, neither separate class time with students nor shared breaks during the day bring teachers together in ways that support talk about teaching.

Is this structural isolation replicated in other fields? Doctors pass each other in hospital corridors daily and consult about patients. They attend grand rounds weekly and hear colleagues present cases, share new techniques, and discuss alternative solutions. Clearly that's not a sometime thing for doctors, not an option, not a one-shot course or workshop. It's an ongoing part of the culture of being a doctor. Research scientists, lawyers, athletes, numerous other fields have organizational structures and mutual expectations that bring them together around the nuts and bolts of their daily practice. But not teachers. Besides these structural reasons, teachers seem to have learned some attitudes of their own that are blocks to professional development.

Protecting Autonomy

Increasing pressure from the public and from administrators in recent years has put teachers under close scrutiny. There is much heard about accountability. It shows up in more and more required curricula, making teachers feel less trusted and less free to pursue the kind of individual or idiosyncratic curricula that they thought were traditionally their right. This is an assault on the one remaining zone of autonomy for teachers—what they do behind closed doors in classrooms with students. They already feel relatively powerless within the school; they are, in fact, usually quite removed from decisions that affect what happens at school and district level. This real "we"-"they" attitude about decisions from above adds to these feelings of pressure and powerlessness and makes teachers even more defensive, more protective of their remaining autonomy in the classroom. That's not the sort of atmosphere that makes teachers want to invite people into their rooms and talk openly about what they do, even with each other.

Timidity about Self-Revelation

Everybody feels qualified to give an opinion about who is a good teacher and who isn't (as they do incidently, about who is a good parent and who isn't). Why is that? Perhaps it's because everybody has experienced teaching and parenting on the receiving end. The result is that teachers are always being judged, often behind their backs. That's a pretty sticky professional climate, and it contaminates teachers' relations with each other. This climate suggests that, as teachers, the kindest thing we could do for each other is say nothing, leave the other guy's teaching alone, it's his! That translates into teachers not talking with each other about teaching lest they *seem* to be judgmental.

Another contributing factor is the seemingly nontechnical nature of teaching. When you sit in the lunch room at Kennecott Copper Company, as I did for a week in between workshops I was giving there for managers, you're likely to hear one metallurgist say to another, "What the hell have I missed? Why are these stress lines crossing like this?" They find it easy to talk to each other about their difficulties and their successes. Perhaps the "scientific" nature of their field allows them to reveal things they're doing without feeling they're risking their inner selves. To talk about one's teaching is far harder. There are two attitudes one can see at work here, and sometimes they appear simultaneously within the same person. On the one hand there's the belief that good teachers are born, not made; it's intuition (attitude 1). On the other is the belief that you've seen it all before and you already know everything that's important to know about teaching (attitude 2).

If good teachers are born, then to confess problems to colleagues is to risk being thought inferior. If a metallurgist has a problem, it's a technical matter to be worked out. Skills and knowledge are brought to bear. If a teacher has a problem there's something wrong with him; he's not good enough. Baloney? Of course its baloney! But as an attitude, an insidious and debilitating attitude, it's as real as rulers and chalk in the profession.

Regarding attitude 2, if one already knows all there is to know about teaching, then slow student progress is the students' fault; one can blame them and avoid self-examination. There's no need to talk about adjusting instruction.

More often, though, teachers tend to take their problems personally, to blame themselves and feel inadequate. They don't have a job culture that treats these as professional problems, and they rarely have anyone to go to for help. They're like some parents with problem children who feel guilty and pretend everything is fine. Both parents and teachers are accused of blaming the kid when things aren't going well, academically or behaviorally. And that happens often enough for us to self-examine about it from time to time. But you don't hear the critics of teaching recognizing how often teachers blame themselves and what psychic and professional costs accrue from the resulting timidity and loneliness teachers impose on themselves.

These obstacles to teacher-talk about teaching are very deep-rooted in the climate and structure of schools themselves, and need, I feel, direct confrontation by those involved with staff development and school administration. But they also need to be addressed by teachers themselves. The culture of the profession is passive with regard to teacher growth as a competent professional. As Joyce says, we need a new attitude that allows "everyone [to be] a student of teaching" (Joyce & Weil, 1980). The position I'm taking is that teachers need an aggressive stance toward research and toward their own professional development, an attitude that lets them reach out to the research, to cull it, to feel free to throw away the junk, the shoddy, the irrelevant, to expect to do so with much of it, but to know that the nuggets they find can improve their teaching and are worth searching for. That attitude would enable teachers to see themselves more as members of a profession which, like other professions, has advancing frontiers of knowledge, hard questions, and orderly and rigorous ways of working on those questions. What conditions might make this stance possible?

TEACHERS AS RESEARCHERS: A NEW SELF-IMAGE

There is much that can be said about the promise and possibilities of teachers as researchers of their own teaching. First, I think we have learned that the collaboration of researchers and teachers on classroom issues is quite productive (Tikunoff & Ward, 1980). The teachers keep the researchers anchored to earth and the researchers bring methodology and analytical capability to sort data and clarify relationships. These collaborations have produced practical results in identifying problems and indicating solutions. Elsewhere in this volume there are good examples of this productivity (Chapter 11, by Claryce Evans and Chapter 13, by Richard C. Carter).

Second, I think we have learned that many teachers have tacit knowledge about aspects of their practice, especially classroom-management behaviors. In one of my studies (Saphier, 1980), I found that in comparing interviews with observations, teachers "knew" far more than they could say about how to gain and maintain student attention and anticipate blocks to momentum. They used moves and techniques that they could not describe in interviews, but that were part of their repertoires when observed. When their attention was drawn to these moves in videotapes, their reaction was, "Oh, I *do* do that." The study of their own teaching with a researcher brought to consciousness things they already did but for which they had no label.

Third, in my study, profiling teachers' behaviors in terms of the areas of teaching listed earlier in this chapter did another thing: it showed them a lot of things they were *not* doing. They were able to compare their behavior with the universe of options for that area of teaching (whether it be ways to maintain momentum or use different models of teaching) and to use that data to make decisions about whether to expand their range. This kind of activity with researchers induced teachers to be more self-analytical and reflective about their practice in a supportive environment. Their universal reaction was that they had (1) learned something about what they already do—acquired some new language and concepts for describing their practice; and (2) had a look at some interesting options for broadening their repertoires.

Fourth, the range of options for teacher behavior on each parameter or area of teaching was constructed with input from the research literature and from the teachers themselves. In my study I brought the categories to the teachers, but they filled out the range of options by what they said (interviews) and what they did (observations). Thus they were vital partners in building the knowledge base.

In sum, what has been demonstrated by this line of work is that teachers themselves are a resource for the knowledge base on teaching, that they can be systematic and reflective about their practice, and that they can use this reflection to choose to expand their repertoires in productive directions. But what is equally apparent to me is that simply urging teachers to take the bull by the horns and *be* that way is not enough. The culture and the climate of the school must support that attitude, that definition of professionalism. In the end, the inquisitive, open attitude of teachers toward one another and toward educational research that I am advocating can only come through sound professional development programs. We cannot expect teachers to seize themselves by the neck and shake themselves out of a debilitating culture alone, individually, and without change from the very institutions that have fostered the culture to begin with.

By the same token we must see more sophisticated research that recognizes the complexity of successful teaching—recognizes it by studying multiple variables *in context*, and at various levels of abstraction simultaneously. We're not going to get anywhere anymore with correlation studies of isolated teacher behaviors and student outcomes. They served their purpose but the purpose is past. Researchers need the collaboration of teachers to steer clear of the trivial and increase the savvy and sophistication of their questions. Researchers, incorrectly stereotyped as convoluted and esoteric in their thinking, need teachers to *complicate their thinking appropriately* and to inform their question asking. It is around forming these questions and around sorting through the existing knowledge base that teachers and researchers must come together.

NOTES

1. I wish to acknowledge the collaboration of Robert Gower, many of whose ideas appear in this section and in Saphier & Gower, 1980.

2. This list was modified from Dunkin & Biddle, 1974.

3. Something a teacher says or does, taking a second or less, often both a solicitation (question) and a response.

4. A multispeaker unit consisting of one or more exchanges that comprise a completed verbal transaction between two or more speakers.

5. More than one episode about a single topic having a single content objective.

6. These categories were derived by the author from a survey of the literature on the study of teaching and from several observational studies carried out in 1976, 1977, and 1979. Explanations and specifics are described in Saphier & Gower, 1980.

7. "Improving Instruction," Address to Association for Supervision and Curriculum Development, Houston, 1977.
8. Enlisting: "moves that tend to captivate students in the interest or excitement of the activity, e.g., suspense, challenge, novel prop" (Saphier & Gower, 1980).
9. Alerting: "moves that keep students on their toes," e.g., startling, incomplete sentences, circulation (Saphier & Gower, 1980).

REFERENCES

Ausubel, D. P. *The psychology of meaningful verbal learning.* New York: Grune & Stratton, 1963.

Bellack, A. A., Kliebard, H. M., Hyman, R. T., & Smith, F. L., Jr. *The language of the classroom.* New York: Columbia University Press, 1966.

Berliner, D. C. Impediments to measuring teacher effectiveness. In Borich, G. (Ed.), *The appraisal of teaching.* Reading, Mass.: Addison-Wesley, 1977.

Blanchard, K. H. & Hersey P. *Management of organizational behavior.* Englewood Cliffs, N.J.: Prentice-Hall, 1977.

Brophy, J. E. & Evertson, C. M. *Learning from teaching.* Boston: Allyn & Bacon, 1976.

Brophy, J. E. & Good, T. L. *Teacher-student relationships: Causes and consequences.* New York: Holt, Rinehart & Winston, 1974.

Bruner, J., Goodnow, J. J., & Austin, G. A. *A study of thinking.* New York: Science Editions, Inc., 1957.

Bugelski, B. R. *The psychology of learning applied to teaching.* Indianapolis: Bobbs-Merrill, 1971.

Clifford, G. J. A history of the impact of research on teaching. In Travers, R. M. W. (Ed.), *2nd handbook of research on teaching.* Chicago: Rand McNally, 1973.

Coker, H., Medley, D., & Soar, R. How valid are expert opinions about effective teaching? *Phi Delta Kappan,* 1980, **62,** 131–134.

Dunkin, M. J. & Biddle, B. J. *The study of thinking.* New York: Holt, Rinehart & Winston, 1974.

Ebbinghaus, H. *Memory: A contribution to experimental psychology.* New York: Dover Publications, 1964.

Gordon, W. J. *Synectics.* New York: Harper & Row, 1961.

Gower, R. R. *Developing criterion measures for assessing model-relevant teaching competency.* Unpublished doctoral dissertation, Teachers College, Columbia University, 1974.

Hiller, J. H., Fisher, G. A., & Kaess, W. A. A computer investigation of verbal characteristics of effective classroom lecturing. *American Educational Research Journal,* 1969, **6,** 661–675.

Hunt, D. E. *Matching models in education.* Ontario: Ontario Institute for Studies in Education, Monograph No. 10, 1971.

Hunt, D. E. & Sullivan, E. V. *Between psychology and education.* Hinsdale, Ill.: The Dryden Press, 1974.

Hunter, M. *Improving the quality of instruction.* Audio tape. Alexandria, Va.: Association for Supervision and Curriculum Development, 1977.

Hunter, M. *Teach for transfer.* El Segundo, Calif.: T.I.P. Publications, 1971.

Hunter, M. *Teach more—faster.* El Segundo, Calif.: T.I.P. Publications, 1969.

Hunter, M. *Motivation.* El Segundo, Calif.: T.I.P. Publications, 1967.

Hunter, M. *Reinforcement.* El Segundo, Calif.: T.I.P. Publications, 1967.

Hunter, M. *Retention.* El Segundo, Calif.: T.I.P. Publications, 1967.

Johnson, D. W. Student-student interaction: The neglected variable in education. *Educational Researcher,* 1981, **10,** 5–10.

Johnson, D. W., Maruyama, G., Johnson, R., Nelson, D., & Skon, L. The effects of cooperative, competitive and individualistic goal structures on achievement: A meta-analysis. *Psychological Bulletin,* 1981, **89,** 47–62.

Joyce, B. & Weil, M. *Models of teaching.* (2nd ed.) Englewood Cliffs, N.J.: Prentice-Hall, 1980.

Joyce, B. & Weil, M. *Information processing models of teaching, social models of teaching, personal models of teaching.* Englewood Cliffs., N.J.: Prentice-Hall, 1978.

Joyce, B. & Weil, M. *Models of teaching.* Englewood Cliffs, N.J.: Prentice-Hall, 1972.

Kounin, J. *Discipline and classroom management.* New York: Holt, Rinehart & Winston, 1970.

Lawton, J. The use of advance organizers in the learning and retention of logical operations in social studies concepts. *American Education Research Journal,* 1977, **14,** 25–43.

McDonald, F. J., Elias, P., Stone, M., Wheeler, R., Lambert, N., Calfee, R., Sandoval, J., Ekstrom, R., & Lockheed, M. *Final report on phase II beginning teacher evaluation study.* Prepared for the California Commission on Teacher Preparation and Licensing. Princeton, N.J.: Educational Testing Service, 1975.

McKibbin, M. *The application of three interaction analysis systems to investigate models of teaching.* Unpublished doctoral dissertation, Columbia University, 1974.

Mosston, M. *The spectrum of teaching.* Unpublished manuscript. Trenton, N.J.: Center on Teaching, 1976.

Nuthall, G. & Snook, I. Contemporary models of teaching. In Travers, R. M. W. (Ed.). *2nd handbook of research on teaching.* Chicago: Rand McNally, 1973.

O'Donnell, K. *Natural teaching styles and models of teaching: The production of unusual classroom teaching behavior.* Unpublished doctoral dissertation, Columbia University, 1974.

Oliver, D. & Shaver, J. P. *Teaching public issues in high school.* Boston: Houghton Mifflin, 1966.

Peterson, P. L. & Clark, C. M. Teachers' reports of their cognitive processes during teaching. *American Education Research Journal,* 1978, **15,** 555–566.

Peterson, P. L., Marx, C. W., & Clark, R. M. Teacher planning, teacher behavior and student achievement. *American Education Research Journal,* 1978, **15,** 417–432.

Pierson, C. Can you keep quiet for 3 seconds? *Learning Magazine,* February 1980, 40–43.

Rosenshine, B. & Furst, N. The use of direct observation to study teaching. In Travers, R. M. W. (Ed.), *2nd handbook of research on teaching.* Chicago: Rand McNally, 1973.

Rowe, M. B. *Wait-time and rewards as instructional variables: Their influence on language, logic and fate control.* Paper presented at the National Association for Research on Teaching, Chicago, 1972.

Rude, E. *The analysis of the intersection patterns characteristic of phases of models of teaching.* Unpublished doctoral dissertation, Columbia University, 1973.

Ryans, D. G. *Characteristics of teachers: Their description, comparison, and appraisal.* Washington, D.C.: American Council on Education, 1960.

Saphier, J. D. *The parameters of teaching: An empirical study using observations and interviews to validate a theory of teaching by linking levels of analysis, levels of knowing, and levels of performance.* Unpublished doctoral dissertation, Boston University, 1980.

Saphier, J. D. & Gower, R. *The skillful teacher.* Newton, Mass.: Research for Better Teaching, 1980.

Scriven, M. The evaluation of teachers and teaching. In Borich, G. (Ed.), *The appraisal of teaching.* Reading, Mass.: Addison-Wesley, 1977.

Sharan, S. Cooperative learning in small groups: Recent methods and effects on achievement, attitudes, and ethnic relations. *Review of Education Research,* 1980, **50,** 241–272.

Sharan, S., Hare, P., Webb, C. D., & Hertz-Lazarowitz, R. (Eds.), *Cooperation in education.* Provo: Brigham Young University Press, 1980.

Shultz, J. & Florio, S. *Stop and freeze: The negotiation of social and physical space in a kindergarten/first grade classroom.* Occasional Paper #26. East Lansing, Mich.: Institute for Research in Teaching, 1979.

Slavin, R. E. Cooperative learning. *Review of Educational Research,* 1980, **50,** 315–342.

Smith, B. O. & Meux, M. O. *A study of the logic of teaching.* Urbana: University of Illinois Press, 1962.

Smith, B.O., Meux, M. O., Coombs, J., Nuthall, G. A., & Precians, R. *A study of the strategies of teaching.* Urbana: University of Illinois Press, 1967.

Soar, R. S. Teacher assessment problems and possibilities. *Journal of Teacher Education,* 1973, **24,** 205–212.

Soar, R. S. An integration of findings from four studies of teacher effectiveness: Teacher assessment problems and possibilities. In Borich, G. (Ed.), *The appraisal of teaching.* Reading, Mass.: Addison-Wesley, 1977.

Stolurow, L. M. Model the master teacher or master the teaching model. In Krumbholtz, R. (Ed.), *Learning and educational process.* Chicago: Rand McNally, 1965.

Taba, H. *Teacher's handbook for elementary social studies.* Reading, Mass.: Addison-Wesley, 1967.

Tikunoff, W. J. & Ward, B. A. *The IR and DT Experience.* Paper presented at the American Educational Research Association Annual Meeting, Boston, April 1980.

Wald, R. *The effects of models of teaching as a program for the training of teachers.* Unpublished doctoral dissertation, Columbia University, 1972.

Weil, M. Deriving teaching skills from models of teaching. In Houston, R. (Ed.), *Assessment in competency-based teacher education.* San Francisco: Jossey-Bass, 1974.

Chapter 8

Methodology: Considerations for Classroom Research

Teresa M. Amabile

Much of the disagreement between academic researchers and practicing educators in their views of classroom research, and much of the difficulty associated with conducting such research, can be traced to methodological issues. Several excellent treatments of educational-psychological research have been published in recent years (see the annotated bibliography included at the end of this chapter). These volumes, however, tend exclusively to address either audiences who have no acquaintance whatsoever with research methodology, or audiences who have already achieved some level of sophistication in considering experimental design and statistical analysis. In this chapter, I will address both groups with the aim of achieving three goals: first, to acquaint teachers with some of the fundamental methodological considerations of formal research; second, in so doing, to provide researchers with a guide they might follow in discussing methodology with teachers; and third, to outline some special features of classroom research that even rather experienced academic researchers might not take adequate account of. Throughout, I will review some of the most commonly employed designs for classroom research, noting their appropriate provinces of application.

FUNDAMENTAL CONSIDERATIONS: A BRIEF GUIDE FOR TEACHERS

At several points in the present volume, and in many other publications on classroom research, it is clear that even educators who have given a great deal of careful thought to questions of research sometimes seem unsure of a number of research issues, including: the nature of research designs and statistical inference; the relative importance of questions of validity; the sources of threats to validity in classroom research; the role of control groups and random assignment in research methodology; and the relative merits of longitudinal and cross-sectional designs. These fundamental principles of research methodology are "second nature" to properly trained researchers. Often, however, educators may remain unaware of these principles, or misunderstand them, or understand but reject them. If teachers and school administrators do wish to become full collaborators in the research endeavor, they must become familiar with important methodological issues. The burden cannot be placed solely on educators, however; it should be the responsibility of researchers who wish to work within classroom settings to discuss these considerations of design and methodology with teachers.

The Nature of Research Designs and Statistical Inference

A Continuum of Designs. Psychological researchers and laypersons alike tend to use the word "experiment" rather loosely in common discourse. Formally, however, a "true experiment" is quite narrowly defined; it is a study in which the experimenter systematically manipulates conditions and randomly assigns subjects to those conditions. Since it is often impossible to conduct a true experiment, there are a variety of research designs from which to choose. These designs can be categorized according to a rough continuum of experimental rigor—the degree to which the experimenter controls treatment conditions and subjects' assignments to those conditions (see Isaac, 1971, p. 14)—from least to most rigorous: *case studies*, exemplified by many current teachers' seminar groups, used to study intensively the background, current status, and change over time of individual units such as persons, classes, schools, or communities; *action research*, exemplified by many staff-development programs, designed to develop new skills or approaches to solving problems for direct application in the classroom; *correlational research*, an observational technique often used in educational assessment, designed to investigate how closely one behavior or attribute is correlated with another; *quasi–experimental research*, often the best research on causality that can be done in an educational setting, encompassing a wide range of designs in which the experimenter has less than complete control over treatment conditions and subject assignments; and true *experimental research*, in which causal relationships are investigated by randomly assigning subjects to carefully controlled treatment conditions.

Most simply, an experiment can be considered to be a systematic attempt to account for the variability in a group of scores. Scores on the dependent variable—the behavior or characteristic of interest—are different from one another; they vary from one another. This *variance* comes from three sources: (1) systematic variance caused by the independent variable (the variable the investigator is manipulating); (2) systematic variance caused by other, extraneous sources; and (3) random or error variance coming from any of a large number of known and unknown sources. The purpose of experimental design is to *control the variance*: to maximize the systematic variance caused by the independent variable, by making its manipulation as strong as possible; to control extraneous sources of systematic variance by ensuring that nothing but the independent variable varies systematically between conditions; and to minimize error variance by controlling, as much as possible, the circumstances under which the experiment is conducted (Kerlinger, 1973).

In the most straightforward case, the experimenter begins with a *motivated hypothesis* that two groups will, if placed under different conditions, behave differently on some crucial measure. The opposing hypothesis, which is always at least implicitly a part of the experimental plan, is the *null hypothesis*—that the two groups will not differ, that the independent variable will have no effect. It is important to note, however, that the hypotheses cannot, strictly speaking, ever be proven. That is, if the dependent variable measures fail to show a reliable difference between the groups tested, we cannot take this as proof of the null hypothesis. We cannot assume that the groups were the same for the same reason, since groups may show the same behavior for different reasons. (For example, one group of children might work quietly because of a deep interest in the work, but another might work quietly because of a fear of punishment). Likewise, we cannot take the lack of significant differences between groups in any one experiment as proof that the treatment is ineffectual. There may have been any number of flaws in the procedure that masked any potential effects. If, however, we know that the experiment was conducted correctly, and there *are* statistically significant differences on the dependent variable, we can safely conclude that the treatment did cause that difference. But we can never be absolutely sure.

Statistical Significance. Two important points, often misunderstood by educators and other "consumers" of classroom research, are the meaning of statistical significance and the probabilistic nature of results. A statistical test pits the systematic variance—the average difference between groups in an experiment—against the unsystematic error variance. A "statistically significant" result at, say, the "$p < .05$ level" means that there is less than a 5 percent chance that the observed difference between groups was just caused by chance (by random variation) rather than by the independent variable. The most reasonable thing to conclude is that the independent variable caused the observed effect; it is never, however, a certainty, even with the very high levels of statistical significance of $p < .01$ or $p < .001$.

In Defense of Experimentation. It is a prevalent view among educators that carefully and thoughtfully documented case studies are far superior to experimental methods for answering questions about classroom behavior, child development, and pedagogical practice. There are a number of possible reasons for this disenchantment with experimentation, including: a sense that the independent variables manipulated and the dependent variables assessed in experiments are too far removed from the events and behaviors that teachers believe to be most important in the classroom; a belief that the phenomena that need to be studied in classrooms are much too complex to be tackled experimentally; a doubt that the results of particular experiments are ever widely generalizable; and a disappointment with the equivocal results produced by most experiments and the necessarily tentative conclusions that can be drawn about classroom practices.

Other observational methods besides the case study, such as straightforward correlational studies—in which one naturally occurring behavior or attribute is correlated with another—are also commonly preferred over experiments by educators. One primary reason for this preference seems to be the "natural" quality of these observations, and the absence of any manipulation of factors such as teaching techniques, physical environments, student groupings, and so on. To be sure, as is discussed below, there are potential problems with the manipulation of variables. Nonetheless, the preference for observation over experimentation suggests an incomplete appreciation of the important differences between *correlation* and *causation*, between the research functions of *description* and *inference*. Only in an experiment, where the experimenter systematically varies the independent variable, can we confidently infer that differences measured in the dependent variable were *caused* by differences in that independent variable—and, even then, only if certain operating procedures are followed.

If a teacher randomly assigned half of the children in a large class to spend two hours per week in a special "discovery room" where they could individually perform simple science experiments, and the other half to read for two hours per week about the same science topics, any superiority of the first group in science achievement at the end of the year could reliably be attributed to effects of the "discovery room" (assuming that the two groups' experiences were the same in all other respects).

On the other hand, if the teacher simply kept track of the amount of time each student in the class spent in the "discovery room" throughout the year, and then found a positive and significant correlation between time in the room and science achievement at the end of the year, he would have no basis for assuming that use of the "discovery room" led to improved science achievement. The direction of causality might be just the opposite—doing well in science might lead students to want to use the "discovery room." Or it might be that both behaviors were caused by some third factor, such as the students' general intelligence.

Nonetheless, correlational studies can serve a useful descriptive function. The discovery of a significant correlation tells us that two variables *are* related, and allows us to predict a person's standing on one of those variables if we know his or her standing on the other. Moreover, there are ways in which sophisticated correlational analyses can point toward causation— but not with the level of certainty attainable with experimentation. And, while good case studies are superior to most experiments in their ability to capture teachers' intuitions and provide insights on day-to-day classroom experiences, they are infinitely worse than experiments in their inability to sort out complex phenomena meaningfully, their lack of generalizable results, and the equivocal nature of their findings. Indeed, Campbell and Stanley (1963) have defended the experiment

> as the only means for settling disputes regarding educational practice, as the only way of verifying educational improvements, and as the only way of establishing a cumulative tradition in which improvements can be introduced without the danger of a faddish discard of old wisdom in favor of inferior novelties. [p. 2]

Even given the limitations of nonexperimental and quasi-experimental methods, however, there clearly are circumstances in which they may appropriately be applied. If it is impossible in a particular situation to do an experiment, it is undoubtedly better to use whatever quasi-experimental or nonexperimental design might be feasible than to let an interesting and important phenomenon slip by unstudied. The point is that the entire range should be considered, and the most powerful design that is appropriate to the particular situation should be applied. In this view, the advancement of knowledge in education is seen as an extremely slow process in which there is a gradual accumulation of understanding based on the collection of individually tentative conclusions drawn from a variety of methods.

Validity

A complaint that educators commonly voice about classroom research is that the results of specific experiments cannot be generalized to other classrooms, other groups of children, other teachers or experimenters. They are saying, in essence, that these experiments lack *external validity*. It is much less common, however, for educators to express concern about *internal validity*: the degree to which the differences obtained in an experiment can be considered as caused by the independent variable. Nonetheless, although the external validity question is extremely important in classroom research and teachers' concern with external validity is completely justified, internal validity is even more important; if we do not know what caused the differences we observe, there is no point in wondering if the results we obtained—whatever they may mean—are generalizable. Internal validity is a prerequisite for external validity.

Several methodologists (e.g., Campbell & Stanley, 1963) have provided detailed lists of factors that threaten internal and external validity in experimental and quasi-experimental studies. Some threats to internal validity that are most common in classroom research involving pre- and post–tests are: (1) *experience* (also called *history*), specific, extraneous events that may occur between the first and second measurement; (2) *development* (also called *maturation*), processes that occur over time (such as cognitive development or the onset of boredom) and are separate from the independent variable; (3) *testing familiarity*, the effects of having taken the first test on performance on the second test; and (4) *instrumentation* changes—for example, changes in the observers or scorers used.

In all experimental designs, internal validity becomes questionable when there are (5) *differential mortality rates*, or drop-out rates, of subjects in different conditions of the experiment. For example, experimental treatment #1 might be much more stressful than treatment #2. If many more subjects dropped out of #1 than out of #2 before the experiment ended, those who did stay in treatment #1 would probably be very different people from the subjects in treatment #2; they might, for instance, be more tolerant individuals. Thus, the goal of equating the two groups in all ways would have been undermined.

In addition, errors in sampling may result in (6) *statistical regression* effects, where subjects who were chosen for their extreme scores on some premeasure would have naturally been expected to become less extreme on the postmeasure, even without any experimental treatment. For example, children might be administered some school readiness test as preschoolers. Scores on the test are not perfectly reliable; a child scoring 56 one time might just as easily score 53 or 62 another time, without any real change in his ability. Thus, if children scoring at the extreme lowest end of the scale on this test (say, the lowest 5 percent) are chosen for a study and then, as a group, they score somewhat above the lowest 5 percent on the test after the study, that change could well be due solely to "regression toward the mean"; they couldn't possibly go any lower, and random variability in testing would cause their average score to move somewhat closer to the population average. Their scores would probably have improved even if they hadn't been in a study.

Finally, one of the most widespread and serious threats to internal validity can arise through a variety of (7) *selection errors*. These errors can enter into the sampling of subjects for the various groups of an experiment. If the selection process is not truly random, there may be important initial differences between the different groups, even before treatments are ever implemented.

External validity, although its distinction from internal validity is not always clear, can be seen as most commonly threatened by (1) the *reactive or interaction effect of testing*, whereby people in the "real world," who hadn't had the experience afforded by a pretest, would react to the posttest differently from people who received the pretest as part of the experimental procedure; and by (2) the *reactive effects of experimental treatments*, whereby any of several features of taking part in an experiment may cause subjects to respond differently to an independent variable from people who had been exposed to that variable in the "real world."

Many of the threats to validity can be traced to either the person doing the study (*experimenter bias*) or to the persons being studied (*subject bias*). Obviously, *characteristics of the experimenter*, such as physical appearance, age, sex, warmth, and so on, may influence subjects' responses. Worse yet, they may interact with the experimental treatments. For example, children might respond very positively to a young experimenter under one set of conditions, but very negatively under different conditions. Beyond such relatively uncontrollable features, however (which can only be accounted for by using more than one experimenter), there are a number of more subtle experimenter factors that might bias the results of an experiment: *rating errors*, by which an experimenter tends to rate everyone favorably, or everyone unfavorably, or everyone toward the middle of the scale; the *halo effect*, whereby raters tend to be overly influenced by one very positive or negative characteristic in their ratings of other unrelated characteristics of that person; and *self-fulfilling prophecy*, whereby an experimenter consciously or unconsciously behaves in ways that lead subjects to confirm the experimenter's expectations. These sources of experimenter bias can be reduced by using experienced raters who do not know the subjects and who are, as much as possible, blind to subjects' experimental conditions. In addition, again, it is helpful to use multiple experimenters.

Factors contributing to subject bias are perhaps even more subtle than those leading to experimenter bias. Most important among these are: the *guinea pig effect*, whereby the subject, aware of being tested, behaves in an artificial manner; the *Hawthorne effect*, whereby virtually any changes in subjects' environments can improve their performance (perhaps because the changes introduce novelty), regardless of the specific nature of those changes; and *role playing*, whereby the subject attempts to adopt the role of the "good subject" and produces whatever responses he or she believes the experimenter wants. The primary technique for eliminating or reducing each of these sources of bias involves keeping subjects unaware that they are in an experiment or, at least, unaware of the experimenter's hypotheses and dependent variables of interest. Clearly, such unobtrusive and actively or passively deceptive methods raise ethical questions about subjects' informed consent and rights to privacy. This is an important issue, and researchers must consider ways of striking a balance between unethical procedures that can lead to completely unequivocal results, at one extreme, and ethically unquestionable but scientifically useless procedures at the other extreme.

In all studies, of course, including nonexperimental, quasi–experimental, and experimental, the results become more meaningful as the dependent measures become more clearly specified and the observational settings become more carefully controlled. The better able a researcher is to convert a global conceptual variable, such as a child's anxiety level, into concrete, easily measured behaviors such as number of nail bitings or hair manipulations, the more likely it is that other researchers will be able to replicate his or her findings and that those findings will be generalizable to other settings. It is perhaps at this level that researchers are most in need of advice and ideas from teachers. There is no foolproof method for operationalizing a conceptual variable, and few people would have better notions than teachers about how to assess something presumed to be present in the classroom, such as a child's anxiety or comprehension of a mathematical theorem. Moreover, teachers can assist researchers in developing measures that have *face validity*, measures that seem intuitively to capture the underlying concept; face validity of measures can be important in determining educators' response to and utilization of research findings.

Perhaps the most powerful guarantee of both internal and external validity is the use of random assignment. External validity can be bolstered by randomly choosing subjects for the experiment from the entire population to which the researcher wishes to generalize (for example, all schools or teachers in a district). Internal validity can be enhanced by randomly assigning members of that subject pool to experimental and control conditions in the experiment.

Random Assignment and Control Groups

When told of a particularly startling research result, students and others unfamiliar with research methodology often object by saying, "But what if the subjects in Group 1 were *initially* smarter [or kinder, or more aggressive], and that's why they scored higher on the post–test [or were more willing to help people, or were more aggressive]?" This objection to experimental research findings is a cogent one *if* subjects had not been assigned to conditions of the experiment on a truly random basis. The objection loses force, however, if subjects were randomly assigned—as they always should be, whenever possible. Surely, there are initially large individual differences between subjects, some of which could importantly influence performance on the dependent variable. By randomly assigning subjects to conditions, however, the experimenter can be pretty certain that these differences will cancel out—that, for example, there will be just about as many very smart people in condition 1 as in condition 2. Certainly, there is a chance that such factors will not be equalized initially. It is, however, a small chance, and the level of statistical significance (e.g., $p < .05$) tells us just how small that chance is.

This discussion of assignment of subjects to conditions assumes, of course, that there *are* different conditions in an experiment. One essential principle of experimental design is that of *control* over extraneous sources of variability, control that can be gained, in large measure, by the use of random assignment. The other basic principle is that of *comparison*. No matter how carefully devised and collected the dependent measures in a study are, no matter how unbiased the subjects and experimenter, the results are meaningless unless there is some basis for comparison, unless there is some way of knowing how the subjects would have behaved if they had not been exposed to the independent variable. This is the function of *control groups*. In the simplest case, subjects are randomly assigned to a control group or an experimental group, and only the experimental group receives the independent-variable manipulation.

Designs that lack proper control groups are quite common in classroom research. The first three of these designs must be considered nonexperimental or "preexperimental" at best, because they are incapable of providing clear information about causality: the *one-shot case study*, the *one-group pretest-posttest design*, and the *static-group comparison* (Campbell & Stanley, 1963). In the one-shot case study, a single group is observed during and/or after the introduction of some independent variable, and the seeming effects of that independent variable on some dependent variable are recorded. The observations, of course, tell us nothing about a possible causal relationship between independent and dependent variable, because we have no way of knowing whether the subjects would have behaved this way even if the independent variable had never been introduced; indeed, they might have behaved this way even before the variable was introduced. In other words, such a study has no internal validity.

The one-group pretest-posttest design seems to get at this before-after comparison, and it is quite common in educational research. It too, however, is of extremely limited use because of questionable internal validity. If we give a group of children some pretest, introduce an independent variable, and then find a change on the posttest, we cannot know if we should attribute the change to the independent variable or to any of a thousand other variables that might have changed over that same time period. Thus, although it is somewhat better than the one-shot case study, this design is not really desirable.

In the static-group comparison design, two different groups are chosen, one is exposed to the independent variable, and then both are tested. For example, Mr. Williams's Grade 4 might serve as the control while Ms. Harper's Grade 4 is given a brief course to improve reading comprehension. If, however, a difference is found between the groups on the posttest, we do not know if we should attribute it to the independent variable (the reading course), to initial differences that might have existed between the two grades, or to any other factors that might have differentiated the two classes during the testing period.

The ideal "true" experiment to test this reading course would have involved randomly selecting children for the study from the entire population of interest (all fourth-graders in the USA?), and then randomly assigning members of that sample to experimental and control conditions. Clearly, however, this is not possible in most school settings and, strictly speaking, it is not even possible in most laboratory settings—although there we might come closer. Nonetheless, there are a number of quasiexperimental designs that can be used in schools as next-best approximations to true experiments, and can enable the researchers to make some tentative statements about causality.

For example, in the *time-series design*, the same group is observed on a large number of different occasions over time. On one of those occasions, the independent variable is introduced, and use of appropriate statistical techniques can allow the researcher to make inferences about the effect of that independent variable. Or, better yet, in the *equivalent time-samples design*, over a period of several observations the independent variable is introduced and withdrawn *several* times. (These two designs, of course, can only be used if the effects of the treatment are expected to be relatively temporary.)

Another useful quasi–experimental design is the *nonequivalent control group design*. Similar to the static-group comparison in that a second nonrandomly chosen group is used as a control, this design represents an improvement in that *both* groups receive both a pretest and a posttest. Finally, the *multiple time-series design* combines elements of several of the others. *Two* groups (nonrandomly assigned) are followed through several observations over time; during that sequence, the independent variable is introduced and withdrawn several times.

As noted earlier, subjects should, if possible, be assigned to experimental and control groups randomly. Beyond this initial selection, however, there are a number of precautions to take in dealing with the different groups to ensure maximum control over extraneous factors. Most important, the experimenter should make an effort to ensure that the experimental and control groups are treated identically in every respect, *except* for the independent variable. Thus, if the independent variable manipulation involves having members of the experimental group spend a half-hour watching a *fantasy* film, it would be inappropriate for the control group to spend that half-hour alone in an empty room with nothing to do. Instead, it might be appropriate for the control group to watch a half-hour nature film. Certainly, depending on the nature of the theory being tested, it might be necessary to use more than one control group to rule out a number of different alternative explanations that might be proposed. In general, however, maximum control over confounding variables is achieved when the experiences of the experimental and control subjects "take the same amount of time, involve interaction with the same people, require the same information, and include the same activities, except for the introduction of the treatment" (Carlsmith, Ellsworth, & Aronson, 1976, p. 241).

Certainly, this is an ideal that can never be perfectly achieved, as is true of nearly all design criteria. Researchers should not claim to be able to achieve more than they can but, at the same time, teachers should realize that researchers can only approximate the ideal experiment even under the best of classroom conditions.

Longitudinal versus Cross-sectional Designs

Many educators appear to believe that only longitudinal studies (studies that follow the same children over a long period of time) can provide useful information about teaching, learning, school environments, or the attitudes, behaviors, and aptitudes of students. There are many areas of psychological and educational inquiry, however, for which cross-sectional studies (one-time studies involving two or more groups) are entirely appropriate—for example, questions about personality, memory, attitude formation and change, motivation, perception, and responses to different techniques of instruction and discipline. Teachers are quite correct, however, if they feel that cross-sectional methods are inadequate for answering certain questions about human development.

Certainly, cross-sectional studies can tell us something about true developmental change, if we can assume that observed *differences* between two different age groups are analogous to *changes* that occur in children from the first age to the second, but this information holds only at the level of group averages (Baltes, Reese, & Nesselroade, 1977). Only longitudinal studies of the same children over a relatively long period of time can provide information about crucial *intraindividual* changes, as well as *interindividual* differences.

Observed differences between age groups in cross-sectional studies are completely confounded with *cohort* effects—differences between groups of children born in different years, differences due to societal, cultural, political, and historical differences. To be sure, cohort effects are a more serious problem if the groups compared are very different in age—say 30-year-olds and 50-year-olds, than if they are close—say 4-year-olds and 6-year-olds. Nonetheless, the problem must always be considered. Straightforward longitudinal research, however, does not avoid this problem, either. If only one group is studied, we have no way of knowing whether changes observed over time are universal developmental changes, or shifts due to external historical factors. Thus, the external validity of a simple longitudinal study is limited. In addition, there are some measurement problems in longitudinal studies. Test familiarity might be a problem if children are given the same tests repeatedly over a period of time. And, if the subjects are initially chosen for study because they are extreme on some variable, by statistical regression we would expect their scores to become somewhat less extreme over time, independently of any developmental processes.

It has been suggested (Baltes, Reese, & Nesselroade, 1977) that, in order for developmental researchers to solve these dilemmas, they use careful selection procedures, employ a wide variety of measures, and create designs that combine features of both the longitudinal and the cross-sectional designs. These designs, though somewhat more difficult to implement and to analyze in their complexity, are probably the best way to ensure reliable conclusions about the nature of developmental change.

SPECIAL FEATURES OF EDUCATIONAL RESEARCH: A BRIEF GUIDE FOR RESEARCHERS

Academically trained researchers who move into classroom settings encounter a wide range of difficulties that are absent or less serious in traditional laboratory research. Many of these are common to most types of field research, but some are specific to educational settings.

Divergent Views of the Purpose of Research

Quite justifiably, teachers see academic researchers as exclusively or primarily concerned with theory building rather than evaluating classroom settings and practices and providing sound recommendations for change. Although good theoretical research should, ultimately, serve to inform practice, it is true that much of it cannot be used directly and immediately in classroom settings. Teachers daily use informal observations and analysis of case studies to inform their daily classroom decisions, but it may be years or decades before a given piece of theoretical research can be directly applied to classroom practice. Because of this, teachers may come to doubt the worth of basic research.

Academic researchers, on the other hand, suffer from their own set of misconceptions about the utility of research. While educators are probably not sufficiently concerned with the design factors required to ensure the internal validity of research, researchers are often not sufficiently concerned with its external validity, the generalizability of its conclusions. Single small studies in single research settings can often produce interesting, informative, and clear results, but those results can seldom be generalized to other settings or to general educational practice without successive modifications and replications.

In addition, researchers may not give sufficient consideration to the difference between *statistical significance* and *practical significance*. A relatively small absolute difference between groups might, though statistically significant, be too small to justify any changes in educational settings or practice. Isaac (1971) identifies *principal criteria* and *modifying criteria* for evaluating classroom research. Principal criteria have to do with the internal and external validity of the study: what do we know about processes, about cause and effect in this and other settings? Modifying criteria, on the other hand, include the practical considerations that can be crucial determinants of decisions to be made on the basis of research: cost of implementing a change, time involved, convenience, personnel training required, and educators' preferences. In general, it can be assumed that if the principal criteria are met and the modifying criteria present no obstacles, a change based on the research will usually be adopted. The modifying criteria, however, become the only bases for decision making when the principal criteria reveal no differences between alternatives. When a statistically significant difference is so small that its educational significance is questionable, modifying criteria might outweigh principal criteria. And, even when a difference appears to be both statistically and educationally significant, modifying criteria might mitigate against any changes in practice being implemented.

Special Sources of Bias

Researchers who are unaccustomed to working in educational settings might, if they fail to acquaint themselves with the classroom or school as a research environment, either fail to take into account some important contextual variables or misinterpret behaviors and, consequently, draw erroneous implications from their findings. As a simple example, a researcher who blindly assumes that going outdoors at recess time is a powerful positive reinforcement for all children will be seriously mistaken if he conducts a study using recess as a reward in a school where staying indoors and tending the school's animals constitute the *real* privilege.

In addition, researchers need to take into account other sources of bias that might be peculiar to school settings. It is important, for example, to be aware of the extent to which children and teachers in a given school or classroom have participated in research in the past. We worry about college sophomores being overly researched and, consequently, being particularly susceptible to subject bias in the form of the "guinea pig effect," but this problem is probably even more serious when subjects are repeatedly drawn from a lab school or a very cooperative public or private school. Other factors, such as the "learning to learn" phenomenon, whereby often-tested children develop an unusual facility with some types of performance, might bias results in such settings. And, finally, the role of the teacher must be taken into account. Even when teachers are not directly involved in treatment implementation or data collection, their attitudes toward the research may be communicated to students in a variety of ways and may importantly influence the students' behavior in unpredictable ways.

Obstacles to True Experiments; Considerations for Quasi-Experiments

Aside from the purely practical problems involved in attempts to implement true experimental designs in classroom settings, academic researchers often encounter obstacles in the form of educators' attitudes toward the use of random assignment and control groups. There are generally two objections: first, that in assigning children to treatments, need or ability are better criteria than purely random assignment; if a particular treatment is supposed to improve self-concept or academic achievement, then why not apply it to those who need such improvement the most? Second, there is the objection that it is simply wrong to treat children differentially, that any treatment—especially treatment that promises improvement—should be administered to everyone equally. This second objection, of course, goes beyond a rejection of random assignment; it involves a rejection of the concept of any sort of control or comparison groups.

There are a number of ways in which researchers might attempt to deal with these objections. In some situations, where the experimental treatment involves an application of strictly limited resources, it might simply be impossible to administer the treatment to everyone; in such cases, random assignment might be accepted. Or, the researchers might make it possible for the control group, instead of receiving no treatment, to receive a type of treatment that is worthwhile but distinctly different from that received by the experimental group. In any case, the researchers should promise, whenever possible, to administer the experimental treatment to all subjects from the control group after the experiment, if indeed the treatment proves to have positive effects.

Beyond these measures, it might be possible to convince educators of the appropriateness of using control groups and random assignment (see Cook,

Cook, & Mark, 1977). Researchers should discuss the threats to internal and external validity presented by nonexperimental designs, and should point out that school boards, citizens, and funding agencies will only be convinced by unambiguous causal evidence. In addition, it can be pointed out that perhaps the measures taken to identify subjects of greatest need are faulty, or, even more important, perhaps the experimental treatment does *not* have the hypothesized effects; that can only be ascertained by conducting an experiment. Finally, researchers can point to examples of successful randomized experimentation in classroom research.

As in all field settings, there are problems in classroom research associated with members of the control group becoming aware of the experimental treatment to which others are being exposed. A number of "contamination" effects are possible, and it is difficult to predict which will occur. The treatment effects may "diffuse" to subjects in the control group, or those in the control group may try harder to compensate for whatever it is they are not being given, or they may become demoralized and perform more poorly than a group that did not know about the treatment. In addition, if institutional administrators discover the differences in treatment, they may wish to compensate the control group by providing them with whatever they are not receiving (or the administrators may be forced to do so).

Thus, a number of confounding factors might enter in when researchers attempt to assign children randomly in a given classroom (or even a given school) to different treatment conditions—especially when the treatments are long term and potentially significant. A reasonable compromise solution is to assign randomly larger units, such as classes, to treatments, trying to match the units as closely as possible on potentially important extraneous variables, and using pretesting to determine the initial equivalence of the units.

Quasiexperimental methods such as this are certainly preferable to the nonexperimental methods that would have to be used in their place. In devising and implementing such methods, a great deal of creativity is often required. For example, if it is not possible at a given time to use a control group, it may be reasonable to use two or more levels of the treatment within the experimental group, and then to use a cohort (for example, next year's class) for comparison. Also, if it is possible to control suspicion or resentment about the repeated introduction and removal of treatment, a time-series design might be used in the absence of a control group. Another possibility in such a situation is to use *nonequivalent dependent variables*—additional dependent variables that are similar to the primary dependent variable but, according to the theory being tested, should be affected somewhat differently from that variable. In this way, it might be possible to rule out other alternative explanations (see Cook, Cook, & Mark, 1977). In any event, whenever quasiexperimental designs are used, the researcher should explicitly consider and attempt to eliminate each of the threats to internal validity.

Developmental Considerations

Academic researchers who are accustomed to working primarily with adult subjects should acquaint themselves with special developmentally relevant issues before conducting research in school settings, even when their hypotheses are not developmental. It may seem obvious that a given task may mean something very different to a child subject than to an adult experimenter. Nonetheless, it is important for researchers, even those experienced in working with children, to pilot-test any new measures and procedures thoroughly, and to solicit teachers' advice on their use. Moreover, researchers should be alert to the possibility that particular age groups of children might show floor or ceiling effects on particular measures, thus masking or distorting independent-variable effects or developmental trends.

In research that is developmental in nature, the problem of task equivalence for different ages of children becomes a serious one. Although using the same task for widely differing age groups is in many instances clearly inappropriate, using different tasks that seem to equate across the ages is quite risky, since the tasks may actually have different meanings and require different processes. The best solution for this problem probably involves *control by systematic variation*: having several versions of a particular task and administering each to each age group tested (see Baltes, Reese, & Nesselroade, 1977, p. 216).

ANNOTATED BIBLIOGRAPHY

So that researchers and educators may share common understandings about research methodology and the nature and functions of research, it is necessary not only for educators to become acquainted with the fundamentals of research design independently and with the aid of researchers, but it is also necessary for researchers to become acquainted with the special validity problems in classroom settings, and the methodological considerations peculiar to working with children and with schools as institutions. Several excellent sources are available for those wishing to explore each of these issues in more detail. The first four provide good introductory reviews of research design and methodology, and the remaining four present more advanced considerations of design.

Introductory

Carlsmith, J. M., Ellsworth, P. C., & Aronson, E. *Methods of research in social psychology.* Reading, Mass.: Addison-Wesley, 1976. A readable introduction to experimentation in general and social–psychological experimentation in particular; includes chapters on ethical issues, deception, and the avoidance of bias.

Isaac, S. *Handbook in research and evaluation.* San Diego: EdITS, 1971. A well-organized, clear, complete but concise (186 pps.) guide to all types of research and data analysis; an invaluable aid to anyone with no training, rudimentary training, or long-forgotten training in research.

Katzer, J., Cook, K., & Crouch, W. *Evaluating information: A guide for users of social science research.* Reading, Mass.: Addison-Wesley, 1978. A very basic, enjoyable treatise on evaluating social-science research; considers errors in research and how to decide whether research reports are trustworthy and useful.

Moursund, J. *Evaluation: An introduction to research design.* Monterey, Calif.: Brooks/Cole, 1973. A practical, nonstatistical treatment of the problems involved in constructing and carrying out evaluative research.

Advanced

Campbell, D. & Stanley, J. *Experimental and quasi-experimental designs for research.* Chicago: Rand McNally, 1963. The "classic" guide to experimental designs and the many variations that approximate them; discusses statistical treatments for each design presented.

Cook, T. & Campbell, D. *Quasi-experimentation: Design and analysis issues for field settings.* Chicago: Rand McNally, 1979. A complete discussion of the important issues in field experimentation, including causal inference, validity, and statistical analysis.

Hamilton, D., MacDonald, B., King, C., Jenkins, D., & Parlett, M. *Beyond the numbers game: A reader in educational evaluation.* Berkeley: McCutchan, 1977. A good introduction to the educator's point of view on experimentation; the section on alternative methodology is particularly helpful.

Wohlwill, J. *The study of behavioral development.* New York: Academic, 1973. An advanced but well-reasoned consideration of the study of human development, including an evaluation of the various methods that can be used; not a "how-to" book, but useful nonetheless.

REFERENCES

Baltes, P., Reese, H., & Nesselroade, J. *Life-span developmental psychology: An introduction to research methods.* Monterey, Calif.: Brooks/Cole, 1977.

Campbell, D. & Stanley, J. *Experimental and quasi-experimental designs for research.* Chicago: Rand McNally, 1963.

Carlsmith, J. M., Ellsworth, P. C., & Aronson, E. *Methods of research in social psychology.* Reading, Mass.: Addison-Wesley, 1976.

Cook, T., Cook, F., & Mark, M. Randomized and quasi-experimental designs in evaluation research: An introduction. In Rutman, L. (Ed.), *Evaluation research methods: A basic guide.* Beverly Hills: Sage, 1977.

Isaac, S. *Handbook in research and evaluation.* San Diego: EdITS, 1971.

Kerlinger, F. *Foundations of behavioral research.* New York: Holt, Rinehart & Winston, 1973.

Part III:
Practitioners' Roles
in Research

Introduction to Part III

Many academic researchers do not consider the educational practitioner's role in research as extending much beyond a passive acceptance of the researcher in her classroom or a submissive agreement to implement the researcher's experimental procedure in the teaching practice. There are, however, some teachers who take an activist's stance toward practitioners' involvement in and evaluation of research. Representing a radical position on this issue, Hull (Chapter 9) maintains that customary forms of academic research cannot be useful to teachers. He proposes, instead, that teachers engage in "personal research," a program involving careful observation of and reflection on children's behavior in the classroom, followed by a discussion and integration of these reflections with other teachers. In defending his view of research, Hull describes the personal and professional experience that led him to it.

In Chapter 10, Watt and Watt take an equally radical stance toward the use of traditional research designs in classrooms. They advance the view that all research must have direct benefits for the participants, that deception should never be employed, and that experimental manipulation of conditions should be eliminated. Watt and Watt justify their position by arguing that the sense of trust between teachers and students must be preserved, the respect for teachers' control over their classroom environments must be maintained, and the complexity of the classroom situation must be acknowledged. They then present examples of classroom research that meet their criteria.

Proposing that teachers must evaluate research and make greater use of research which meets their criteria, Evans (Chapter 11) outlines her own criteria for research, including the rule that research reports be comprehensible to and directly useful for teachers. Evans acknowledges differences between her criteria and those of researchers, presents her own favorable evaluation of several research projects, and ends by giving examples of teachers applying her criteria in informal research in their own classrooms.

Despite some hostility toward academic researchers and their methods, many educators are genuinely interested in and sympathetic toward psychological research in classrooms. In Chapter 12, Dwinell and Berman present a practical guide to the criteria used by a particular public school system in evaluating research proposals, including a discussion of preferred topics, criteria for research designs, and ethical and social issues. Addressing themselves to researchers who wish to work in public school systems and to administrators of such systems who wish to devise their own evaluation procedures, Dwinell and Berman describe the functioning of one research evaluation committee in detail.

Chapter 9

Personal Research

Bill Hull

Since the early 1970s I have been exploring ways of encouraging classroom teachers to investigate children's thinking in the classroom, which has been my own central interest for over 30 years. The methodology that has evolved out of our joint undertaking is sufficiently different from traditional research in its assumptions and procedures that another name is needed. I have been calling it "personal research" to distinguish it from customary forms of academic research that I had not found to be very useful when I was a teacher of young children.

One form of personal research is represented by Teachers' Seminars on Children's Thinking, first organized according to our current guidelines in 1972. The continuing interest of teachers in these seminars has resulted in the formation of an informal network of people who continue to meet with each other and to share their insights through writing for members of other seminar groups.

Our way of working is unusual, and its apparent simplicity may be misleading. Since its antecedents go back a good many years I will use a personal narrative form to discuss the style of inquiry that has evolved, some of the assumptions embodied in the organization of the seminars, and the reasons why this approach appears so promising.

During my last year in college I met with a small group of children at a local settlement house once a week to work on various craft projects. This provided such a good setting for me to observe their interactions that I decided to do an undergraduate thesis based on these sessions. Since there was no tape recorder available I developed the practice of listing all the events I could remember as soon after each session as possible. Later I would write as complete an account as I could, expanding on the list I had made. I was amazed to discover that so much was happening in my mind without my being aware of it. Finding that I could retrieve what was there, provided I went about it in a disciplined and patient way, was a significant discovery upon which some of the assumptions and methodology of personal research, as exemplified by the Teachers' Seminars on Children's Thinking, are now based. Writing helped me to recall instances and to become aware of patterns that I would otherwise have lost. It became a cyclical thing: noticing certain events and reflecting upon their significance seemed to lower my threshold for noticing even more.

I think I had always had a strong curiosity about why people behaved as they did. As a camper, and later as a camp counselor, I had wondered a good deal about growth and development—my own as well as that of others. Knowing the same people for a succession of summers, separated by ten-month interludes, forced a recognition of continuity underlying the many changes that were taking place in all of us. I assumed, therefore, that if I wanted to study my own thinking, or that of others, I would need to do so over an extended period of time.

After college I continued to develop my skills of recall and reflection as an apprentice teacher in a nursery-school class, which was a far more varied and complex setting for children than any I had previously experienced. I was strongly impressed with the skills my directing teacher had for keeping track of a great many interactions, while at the same time providing appropriate support and guidance to help a group of 20 four-year-olds have a happy and productive experience together. I had not expected that young children would be so mentally active in trying to make sense of their world or that they would be such interesting people so early in their lives. Trying to keep track of what was happening, and to find appropriate ways of thinking about it, while at the same time learning to be a teacher, was one of the greatest intellectual and personal challenges I had ever faced. Although I had majored in social psychology in college with the expectation that I might want to continue graduate work in psychology, I found that working with young children was so stimulating and gratifying that, after completing my apprenticeship, I accepted a job as a teacher of a third grade. To keep my options open and help keep a broad perspective on learning, I also held a job as a proctor for college freshmen during my first three years of teaching.

I was very fortunate in my choice of apprenticeship and first teaching assignment. A beginning teacher has so much to learn, so many basic readjustments to make in both perception and behavior, that it would have been overwhelming had I not had the help of teachers whose experience and expertise were far greater than my own. I began to realize that the fabric of complex interrelationships in well-functioning classrooms is sustained by tacit knowledge expressed in behavior, and that this knowledge need not be verbalized to be useful. It is indeed possible to do highly complex things without ever having said how it is we do them. The words we use to illuminate aspects of a child's reality are inevitably inadequate, conveying far less than the reality itself. The skills necessary for being a sensitive and responsive teacher may even, at times, be at odds with those that are necessary for talking in logical and coherent ways about what has happened. Successful teachers of informal classrooms have learned to notice and to interpret forms of behavior which the less skillful simply do not see. Their behavior is often labeled "intuitive" when it encompasses a great range of variables, many of which have not been analyzed explicitly. The capacity to sense those signals from a child that are of particular importance and to handle large quantitities of information that interrelate in complex ways requires a high level of intelligence. Unfortunately, it is a style of mental organization valued far less highly than it deserves.

I developed a very deep respect for teachers who had learned practical ways of supporting children's learning, even when they were not particularly articulate in talking about what they were doing. My apprenticeship forced me to question some of the assumptions I had been making about the relation of theory to practice. Some things come to seem practically self-evident from the perspective of a practitioner immersed in the complexity of a demanding profession. They can be very difficult to explain to others who have not themselves experienced the challenge of working with groups of young children. The four-year-olds I had been with were vitally concerned with some of the deep and central problems of the world and, through their play, were inventing productive ways of anticipating and re-creating experiences which they were struggling to understand. I only gradually began to realize how much was going on and that a fair amount of skill was required in order to be able to see it. The same deep wondering and eagerness to explore were still there in the third-graders I later taught. I was surprised to find that their intellectual lives were so fascinating, and that there were ways in which their learning, and my own, could become the subject of a lifelong investigation. The things I said, the way I behaved, the person I was, could make a difference in what these children noticed and the choices they made for themselves. I began to realize that children's thinking needed to be taken seriously and that the biggest challenge to me, if I were to study it from the vantage point of a teacher, was to become a more sensitive, responsive, and reflective person.

About 30 years ago I decided to become a researcher in education. At the time it seemed obvious that this would be the best way to pursue my own interests. I expected that I would continue to be able to work with children in ways I had been finding so stimulating and gratifying. My head was so full of wonderings and suspended questions from being with young children that I was ready to commit myself to a long-range study of children's thinking, to find out all I could about what other people knew, even if it meant doing some of those disagreeable things necessary for accreditation. Since I had continued part-time graduate work during my apprenticeship and first years of teaching, it was, in a sense, a continuation of what I had been doing all along.

I studied experimental design and statistics, read widely in psychology, and searched for studies that would help me to a better understanding of children's thinking and greater skill as a teacher. After five years as a full-time third-grade teacher and a part-time graduate student, I took a year off from teaching children to be a research assistant in psychology and an instructor in a school of education. During this year I was also able to conduct exploratory investigations with some of the fourth-graders whom I had first known as four-year-olds and then taught as third-graders.

The game of researching was interesting for awhile. It was intriguing to isolate variables and to look for relationships, even when there wasn't any connection to the skills of being a teacher. It was fun to work out new ways of thinking about all this input even when it meant juggling the observations and formulations of other people that were often not relevant to my own teaching experience. But laboratory or controlled classroom studies paled in comparison to being with children and using whatever resources I had to understand what was happening and to improve on what I was doing.

I didn't give up completely on traditional forms of psychological research when I returned to full-time teaching and I did try using some of the methodology I had been learning in my own classroom. A few controlled experiments, with approved statistical analyses, convinced me that this was not an appropriate way for me to find out the things I most wanted to know, nor was it likely to reveal ways of helping children become better learners. As a teacher I was making changes all the time, based upon my own recall and reflection. My choices were made on the basis of feelings, my sense of the total situation. While my own mental activity was often very intense, it didn't have to be forced into a verbal/analytical form. I realized that I had to face my concerns in all their complex and subtle interrelationships and to judge my success by the condition of the class for which I was responsible, not by what I could say. My way of working seemed completely antithetical to that of carrying out separate research studies. Most of those I had studied in education and in psychology seemed trivial, misguided, or pretentious to me, when judged in terms of their usefulness in the classroom.

My personal research was concerned with all kinds of mental activity because I knew that the style and the skill that children had developed had a continuity that could be observed in many of the things which they did. I was particularly interested in the learning of mathematics, for it provided a good vantage point for observing, over time, the strategies children were using. The way they had been learning often determined the way they would go on learning in the future. Those who concentrated on remembering what they were supposed to do often prevented themselves from grasping the underlying structure of the subject. Mathematics, for them, became increasingly difficult and distasteful. I had been such a student myself. It was not until I had been studying children's thinking for several years that I began to realize that my own education had not prepared me to think effectively about new problems. It was traumatic to have to acknowledge that my own understanding of mathematics was deficient, even for being a third-grade teacher. Now I know that I was not exceptional; most adults do not really understand the mathematics they have been taught in elementary school. To demonstrate that this is so, it is only necessary to ask "transfer questions" that call upon the same understandings, but in a different context from that in which they were originally taught. Many of us have learned to follow patterns, or recipes, which cover up our lack of grasp; we were judged to be good students if we remembered them. I have demonstrated to my own satisfaction that even the "top" students in a class of "exceptionally able" fifth-graders, selected for a special program because they had scored above the 95th percentile nationwide on a standardized achievement test, were scarcely better off.

I had been experimenting with various materials, things for children to "think with," from my first years in teaching. Eventually I found that varied systems of representation could be used to reveal the underlying structure of mathematics, its beauty as well as its complexity. These were exciting years, for the work in mathematics brought me into touch with other teachers outside my own school who had also been finding that children could learn much more effectively under appropriate conditions. The vitality and freshness of thought that we had been finding, though, could not be sustained when it was translated into lesson plans for uniform group instruction or into standardized work sheets. We needed a different climate in which children's initiative was encouraged and in which they could experience the satisfaction of taking responsibility for their own learning. I began to realize that curriculum must be considered as part of the total style and organization of the classroom because basic approaches to learning developed within a total climate in which expectations were being communicated by one's peers as well as by parents and teachers. This insight as well as the later experience of being a science-curriculum developer convinced me that trying to proceed in any other way was likely to be self-defeating. Good materials could be a great help, but unless a teacher was free to depart from formal methods of instruction and to tune into the thinking the children were actually doing, not much would be accomplished.

Max Beberman, a pioneer curriculum specialist in high-school mathematics, was strongly concerned with this problem at the time of his death in 1971. He had located a number of infant and primary schools in England where progress in certain subjects seemed to have passed some kind of threshold. In one school the quality of writing was outstanding; in another, mathematics had progressed much farther than usual. There were other schools where exceptional progress had been made in art, physical education, or science. He was impressed that what was happening in these schools was qualitatively different from what was going on elsewhere. It had been his intention to try to analyze what was happening in each of these schools so that the best of each might become available for other schools. While his observations were similar to my own I disagree with his formulation about trying to transplant materials and procedures. As subsequent experience has demonstrated, it was not at all easy to introduce these admired practices to schools in the United States. Concentrating on the product without studying the process, in the hopes of producing quick results, is rather like trying to plant cut flowers. Curriculum development, considered separately from the total setting and climate of assumptions and expectations in which children are operating, is not likely to be very successful.

Focusing on mathematics learning in my own classroom led me to be suspicious of the strategies that students were developing when they felt under pressure, no matter what the subject was. Fifth grade in our school had a long reputation for being especially challenging. Graduates were often quoted as saying that it was the toughest grade in the school, that the rest was easy if you made it past the fifth grade. The curriculum, based on the study of world geography through the explorers, was formidable. One requirement was to draw a map of the world, entirely from memory, at the end of the year. When I tried to carry on the curriculum I had inherited I began to notice surprising differences between third-graders and fifth-graders. The *same* children who had been lively, inventive, and spontaneous as third-graders were dutiful, industrious, and compliant when faced with masses of assignments. It was impressive to see how hard they were ready to work, but I kept wondering why it was that they seemed intellectually irresponsible, why they were having so much trouble with problems for which they had not been supplied recipes. I was greatly puzzled by this change, which did not seem at all healthy, and continued to explore it by watching how children went about coping with various problems.

Eventually I realized that many students were meeting the school's strong pressures for production by developing strategies for getting things done as quickly and as painlessly as possible. Our program was rewarding children who were facile in the use of language and dutiful in completing detailed assignments, but the students who were good at this were often not very curious or thoughtful. I was also surprised that these "successful" students, those who were good at getting their work done and scoring well on tests, were frequently the ones who had the most trouble when they encountered new problems for which they did not have standard solutions. On the other hand, some of the "slower" students often demonstrated that they were very able when dealing with higher levels of complexity. I analyzed what was happening in terms of the strategies that children were developing to meet the expectations of a high-powered and ambitious school and cited Piaget's work in an attempt to show that this form of schooling was not conducive to good intellectual development in a paper called, "Learning Strategy and the Skills of Thought" (Hull, 1958).

My conclusions were difficult to explain; few people seemed ready to understand or accept their implications. I am sure that my perceptions were different from those of my colleagues because I knew these children quite well, in classroom settings, over a seven-year period. Being a parent of four school-aged children, and having a wife who also shared my fascination with the children's growth and development, also contributed to my thinking enormously. While I was not always comfortable about holding views that were sharply divergent from others working in the same field, I have come to realize that, like various forms of expertise, personal knowledge gained from particular experiences should not be discounted.

After my paper was printed, someone did me the very great favor of asking me how I knew I was right. It was a nonhostile query at a time when few people were ready to give serious consideration to the evidence I was reporting, and an important one for me because it allowed that I might be right in criticizing an ambitious, polished, and highly admired form of schooling. It may sound simplistic to say that I knew I was right because I had been looking very closely at the thinking children were doing in various classrooms over a period of years, but I believe this to be the case. I had developed an unstandardized form of evaluation that I could personally trust, though I didn't know any way of presenting it in convincing form to others.

I had to discover these things for myself. My perspective grew out of my own investigations, not from traditional forms of research. Now I realize that our school, once an innovative and progressive institution, had been caught in a reactionary cycle in which uniform, direct instruction was spreading from the upper grades to the lower ones in response to a general climate of anxiety. The curriculum and style of the middle and upper grades were as harmful to those who were successful in completing masses of detailed assignments as it was for those who lost confidence in themselves because they were unable to keep up with ever-increasing demands for production. Superficially, though, it seemed so successful that some parents and teachers began wondering if the younger children were not having too good a time in school. "If you would only make it tougher for them in the early grades then they wouldn't dislike so much what we have for them later on" was a view expressed in so many words by a teacher of the older students. The easy defense against the anxieties and criticism of parents who were worrying about test results and getting their children into the next school was to move even more strongly toward "stiff requirements" and "high standards." Then failure could be blamed on the students who were not able to measure up, rather than on the school.

"What the wise and good parent will desire for his own children a nation must desire for all children" is a stirring phrase, quoted in the Plowden report, *Children and Their Primary Schools (1967)*. The "wise and good" parents among the professional, academic, and business communities during the time I was a classroom teacher were outnumbered by parents who had such a high investment in their children's success that they could not see the damage being done. Parents who feel under economic and social pressures, whether they are highly paid professionals or members of minority groups striving for a better life for their children, seem all too ready to opt for "high standards" and "stiff requirements" and to disregard the evidence that there might be something wrong.

I don't think it took any special talent to see what I was seeing; I was simply curious enough to keep on looking, wondering about what I was seeing and making modifications when it seemed that they might help. I didn't start with a self-conscious theory that I was going to investigate or even a list of priorities to reflect upon. I just began noticing things, watching changes in children over time and paying particular attention to contrasts. As I learned to tune myself to things that seemed most interesting or puzzling, I began to be aware of relationships and possibilities that had escaped me previously. I spent a lot of time listening to children and talking with them about a wide range of topics. It couldn't be called "research" in the traditional sense. There was no orderly collection of data determined in advance, no experimental design.

There is a feeling of involved detachment that comes from doing something you know is important, from being ready to look at the whole situation and to accept your own responsibility for what is happening. If you are mistaken you want to know it; you have no wish to fool yourself even when you are caught up in the excitement of what seem to be new insights. I had confidence in my style of investigation. Still I had many doubts and uncertainties that weren't diminished by my relative isolation or the fact that what I was finding was not at all what people wanted to hear. My questioning led me to be very critical of my own classroom, but it wasn't possible to talk about this with fellow teachers. I really didn't know how far I could trust my own constructions. I remember reminding myself more than once that it was dangerous to generalize on the basis of one class of children and that the patterns I was seeing might be attributable to their particular characteristics. Some patterns did seem to change significantly from year to year. I really didn't know, therefore, how far my formulations could be generalized or whether I might be mistaken on some fundamental issues. I needed the perspective of teachers who were working along similar lines in other schools.

There was another feature of the way of working that I had been evolving which did provide more perspective and has helped me see that there are ways in which classroom teachers can become engaged in an important form of nonstandard research. Our school had an excellent apprentice program. Having been both an apprentice teacher and a graduate student, I had no doubt that the apprenticeship was far more important for learning about the complexities of teaching and for sensitizing me to problems of high priority than graduate school. Training apprentices, however, was less rewarding for me because it forced an emphasis on explaining and justifying rather than questioning and trying out new ideas.

When Judy Thomson was assigned to be my fifth-grade apprentice it was soon clear that she could learn all the routines very rapidly and could get along without most of my explanations. After the first few months, she became my unofficial assistant and we shared the teaching and also our perceptions of what was happening in the class. Having two full-time teachers who are interested in looking closely at the whole situation, including the seamy side, can be quite painful, and in our case meant more work than it would have taken to teach the class singlehandedly. Not only did we have time to reflect together upon what we were seeing from our different points of view, we also had the resources to act upon those fringe ideas that seem promising but so frequently get crowded out because there is so much else to do.

That year was so interesting that I couldn't face starting over again every year with a new apprentice. Judy stayed on a second year as a volunteer assistant and we made ourselves interchangeable. After that I was granted the special privilege of not having to have an assigned apprentice. The following year John Holt dropped in for a visit and then came back so frequently that we worked out a similar arrangement for two more years. The opportunity to look openly and critically at the results of our own best efforts and to talk at great length about the details of our own experience was both exciting and productive. I am very grateful for the administrative support we had which made this possible. Teachers' Seminars on Children's Thinking owe their beginnings to these years of learning to see and to share.

I had expected to find in graduate school an organized body of knowledge about learning and teaching that would be more or less directly related to my primary concerns. I thought there would be experts who had more skill than I had and who knew a great deal more about the problems I was encountering for the first time, people who could at least guide me to relevant studies or strategies of investigation that would help me explore my own questions. But the questions I was asking myself were not the ones that interested academicians. The spontaneous and informal investigations I was making on my own were of far more importance for my understanding, and for bringing about changes in my classroom, than anything the university had to offer.

Graduate school was not the help I expected it to be in its people resources, its methodology, or its useful body of knowledge. I have known teachers who were more skillful than I in establishing and maintaining settings that were good places for children to be, classrooms that were humane, comfortable, and stimulating. I didn't find such people in the university, nor did anyone there seem to know that such conditions were even possible. There seemed to be very little relation between academic concerns and enlightened classroom practice during the six years in which I was a part-time graduate student.

It is curious that I have never met any psychologists or researchers who were also skilled in this sense. I have known several who have tried and found that managing a classroom in which there are a variety of options for children was far more challenging than they were able to handle. The skills involved in being such a teacher are apparently of a different order than those that are valued in a graduate school of education. I had experienced a strong sense of indignation when I began to realize that schools for children were practicing a form of intellectual discrimination no less damaging than racial discrimination, though few people seemed to realize that there were strong qualitative differences in personal mental organization. The same pattern of overvaluing facility with language and undervaluing competence in problem solving expressed in action discriminates against many able teachers whose skills are demonstrated in action better than they are in words.

I had been excited to discover Piaget's work during my year of apprentice teaching. His experience supported my own growing awareness that what is happening in children's heads is often very different from what the casual observer is likely to notice. His observations had strengthened my own resolve to look even more closely at what was happening in my own classroom and to be prepared for surprises. Piaget, though, was not very much in favor at the time. When my adviser at the Harvard Graduate School of Education told me that Piaget could not be considered for a degree at that institution because his work was not considered "academically respectable," I dropped out, not because I wanted to use Piaget's methodology, but because I could no longer respect a tradition that was so restricting.

As a supervisor of student teachers I had been able to visit a variety of public school classrooms. Since I had already been teaching for five years, and wondering a good deal about the conditions that supported good learning, I saw them very differently from other observers. With few exceptions, they did not compare favorably with some of the primary classrooms in the independent school in which I had been teaching, even though they had been selected as representing among the best in the area. It was strange to find a school of education supporting, and indeed promoting, practices that I found unenlightened. Student teachers were offered the example of classrooms that, with few exceptions, were taught by methods of uniform group instruction, with textbooks containing systematic guides for teachers. I found few classrooms where teachers were ready to question what they were doing or willing to depart from customary practices. There was also direct, or at least tacit, support for standardized achievement testing, which in my own experience was one of the most misleading and destructive influences operating against the development of more enlightened forms of educational practice.

Despite the tremendous diversity in values and styles of the classrooms I visited, I felt that I could judge which situations were favorable for children's intellectual growth and which were not. Because I had taught children of the same ages, and thought a good deal about how they were using their heads, I could penetrate beyond surface appearances and observe a number of things that apparently were not at all obvious to others. I was surprised to find that I was quite confident in judging the quality of these classrooms by looking at the kinds of mental activity being encouraged, because there were a great many other things that I did not understand at all well.

I had hoped to find in graduate school people who had a broad perspective on education, who could help in illuminating the conditions most favorable for learning or guiding prospective teachers on the choices they would soon face. There was not the wisdom, the expertise, or the leadership that one would expect to find in a mature profession. I am not suggesting that this was the fault of a single institution, for I have no reason to believe that conditions were much different elsewhere in the United States at the time. It was disillusioning, though, to discover that I was in such a backward profession, that there were not people who were able to look at what was happening in schools and to say that much of it was destructive and limiting to children's growth. Eventually I was able to see what was happening as a manifestation of a larger cultural delusion about the nature of mental activity, a delusion perpetrated by universities as well as schools, because it was an integral part of the heritage of all of us who had been to school. It is an unfortunate academic heritage, particularly in the fields of education and psychology, that values the ability to say much more highly than the ability to do. Perhaps it is because few people have been ready to look closely enough or long enough at what is happening in the mental lives of children, that we have a persisting cultural delusion about the nature of thinking and learning that has gone unchallenged for so long.

I have continued to wonder a good deal about the university-based research of the 1950s, during the time I was a part-time graduate student. Where were the researchers whom one might expect to understand the larger picture? Why couldn't they see that the strongly directed, pressure-cooker style of education in which uniform group instruction dominated was limiting to the intellectual development of children when it was not outright damaging? Why were they not critical of standardized achievement tests which were fostering such trends? Why were they promoting movements such as "team teaching," "programmed instruction" or "the new math," most forms of which were based on the assumption that education is something you do to children, and that with better organization and planning, better materials, you could to it more efficiently? Could they not see that children who are told what to do, how and when to do it, as a steady diet, are apt to become rather limited people rather than resourceful, independent ones?

I have very strong misgivings about this kind of legacy from traditional approaches to research. It is not just relatively useless, but outright damaging to children when it legitimates practices that restrict children's potential for development. It is worth reminding ourselves of these shortcomings, even to accentuate them, in order to realize how mistaken people can be.

The contrast of enlightened growth being made in some British infant schools in the same period is another way of pointing up the shortcomings of traditional research in bringing about basic, long-lasting changes in schools. It does not seem to be the case that such progress was attributable to research in the conventional sense. Such long-term growth appears to have come about because able people with an intense concern for the welfare of children found the freedom and support to explore their interests in ways that they found natural.

In 1961 I visited a small group of infant and junior schools in the county of Leicestershire to study the progress of approaches to the teaching of mathematics which we had been trying to introduce, with little success, in local classes. The contrast was dramatic. Children of the same age were more relaxed and flexible in their approach, and had accomplished more using the same materials, despite classes being almost twice the size and the children from far less privileged backgrounds than those with whom we had been working in the United States. The differences were not confined to mathematics; the spirit of the schools and the quality of life was different. The English children were more independent, resourceful, and had greater capacity for self-direction. Their work in art and writing was often of higher quality. I found strong confirmation for the perspective that had been growing out of my own study of children's thinking in the classroom: that initiative, perseverance, and the capacity for self-direction are essential for good intellectual development, and that other qualities such as humor, lightheartedness, empathy, and joy in living are not unrelated or irrelevant.

The evidence from England is very important because it made visible some important dimensions which few people in the United States, regardless of profession, had been able to see. Many articles were written in the 1960s by Americans who found schools in England more humane, intellectually interesting, and enlightened than our own. *Two Classrooms* by Tony Kallet (1971) and my report, *Leicestershire Revisited* (Hull, 1971), are examples of some of these early reports. When the Plowden report (1967) was published, it was estimated that about a third of the infant schools were using informal methods. These developments had been proceeding on a much broader front than we had realized and a great many people were ready to recognize that they represented a major advance in educational practice.

First-time visitors to England are usually impressed with the vitality and the freedom of children in classes where the teacher is not a dominating and continually controlling figure. They are apt to miss the complex patterns of constraints and expectations that have been established by the skill and the artistry of a teacher whose own intellectual activity is very high, whether or not she can express in words how she operates. Successful teachers of informal classrooms do learn to respond to subtle variables about which they do not have full information, which requires first of all that they be fully alive and sensitive human beings. Their expertise depends on the ability to develop a feel for the whole situation as it is changing and to react spontaneously in ways that will encourage certain kinds of activity while limiting others. They must have a feel for how a great many factors are interacting, whether or not they have been consciously identified or analyzed.

I believe these accomplishments were possible because teachers discovered and found support for a way of doing personal research. I didn't find programs directed from a central source, but rather individuals working in loose association with one another. There was an awareness of the accomplishments of particular people or schools and support for this work from people who were highly respected, but there did not seem to be any detailed plan or prescription for what was to be done. It is likely that informal networks existed for the sharing of experience, but I didn't find any strong theoretical base from which they were operating. It all seems to have happened with "precious little theory." People did share a very deep concern for the welfare of children, a readiness to observe closely and to modify what was done on the basis of experience. The strategy of supporting the personal research of teachers who were growing most rapidly may explain the fact that enlightened practices spread quite rapidly when conditions permitted. Teachers, head teachers, advisors, and inspectors with whom I talked emphasized that this evolution had taken a long time, that they owed a great deal to those who had been pioneering before them, and that the work was still continuing.

These then were some of the experiences that contributed to my divergent views about education and eventually to the start of Teachers' Seminars on Children's Thinking: experimentation with recall and reflection which changed my capacity for experiencing, informal research which I carried on while being a full-time classroom teacher, my dissatisfaction with traditional research in psychology and education, sharing my classroom under conditions that permitted informal investigations, collaboration with others in curriculum development in mathematics and science, and studying changes in certain British infant schools.

Long before I visited England, however, I knew there was something drastically wrong with our own schools, even the ones that were being held up as examples of exemplary practice. Repeated cycles of looking closely at children's thinking in my own classroom and then searching for productive ways of thinking about it made such a conclusion inevitable. From my own perspective, gained from years of wondering and experimenting, it seemed self-evident that one could not expect optimum intellectual development in children unless the capacity for initiative and self-direction were strongly encouraged—that no quantity of cleverly constructed materials or curriculum plans could take the place of that. Had I not visited in England and then discovered that there were large numbers of people who understood that what had been happening there represented significant progress, I would have had little support for my convictions. There were no alternatives to traditional education, that I knew of, either from my observation of schools in the United States or my reading of research in education or psychology. My personal research also allowed me to see far more complexity in what was being achieved in a few schools in England than some enthusiastic visitors who learned, to their regret, that what had grown there over a number of years was far more difficult to achieve than might appear on the surface.

I don't pretend to understand the complex mixture of factors that permitted such a favorable growth in British infant schools while schools that had once been progressive in the United States were in strong retreat. It does seem clear, however, that very little (if any) credit can be accorded to traditional forms of research. Michael Bassey (1980) argues persuasively that hypothesis-testing forms of inquiry are not appropriate for educational research. His conclusion that there are no generalizations about teaching which are of consequence to teachers sounds a bit extreme, though I believe it is useful to present the argument in this form.

As much as I admired what I had seen in England, though, I felt that there might be a better way of continuing what had been started. I have been particularly concerned that progress in education has seemed unnecessarily slow and not cumulative. Teachers who had achieved important insights in a lifetime of work have not had good ways of sharing what they have learned. From my own experience I knew that teachers could learn to talk very effectively about what they are doing and to find appropriate levels of analysis that would make sharing very rewarding. Though teachers don't make much use of traditional research it is much more likely that they will be ready to act upon what they have learned from sharing personal research. Sharing what has been noticed creates a flow in which one becomes more skillful in providing information and receiving it; the more one has noticed, the more one is able to see, and the more receptive one can be to others who are having similar experiences.

It is a basic premise of the Seminars on Children's Thinking that long-term growth is possible when able people have the right conditions of freedom, stimulation, and support to work on practical problems of vital importance to them in a style which is in accordance with their natural ways of functioning. These seminars are described in two publications by the North Dakota Study Group on Evaluation, one a progress report (Hull, 1978) and the other an account of the relation between the seminar and one teacher's experience in working with children (Jervis, 1978). These reports provide a much more comprehensive account of the methodology and the assumptions of the seminars than is possible in the brief outline suggested here.

The constraints under which seminars in our network operate are not elaborate, but we have found them to be important. Experienced teachers, each from a different school, meet weekly to discuss specific instances of children's thinking from their own classroom or their own learning experiences. Each discussion is tape-recorded and notes and commentary written for each session. We rely on the well-developed perceptions of highly skilled people who participate on a voluntary basis, motivated by their own curiosity and a strong interest in doing the best job they can with the children they are teaching. Powers of recall are developed through making lists from memory of recent events, writing journals, and presenting instances to the group. We have the opportunity to discover and reflect on patterns that begin to emerge from a great many specifics, selected because they have high priority for the teachers in the group, and to remind each other of observations that continue to be perplexing. By concentrating on specific instances and allowing formulations to arise and be modified on the basis of shared experience, we keep what is being talked about close to what is being done, being guided by the central concerns of the participants whether or not these concerns can be stated explicitly in advance. With such a richness of experience available we find ourselves asking deep, long-range questions about the nature of the intellect and the conditions most favorable for its development.

We feel that it is important to share doubts and uncertainties freely, as well as successes, to continue to question, and to suspend judgment. Teachers who are accustomed to presenting instances from their own classrooms to colleagues for their reactions, and who have reacted to instances that others have presented, tend to develop richer, more differentiated perceptions. They learn to listen carefully to what has been said, to reflect about it when they review it in written form, and to remind each other of useful insights that have emerged. The process encourages experienced participants to explore ideas on the fringes of their awareness which have often been difficult to express. Re-sorting and reexamining what one knows through the process of sharing perceptions with people working in different situations helps develop greater skill in analysis and a trust in one's ability as a problem solver. Hearing about innovations others have made and reporting on one's own also provide easy, nonthreatening ways of keeping up to date. Sharing articles, books, or ways of thinking is another benefit that can sustain growth and the continual renewal of advanced classrooms. Curriculum development and evaluation, therefore, are a part of this undertaking and need not be considered separately. Seminars do function as support groups as well, but I believe the intellectual excitement that comes from fresh understanding or the satisfaction of discovering that important insights come to mind when you need them is even more important.

Teachers who are or who have been seminar members are increasingly interested in sharing what they are learning or what they are wondering about with members of other seminars. As they develop greater familiarity with this form of inquiry, new possibilities emerge. As Molly Watt (1979) says:

> I think the seminars will continue to multiply in their existing forms. I see teachers in the future becoming more vocal about their knowledge. The seminars can serve as a training ground for us to present our material. With a greater sense of professionalism, we will conduct our own research projects, write our own articles and books. We will begin to shoulder more responsibility for in-service training programs and staff development. As we, the practitioners, develop our own ability to organize our knowledge, we can look forward to our schools reflecting that knowledge.
>
> For myself, the group has many ramifications. The most important has been the personal nourishment that comes from stepping outside my daily experience and reflecting on it. I am aware of no other structure which allows the kind of deep thinking mixed with idealism which lured me into teaching. No matter how hassled I may feel from my teaching just prior to the seminar, I return to a state of wholeness and optimism. Even when I have been feeling most stuck, I regain a sense of resiliency, and, yes, HUMOR, about my work as I develop new understandings about my role as a facilitator of children's thinking (pp. 14-15).

Those who are asking questions about their own experience, who, despite their expertise, are willing to share their doubts and uncertainties, are engaged in a form of personal research that can be self-sustaining. Energy seems to come from a variety of sources: the intellectual satisfaction of finding more appropriate ways of dealing with problems and developing greater personal skill and effectiveness, as well as knowing that what one is doing makes a difference in the lives of children. I believe that this form of inquiry has the potential to become an important alternative to more academic forms of research, one that can continue to build on its own results at the same time it is contributing directly to the improvement of educational practice.

REFERENCES

Bassey, M. Crocodiles eat children. *The Theory and Practice of Educational Action Research,* Summer 1980, 16–24.

Hull, W. P. Learning strategy and the skills of thought. In *The ESS reader.* Newton, Mass.: Education Development Center, Inc., 1970.

Hull, W. P. Leicestershire revisited. In Rathbone, C. (Ed.), *Open education in the informal classroom.* New York: Citation Press, 1971.

Hull, B. *Teachers' seminars on children's thinking.* Grand Forks, N.D.: North Dakota Study Group on Evaluation, 1978.

The Plowden Report. *Children and their primary schools.* London: Her Majesty's Stationery Office, 1967.

Jervis, K. *Children's thinking in the classroom.* Grand Forks, N.D.: North Dakota Study Group on Evaluation, 1978.

Kallet, A. Two classrooms. In Rathbone, C. (Ed.), *Open education in the informal classroom.* New York: Citation Press, 1971.

Watt, M. *Thinking about thinking.* Brookline, Mass.: Teacher Center Publication, 1979.

Chapter 10

Design Criteria
for Collaborative
Classroom Research

Daniel H. Watt and Molly Watt

We believe that a school can best be viewed as a community in which teachers, students, and administrators work together to create an atmosphere conducive to learning. Within such a community, an ongoing process of growth and development takes place. The learning environment created results from the balancing of many needs, interests, ideas, values, and constraints, and is continually shifting to reflect new balances among those forces. When an outside researcher enters such a community to introduce and assess changes in school practice, to test a particular psychological theory, or to observe the behaviors of students and teachers in certain settings, all parties should be sensitive to issues and problems that might arise from his or her presence:

The presence of outside observers in a classroom may arouse the curiosity of the students, as well as raise questions for a teacher about whether the observer approves or disapproves of classroom practices.

The researchers' methods, agendas, and time-lines may not have been coordinated with the teacher in whose classroom the research is to take place, thus interfering with long-term plans.

Changes in classroom practice suggested by a researcher, although small in terms of total impact, require replanning by the teacher, and may require that teacher and students adjust to a new routine.

A researcher interested in controlling or observing one particular aspect of classroom practice may not be aware of the subtle ways in which many different aspects of a classroom community are interrelated. Altering one aspect of a classroom may have impact in other areas.

Teachers may not have had the training necessary to understand research methods. Thus the research itself may be surrounded by a special mystique which interferes with cooperation between teacher and researcher.

We believe that the relationship between a researcher and a classroom community should be given the same thoughtful attention and careful planning that is usually given to the content and design of a research project. Our experience leads us to the view that the best way to ensure such a relationship is to offer teachers the opportunity for full collaboration in all aspects of a research project. In the next section we suggest a set of criteria for research design intended to foster such collaboration.

THE DESIGN CRITERIA

Our suggested criteria are based on our own experiences, which include both education research and classroom teaching. From a teacher's point of view, we want the research to benefit the classroom community. From a researcher's viewpoint, we want results that can influence the development of improved classroom practice. We believe that both objectives will be served by collaborative research conducted according to the four criteria we suggest:

1. Classroom research should offer direct benefits to all its participants— teachers and students, as well as researchers. Long-range goals, including the national significance of the findings, although of critical importance to researchers, funding agencies, and ultimately to the schools, do not in themselves justify disruption of the school community.
2. As much as possible, teachers, students, and school administrators should collaborate with researchers in the planning and implementing of school-based research projects.
3. Research should be conducted with honesty, openness, and mutual respect. Research designs should not require misleading or misinforming students or teachers.
4. Observations and data collection should be as unobtrusive and natural as possible, and the participants should be informed of the purposes and methods of those observations. Aspects of data collection that disrupt class routines without being beneficial to students (such as some types of pre- and posttesting) should be minimized.

In elaborating these points, we will draw informally on our own teaching and research experiences, on personal knowledge of other projects, and on published reports of classroom research.

1. The first consideration in any proposed classroom research should be: will the benefits of the process to teachers and students outweigh the disruption caused by the project? While the researchers benefit directly through employment on a research project, enhanced academic or professional standing, and the intellectual challenge of the research, other direct benefits should result for members of the school community. Although we should consider the long-term benefits that might result from the *findings* of the research, those findings rarely benefit the participants directly.

Many research reports indicate to us that some researchers see students as convenient "guinea pigs" to be used in testing their own hypotheses. A number of research designs involve the use of control groups—students who do not directly benefit from a project activity but who are nonetheless required to participate in interviews, respond to questionnaires, or take tests that may themselves be disruptive and time–consuming. Other research designs involve manipulating the classroom environment in ways that may disturb the learning environment without enhancing it. One recent report described how groups of second- and seventh-grade students were subjected to repeated shifts in seating arrangements to see whether there was any change in "study behavior" (Axelrod, Hall, & Tams, 1979). In another study, 72 sixth-graders were subjected to a set of questionnaires designed to measure their anxiety levels. One-third of the students were then given test instructions designed to *increase* anxiety, while others were given neutral or supposedly positive instructions (Trentham, 1979). Such activities could easily disrupt the sense of trust that must exist between teachers and students in a successful classroom community.

Once the principle is established that students and teachers are not merely convenient research subjects, there may be many ways that a research project can offer benefits to school communities in which the research takes place. Students may benefit through participating in new learning experiences that are part of the research activity, or through increased awareness and sensitivity on the part of their teachers. Training provided by a research project can be an important professional growth opportunity for many teachers. A teacher who has learned new skills of teaching or observing will be better able to provision a classroom for student learning. In addition, the researcher can offer more tangible compensations by, for example, donating a book to the classroom library of any class used for research, by presenting a slide show about the research to a school assembly, by offering materials and equipment used for research as a supplement to those already available in the classroom, or even by giving students a party or tickets to a play in appreciation of their participation in the research.

2. Teachers, students, and school administrators should collaborate as much as possible in the design, planning, and implementation of classroom

research. A research project, no matter how beneficial to the students and teachers involved, cannot help but cause some disturbance or disruption to the educational objectives and daily routines of the classroom. Careful negotiations are often required to ensure that benefits are equitably distributed, or that the project does not unduly disrupt the larger community. Involvement of teachers in planning the research is one way to minimize such disruption. Unfortunately teacher participation cannot be assumed. Planning research is not part of a teacher's job description, and teachers may find the time required for careful planning an unacceptable extra burden.

Research projects should be set up to allow teachers a degree of choice as to their involvement in the project—ranging from full collaboration in the project to a more passive yet fully informed participation in the research. Project time-lines should allow for teacher feedback during all stages—planning, implementation, and data analysis. We question the acceptability of research designs, no matter how beneficial, that do not allow the classroom teacher to choose whether or not to participate, or do not provide for some degree of collaboration for a teacher who desires to participate.

3. Research should be conducted with honesty, openness, and mutual respect. Reports of research designed to mislead teachers and students has led to educators' distrust of researchers. Examples of this type of research are regularly reported in education-related journals and magazines. We appreciate that there is a distinction between research in which deliberate falsehood is an essential part of the research design, and research designs in which student or teacher behavior is to be manipulated in ways that preclude an honest description of what the research is about or how the activities are to be conducted. We believe, however, that those who conduct either type of research are not straightforward about their intentions and are therefore harmful to the classrooms in which the research takes place, and to the education research community in general.

Perhaps the most famous example of the use of deliberate falsehood in education research is the study known as *Pygmalion in the Classroom*, designed to determine the effect of teacher expectations on student achievement (Rosenthal & Jacobsen, 1968). By giving teachers false information which indicated that certain students were "late bloomers," about to achieve greater academic success, the researchers attempted to observe the relationship between teacher expectation and student success. The results of student achievement tests led the researchers to claim that when teachers expected a student to do better, the student's achievement increased. This finding corresponded with the previously held views of many educators and psychologists that teachers' attitudes can help or hinder student achievement.

An inadvertant consequence, not considered by the researchers, was the effect that publication of their deceptive research methodology had on teachers' attitudes toward educational researchers. Remembering examples of deception of teachers by researchers, many teachers now distrust researchers who want to investigate any aspect of the teaching and learning process. We believe that it *is* appropriate for a teacher to wonder about a researcher's hidden agenda, and whether there is misleading information, or secret manipulation involved in the research.

More fundamentally, we believe that the results of research based on falsehood are themselves suspect. Researchers who deliberately mislead their subjects cannot be expected to report honestly on the outcomes of their experiments. We have often wondered whether the researchers involved in the *Pygmalion* project might have had another hidden research agenda. Perhaps they were studying the effect of releasing misleading information about education research on public opinion and on the education community. Unless honesty and ethical behavior are an integral part of the research process from start to finish, there is no reason to trust the validity of the research findings or the truthfulness of the researchers.

While the deliberate use of falsehood is regularly reported as a technique of psychological research conducted among college students and adults, such techniques are rarely used with younger students. On the other hand, research in which student behavior is manipulated without explanation is quite common. We believe that such research can have harmful consequences for the classrooms in which it takes place. Students have a right to expect that teachers will deal with them in a straightforward manner in giving reasons for classroom practices, especially when changes are taking place. In our experience, students know when they are being manipulated by adults, or when information is being deliberately withheld from them. Even when students are unwilling or unable to articulate this, such knowledge can have damaging consequences for the sense of community in a classroom, thereby distorting the results of the research.

As an example, consider a research project (Miller, Brickman, & Bolen, 1975) which was a controlled experiment designed to test the effects of two different approaches to modifying student behavior: "persuasion" and "attribution" ("We've got to keep our classroom cleaner!" versus "We *are* a litter-conscious class!"). What were students told about the experiment? Did the teachers suddenly develop a new set of behaviors for six weeks, without discussing the situation with the students? Did the students cooperate out of loyalty for their teachers, or because they were convinced by what their teachers said? Were the students involved ever informed that they had participated in an experiment, or given an opportunity to discuss the results? Did researchers investigate the consequences of the experiment itself for the overall quality of the classroom community? We question whether teachers can participate in such a study and still maintain a position of trust with their classes.

4. Observations and data collection should be as unobtrusive and natural as possible, while ensuring that participants are aware of the purposes and methods of observation. Students are naturally curious about any changes in their classrooms, from a new book or piece of furniture to the presence of a new person. While observers should be careful to minimize their impact on the situations being observed, students should know them as *people* who have names, voices, and ideas. In our experience, a simple introduction and explanation leads to less disruption than an anonymous observer, attempting to remain unnoticed.

Several years ago an observer made regular appearances in Dan Watt's fifth-grade classroom for the purpose of observing students who were participants in a special tutoring program. The students were not informed about who or what was being observed in the classroom or why the observer was present. The observer tried to stay in the background, taking copious notes, and regularly consulting her stopwatch. Despite the care taken by the observer to remain unnoticed, the teacher realized that the students being watched were acutely aware of the observer's presence. One such student resorted to spending his time staring at the observer, paying careful attention to what *she* was doing. Obviously the attempt to capture the child's "natural classroom behavior" had been seriously undermined, along with the normal classroom routine. If the observer had introduced herself to the students, explained what she was doing with her notebook and stopwatch, and taken an interest in their work and classroom, she could gradually have become an accepted part of the class routine, and both she and the students would have been able to work more effectively.

EXAMPLES OF CLASSROOM RESEARCH AS A COLLABORATION BETWEEN TEACHERS AND RESEARCHERS

The involvement of teachers as collaborative partners or initiators of research projects is an encouraging trend in education research. We have been personally involved in several such collaborations and in this section we describe three of them. They include a teacher-initiated research project, a project in which large numbers of teachers were involved in the collection and interpretation of data for a long-term study, and a federally funded, university-initiated project in which an innovative computer-based learning environment was implemented and assessed in a school setting.

As part of a graduate program under the direction of George Hein at Lesley College, Molly Watt initiated and conducted an investigation of how five-, six- and seven-year-olds understand the loss of loved ones through death, divorce, moving, and school-year endings. The research focus was chosen because of her insight that some inappropriate behavior was an indication of incomplete mourning on the part of her students. As an experienced teacher, she wanted to learn how the children's completion of the mourning process could be supported in the classroom in order to allow them to move on in their own learning.

Molly presented the study to her young students openly and simply. "I am studying how some of you feel when your pet dies or a friend moves so that I can learn to be a better teacher to you by knowing how to help you feel better." She took notes on children's conversations, taped class-meeting discussions, and saved children's writings and drawings related to this topic. The methods of documentation were easily integrated with her role of classroom teacher. She documented the children's responses to the losses that occurred in the natural unfolding of the school year: a bird flew into the window and died, the student teacher's internship was finished, a child moved out of district, the iguana died, the bunny died, the school year ended. When children demonstrated curiosity about her work, she shared the information they needed. When children asked, they were allowed to listen to the tapes or look at the collection of writings and drawings.

Immediate benefits for the students included the increased sensitivity and attention to the process of dealing with endings and loss. Molly made reading books for the class library based on the children's own words describing their own experiences with moving, separation, and loss. As students read the books which they themselves had illustrated, their understandings about grief were reinforced as the regular reading program was supplemented. Unanticipated benefits were the ripples of good feeling and mutual trust which grew from the process. It was important for the children to see their teacher as a learner and to begin to understand that learning is part of a life-long process.

Long-term benefits included a workshop on "Saying Goodbye" given for teachers at the Brookline Teacher Center. Some of the data were included in a paper describing a seminar for teachers engaged in research into children's thinking (M. Watt, 1979). (See Chapter 9 for more information on the Children's Thinking Seminars.) An article in *Learning* magazine described ways to build preparation for the end of the year into classroom activities throughout the year (M. Watt, 1980). In these ways some practical aspects of the research were shared with other teachers. A children's book designed to help children and teachers prepare for the end of the school year is now in manuscript form.

Our second example comes from a study of democratic classrooms initiated by Dr. Ralph Mosher of Boston University, and funded by the Danforth Foundation. Public-school teachers from Brookline, Massachusetts, were enlisted as participants in designing a research project to document practices designed to foster democracy in their classrooms, and the relationship of those practices to the process of educating children for responsible citizenship in a democratic society. The teachers were paid by the grant for after-school time spent as researchers, and further supported by access to videotape and photographic documentation. Participants attended biweekly seminars to learn from developmental psychologists and from each other.

The knowledge and experience shared by the psychologists in their presentations and through informal consultations helped the participants develop clearer perspectives about their own research. Some of the teachers prepared presentations of the research they had conducted in their classrooms for workshops and conferences (Lickona, Mosher, & Paradise, 1979). One major outcome of the three-year project will be a book with chapters authored by individual teacher/researchers (Lickona, Mosher, & Paradise, 1981). Significant immediate benefit to the students and teachers resulted from their greater understanding of and sophistication about democratic practices in their own classrooms.

The university-initiated project described in our third example was also designed so that students and teachers enjoyed many direct benefits. Under the leadership of Professor Seymour Papert, the MIT Logo Group has spent a number of years developing a computer language for children and a computer-based learning environment in which children can learn computer programming, problem solving, and mathematics. During 1976–1977, Dan Watt, then a fifth-grade teacher, spent a year on sabbatical leave with the Logo Group at MIT. The following year, the National Science Foundation provided funds for a year-long study of the Logo learning environment at the Lincoln School in Brookline, Massachusetts (Papert & D. Watt, 1978). Dan Watt had a full-time role, supported by the grant, to act as a teacher/researcher and to coordinate interactions among the MIT research team and the students, teachers, and school administrators involved. As an experienced teacher who had already spent a year with the researchers, he was able to be sensitive to the needs and expectations of all project participants.

During the course of the project, several days of release time were provided to the classroom teachers involved, to encourage their collaboration. During the release days, and in many other less formal meetings, the teachers were informed about the progress of the project, received training in computer education, and were able to offer feedback and suggestions about the content and process of the project to the researchers.

Immediate benefit to the students and teachers was a major concern to all participants throughout the project. Project funding was designed to provide for a detailed observational study of the learning experiences of 16 representative sixth-grade students (Papert et al., 1979; D. Watt, 1979). The staff of the school wanted the project to be a more integral part of the school, and insisted that *all* sixth-grade students be offered the same opportunity to participate. This could have placed a severe strain on the tight project budget, but the project staff resolved the issue creatively by finding university students to act as volunteer teachers for all the sixth-graders.

The project benefited its participants in another way. Because the research involved many hours of detailed observations of student learning, the researchers were able to share insights about students' learning styles, strengths, and weaknesses with their classroom teachers. By meeting regularly with the researchers, the teachers were able to take advantage of the researchers' insights to plan for the students' regular classroom work. As a result of this collaboration, it was possible for classroom teachers and specialists to plan new intervention strategies for certain students with severe learning problems.

Subsequently, the school system decided to create its own pilot Logo project, in which computers were placed directly in classrooms. As the school carried out this project, the MIT Logo Group was able to provide support for some additional teacher training and curriculum materials to support classroom use of the computers. The use of the Logo computers is now a regular part of the program at Lincoln School, involving eight classroom teachers and all students in grades four through eight.

Another outcome of the project was a plan to use the methods of the Logo project with learning-disabled students. Noting the success of learning disabled students reported in the original research study (Papert et al., 1979), Dr. Robert Sperber, Brookline's Superintendent of Schools, initiated planning for a new project aimed directly at these students. A committee consisting of university researchers, special-education teachers, and school administrators was formed to plan the project. The joint planning involved ensures that the impact of this project, when it occurs, will be significantly greater than if it had been developed primarily by university researchers (Watt & Weir, 1980).

CONCLUSIONS

In considering the impact of educational research on a school community, we have focused primarily on the potential for collaboration between teachers and researchers. We also feel that there are appropriate roles for students, parents, and school administrators as collaborators in classroom research. Without a consideration of their roles and rights, no analysis of the impact of research on the classroom community could be considered complete.

Finally, we want to reiterate our belief that there is important work to be accomplished in the field of educational research. If the findings are to endure in a significant way, teachers must participate as willing collaborators in the process, adding their own understanding of a classroom community and its needs to the research design. The process itself must be beneficial to the educational community, regardless of any eventual findings. We believe that reliable findings require presenting the project openly and honestly to the school community. We believe that if these criteria were consistently met by researchers, the schism and mutual suspicion that often exists between classroom practitioners and educational researchers could be significantly reduced. We believe that educators and researchers have much to learn from each other. The process of collaboration could lead to more significant research questions and the development of less disruptive research methods. Collaborative research is more likely to lead to new understandings of the complex and delicate issues surrounding the creation of environments to support human growth and development.

REFERENCES

Axelrod, S., Hall, R. V., & Tams, A. Comparison of two common classroom seating arrangements. *Academic Therapy*. September 1979, **15**, 29–36.

Carini, P. *Observation and description: An alternative methodology for the investigation of human phenomena*. Grand Forks, N.D.: University of North Dakota Press, 1975.

Carini, P. Illuminating children's growth: The long and short of it. *Today's Education*, February–March 1980, **69**, 1.

Lickona, T., Mosher, R., & Paradise, J. *Democratic classrooms, theory and practice*. Brookline, Mass.: Teacher Center Publication, 1979.

Lickona, T., Mosher, R., & Paradise, J. (Eds.). *Schools and classroom democracy*. Boston: McCann, in press, 1981.

Miller, R., Brickman, P., & Bolen, D. Attribution versus persuasion as a means for modifying behavior. *Journal of Personality and Social Psychology*, 1975, **31**, 430–441.

Papert, S. & Watt, D. *Assessment and Documentation of a Classroom Computer Laboratory*. Logo Memo #48, MIT Logo Group, 1978.

Papert, S., diSessa, A., Watt, D., & Weir, S. *Final Report of the Brookline Logo Project*. Logo Memos #53, 54, MIT Logo Group, 1979.

Rosenthal, R. & Jacobson, L. *Pygmalion in the classroom: Teacher expectation and pupils' intellectual development*. New York: Holt, Rinehart & Winston, 1968.

Trentham, L. L. Anxiety and instruction effects on sixth grade students in a testing situation. *Psychology in the Schools*, 1979, **16**, 439–443.

Watt, D. A comparison of the problem solving styles of two students learning Logo. *Proceedings, National Educational Computing Conference*, June 1979. Reprinted in *Creative Computing*, 1979, **5**, 86–90.

Watt, D. & Weir, S. Logo: A learning environment for disabled students. *The Computing Teacher*, 1981, **8**, 5.

Watt, M. *Thinking about thinking*. Brookline, Mass.: Teacher Center Publication, 1979.

Watt, M. How to plan for the year's end. *Learning Magazine*, 1980, **9**, 38–39.

Chapter 11

Practitioners and Research: A Practitioner's View

Claryce Evans

As an educator who has long been interested in the relation of educational research and theory to practice, I am encouraged to see the current increased attention to models of collaboration between researchers and practitioners (Carini, 1975; 1979; Elliott, 1976; Florio & Walsh, 1978; Hull, 1978; Peterson & Emrick, 1981; Tikunoff, Ward, & Griffin, 1979). Much of that interest has been stimulated by the widely acknowledged need to conduct research and develop models that will lead to a greater use of research knowledge in school and instructional improvement efforts. Though many efforts at school improvement have been less successful than one might have hoped and current efforts to close the gap between research and practice are still too new for informed judgments, they do offer promising possibilities.

The gap that exists between research and practice is maintained in part, by two related problems. Educational research is based, as it should be, on questions that have arisen from previous research and on the research community's perceptions of the needs of the profession. Researchers, however, often have an inadequate understanding of the needs or potentials of teachers and other practitioners. They are dismayed that teachers continue to teach on the basis of intuition, their own experience as students, and the culture of the school in which they are employed, rather than improving their practices on the basis of analysis and application of current results. Researchers tend to characterize teachers' judgments as insufficiently objective and have too rarely solicited teachers' views on questions to be investigated. In other instances they have been influenced only by initial, sometimes superficial, statements of teachers' needs, problems, and interests.

At the same time, those of us who are practitioners often see the research process as mysterious and beyond our capabilities to do or understand. ("I can't balance my own checkbook—I'm sure I could never understand statistics.") In addition, teachers and school administrators often make only implicit, and sometimes hasty, judgments of educational research. We tend not to join or attend meetings of professional research organizations; we rarely subscribe to or read research journals; whenever possible, we ignore research efforts. The assumption is that educational research is often irrelevant to the concerns of real schools with ordinary people as students, teachers, administrators, and parents. This conclusion is, unfortunately, justified but overgeneralized. There is educational research which is interesting, useful, or encouraging to practitioners. It seems appropriate, therefore, for practitioners to start making public and explicit evaluations of classroom research and defining useful directions for future research.

In an effort to begin to make those evaluations and define those directions, I will present some examples of classroom research that have been of interest or use to me. Then, in an effort to stimulate a continuing professional conversation among practitioners, I will offer some suggestions for ways in which we might take more responsibility for the research agenda.

SOME POSITIVE EXAMPLES:
ALL TEACHING IS RESEARCH

In reviewing educational research that has been of interest or use to me, I have noticed a number of characteristics of importance to practitioners. Among these are the following: (1) the design is one that teachers can easily understand and adapt for investigations in their own classrooms; (2) the procedures employed are respectful of teachers; (3) the researcher attempts to develop measures that will test teachers' informal observations; (4) the report is comprehensible and useful to teachers; and (5) the research supports teachers' efforts to reflect on their practice. Certainly, not every research project must exhibit all these characteristics in order to be useful. This is, however, a beginning list which I suggest both practitioners and researchers consider.

In a good example of observational research that can easily be adapted by teachers, students who had been in an experimental, "hands-on" science program were compared with students who had taken the usual science program based on a written curriculum (Duckworth, 1971; 1978). In one phase of the study, groups of students, twelve at a time, were taken to a room supplied with a variety of materials, including pattern blocks, rice, batteries and bulbs, scraps of metal, pins, paper clips, string, mirrors, and paper. Then they were told they could do what they wished with the materials and were left in the room for 40 minutes with two observers and no teachers. The intent of the study was to determine whether there were differences between the groups with respect to the number of ideas that students had of ways to use the materials, the intellectual quality of the ideas they pursued, and the extent to which they continued to work with the materials rather than sit or watch others work.

This study is of interest for a number of reasons. First, the design of the research allows teachers to adapt the methodology for their own use with relatively little outside help. Teachers who chose to use these techniques would probably not choose to do comparison studies, but rather to collect information about the functioning of their own classes.

Second, the study is a relatively direct investigation of a question which is important to the many teachers who are interested in their students' ability to pose and solve problems for themselves and in the quantity and quality of the curriculum-relevant ideas students have. For such teachers, Duckworth's design gives information which is more direct than a paper-and-pencil test would be.

Third, the design appears to be based on the assumption that the differences between the groups studied will be great enough that relatively straightforward documentation and analysis will identify them. I think most practitioners believe or would like to believe that some of the things they do might have a visible, important impact on some student, class, or school. It is encouraging to see research designs that reflect that hope.

Fourth, the presentation of the research is such that the argument can be followed and judged by someone who has not had extensive training in research methods and statistics. One need not say, "I don't really know how they reached that conclusion, but I guess it must be right since they are better trained than I am."

Finally, the study places students in relatively nondirected situations. I think most practitioners would hope that their work has some impact on students in their "real lives." For example, they hope not only that students can read when assigned a page for reading, but that they will, of their own accord, go to the library, choose books, and read them. Duckworth's study is clearly not "real world," but it comes closer than many educational studies because it places students in a setting in which expectations for their behavior are not clearly and fully defined.

A study of the practical problems faced by teachers implementing an "inquiry and discovery" approach to teaching provides an excellent example of research that is respectful of teachers (Elliott, 1976; Elliott & Adelman, 1975). This example is noteworthy for two reasons. First, the researchers made a deliberate attempt to close the gap between researcher and practitioner. They acknowledged that teachers often view research as irrelevant and that researchers often view teachers as unreliable reporters of classroom practice. They then developed techniques for interviewing intended to decrease the chances that teachers' reports would be biased or distorted. They also developed internal checks for biased reporting, including triangulation methods that would allow them to compare reports by teachers, students, and observers.

Second, in their reports, the researchers discuss explicitly the ethical questions raised by the research design and conclude, on principle, that people have a right to control the data they supply. For example, they propose that teachers ought to control the extent to which other teachers have information about their classrooms and that students ought to control their teachers' access to records of their interviews with researchers.

It seems clear to me that these researchers reach the conclusions they do on data control and on bias and unreliability because they are respectful of teachers. They attempt to close the gap in information and control between themselves and teachers, rather than try to obtain accurate information by conducting a double-blind experiment which keeps teachers ignorant of the real intent of the research.

Reading this work reminded me of an experience I had as a graduate student which led me to question the prevalent assumption of researchers that anonymity provides the most effective and appropriate protection for subjects. In my thesis I did a case study of two successful elementary-school principals in Massachusetts. I dutifully followed the form of inventing new names for the schools, towns, and principals. Having been a subject more often than a researcher, I also sent all my notes for each interview to the person who had been interviewed so that he or she could edit them.

Later, when I made copies of my study available to people in the two schools, it was clear that it was unnecessary and insufficient to have renamed the schools and the principals. "Mr. Marsh" was certainly identifiable by anyone in his school and by anyone in the school system who knew that a study had been done. He would not have been identifiable to anyone in Oklahoma—but then he didn't need to be anonymous there. The two principals were only protected by having had control over the data.

My third guideline for good classroom research was that the researcher should try to develop measures that will confirm teachers' informal observations. Harry Brickell, in "Needed: Instruments as Good as Our Eyes" (1976), reports on an evaluation of a career educational program in which all observers agreed that teachers were teaching career education well and students were learning, but in which the tests designed for students yielded no significant differences with control schools. The evaluation directors chose to assume that the observers' reports, rather than the tests, were correct. With another try and a lot more work, they succeeded in designing a test that yielded results consistent with what had been reported—that the experimental group learned things the control group did not. On their second try they did not rely on the stated goals of the curriculum guides or on statements by administrators or teachers. Observers sat in classrooms and recorded what they thought students were learning. While still in the classrooms, they tried to write test items to match the learning they had seen—items that the program students would be able to answer but control students would probably not be able to answer from their learning about career education from their family and friends or from television. Brickell makes the point:

> Indeed, the finished field-based tests themselves profiled the superior learning of the program students. [p. 12]

> We need such instruments. As evaluators, we need to be able to say to program directors and classroom teachers: "Yes, we can measure what you can see." Otherwise, we may look irrelevant or incompetent or dangerous. [p. 13]

As practitioners we need to say more frequently to evaluators or researchers: "This is what is happening in this school or these classes. Can we work with you to document it for the benefit of other teachers?" or "This is what we think is happening. Can you help us find some evidence to bolster or to check our intuitions and impressions?" Otherwise *we* may look apathetic or incompetent or unprofessional. We may appear to others to be the primary obstacle to the improvement of education.

If researchers are now more willing to search for new methods to document learning and teaching and to confirm observations, and if practitioners become more willing to seek assistance in expressing those things they know about schools and classrooms, then it is also appropriate to consider new ways of presenting the results from school-based or classroom-based research. As an extension of Brickell's, "Yes, we can measure what you can see," I suggest, as a fourth characteristic of useful educational research, "And we can write it so you will want to read it." That is, I propose that each research report be written twice, once in the usual way for standard academic journals, once in a way that would be accessible to teachers and school administrators who have not had extensive research training and who tend to be skeptical of research results. I hope I will not be misunderstood. I do not mean the second report to be a shortened and simplified version of the first on the assumption that the reader who is not trained in research is therefore less capable of complex thought. I do mean that its writers should recognize the differences in training and attitude between researchers and practitioners and assume that readers have little background in research. It would, therefore, delete or explain references to previous research on the topic and would replace a presentation of statistical analyses with an explanation of the analyses that had been done.

The second report would also include more information on the research process and setting. Many school systems allow research to be carried out without approval by, or input from, school staffs. Teachers have often had the experience, therefore, of viewing research conducted on their students or their colleagues' students which appeared to ignore important factors in the classroom, school, or neighborhood. Thus they conclude that research results are often unfounded. In reading a report they would want to know: What was the origin of the question and why was it considered important? What was the neighborhood and school setting? Who participated and who decided they would participate? What was the basic approach to education in the classroom? Careful documentation of the context of the research would allow teachers to judge the points of relevance and irrelevance to their own settings.

There are some excellent examples of researchers attempting to help teachers reflect on their own classroom practice. Several research centers have included classroom teachers in investigations of curriculum and classroom practice (Florio & Walsh, 1978; Peterson & Emrick, 1981; Tikunoff, Ward, & Griffin, 1979) and might serve as models for others who are interested in working with teachers. The work of Patricia Carini (Carini, 1975; 1979; Peterson & Emrick, 1981, pp. 26–31) and Bill Hull (1978) is particularly interesting to me. They have been, for a number of years, developing strategies for investigating classrooms by working with teachers and other practitioners. Carini's work is based on observation and the documentation and analysis of students' work. Hull's work, which he describes in Chapter 9, focuses on "children's thinking." Though there are differences in the methods used by Carini and Hull, they share a number of important strengths:

1. Teachers are encouraged to do research in their classrooms and are supported in that challenge.
2. Teachers initiate the topics for discussion and investigation.
3. Teachers are encouraged to write and to publish their work (Jervis, 1978; Watt, 1979).
4. Teachers meet in peer groups to discuss their observations, without supervisors from their school systems and without evaluation or grading by the leader.
5. The seminars are voluntary.
6. The seminars are not necessarily problem-oriented. Teachers are encouraged to recognize, document, and reflect on their own strengths as well as the strengths of individual students.
7. The seminars are long-term; some of them have been meeting for seven years.
8. Teachers are expected to give detailed, nontheoretical descriptions of students and their work.

One of the groups that has been working with Carini for a number of years is the Philadelphia Teachers' Learning Cooperative. The teachers meet weekly to continue and build on the work done in summer institutes. They are an unfunded, independent group and use the formats developed by Carini and her colleagues to provide structure for their discussions of their classroom observations and documentation. Not only do these teachers study students in their classrooms and their own roles in relation to their classes, they also ask and resolve a number of important questions about the functioning of their group. Undertaking this analysis of group dynamics is an important though often overlooked part of such endeavors. I find their work impressive. They are teachers in "ordinary" public schools in Philadelphia who routinely teach classes of more than 30 students. Yet they find time to meet weekly in their own homes for no additional pay or academic credit and to take responsibility for conducting their own staff-development/teacher-research group, for initiating new members into the group, and for documenting and analyzing that group as they look more carefully at their classroom practices.

There has been, and I assume will continue to be, some dispute over whether such groups are doing "research." As one of the participating teachers explained, "I do research every day in my classroom, just as I taught reading all day when I taught kindergarten." *All teaching is research.*

An academic researcher is likely to assume a different definition and to claim that "no knowledge has been found which can be transmitted and generalized to other settings. These are excellent staff development programs, but *they are not research groups.*"

I am reminded of earlier discussions of whether other teacher seminars were support groups or work groups. The dichotomy was usually phrased, "Are we going to be just a support group or are we going to try to change our classrooms?" In both cases we have an unnecessary, inaccurate separation of function. I don't believe there are effective support groups that do not also have an important intellectual content, though it may not be systematized, academic, or generally recognized. Neither are there groups that allow people to develop and share profound intellectual insights into teaching that are not supportive. Similarly, effective staff development programs should include, as one option for teachers, an opportunity to participate in research; and collaborative research between teachers and academicians need not be classed as inadequate research because it also provides stimulation, encouragement, and challenge to teachers.

Even if we assume, however, that a group can function both as a research group and as a staff-development group, we might ask whether analysis of one's own practice deserves to be called research. If it hasn't been published, is it research? I would extend the definition of research to include such work on the grounds that the function of publication is simply to open one's work to the scrutiny of peers and to allow others to make use of what one has learned. The Philadelphia Teachers' Learning Cooperative has achieved both of these purposes—though not in the standard way since they have not yet published a description of their work. The structure of the meetings assures that individual members present their documentation and observations to the others in the group and, as a group, they have presented their work at summer institutes at the Prospect Center, and, by invitation, at local universities and conferences. Their work is not easily generalized to other settings, but then few research results are. They struggle, as members of Hull's Children's Thinking Seminars struggle, to express in writing what they have learned from their work together.

This selection of interesting research examples is clearly incomplete. It is intended as a beginning that will encourage other practitioners to make their individual reactions to research public and explicit. The selection can also be seen, however, as having certain features that are idiosyncratic to practitioners. Viewed in that way, the list of examples demonstrates, I think, some differences in approach from that which would be likely for a researcher:

1. Teachers are likely to favor viewing important issues in many different, changing ways, while researchers tend to pare concepts down to fixed operational definitions.
2. The selection of desirable characteristics is based on practice, not on theory. It did not start from a defined theoretical framework and is not intended to be part of one. If practitioners generate similar lists, they are less likely than researchers to be interested in analyzing the lists to develop a theory of practitioners' views of research.
3. There is no attempt to specify under which circumstances which characteristics of the research are important. Practitioners are often interested in bits and pieces of information and will make individual judgments about which is likely to be applicable in their settings. Researchers are more likely to try to specify in advance the conditions under which a particular result will be relevant.
4. The discussion is based on positive examples. Practitioners, in contrast with academic researchers, are rarely interested in a definitive analysis of a failure.
5. The descriptions, "interesting" and "useful" are used without defining either one of them.

INITIATION OF RESEARCH QUESTIONS

Practitioners need, however, to go beyond public evaluation of completed research to assume a more active role in defining the research agenda. As suggested earlier, I propose we issue invitations to researchers to help us answer our questions and that we pursue the deeper questions that arise in our work more carefully and fully. That need not mean that we supply a list of questions to researchers who then design and carry out the studies. It may mean that we conduct the research as well as identify the issues.

Terry Denny, in *Story Telling and Educational Understanding* (1978), has argued that there is a need for research that does not require a high degree of technical research training. He describes the methods of ethnology, ethnography, case study, and journalistic documentation, which he calls story telling, and asserts that teachers can help in the important work of problem definition by contributing to good documentation.

> Weak theory comes and goes but superb description survives the test of time. . . . without good documentation, good story telling, we'll never get good educational theory, which we desperately need.

> Simply put, if you know what the problem is you don't need a story teller or an ethnographer. An educational researcher might be able to help discover the probable effects of competing treatments or solutions to a problem. It is not likely, but it is possible. I claim story telling can contribute to our understanding of problems in education and teachers can help. Folks are forever calling for and proposing nifty solutions to problems never understood. Story telling is unlikely to help in the creation or evaluation of educational remedies, but can facilitate problem definition. Problem definition compared to problem solution is an underdeveloped field in education. [p. 5]

The skills Denny identifies as those necessary for story telling are among those that many teachers have already worked to develop.

> I am opting for a heavy investment in lower-skill requirement approaches to searches in education. Literacy in one's mother tongue, reasonable sensitivity to one's informants and environment, and a clear attempt to communicate the important dimensions of an observed milieu are what I ask of a story teller. [p. 16]

Such "story telling" research would not only offer interested practitioners an opportunity to clarify and make available to others the hunches and personal knowledge that they have, but would very likely be more accessible to teachers than many of the current, more technical reports.

A good example of using story telling and other less formal research techniques comes from the Teacher-initiated Research Project at Technical Education Research Centers (TERC) in Cambridge, Massachusetts. This project, supported by a grant from the National Institute of Education, is currently conducting a research seminar for elementary- and middle-school teachers. During the school year, teachers meet weekly for two hours. Early in the year each teacher identifies an area of interest or concern to be investigated in his or her own classroom. Through discussion, other members of the group help to clarify the question, identify the data to be collected, and select the most appropriate, feasible method for collecting the data. In some cases teachers collect the data themselves. In other cases, graduate students visit classrooms to observe, conduct interviews, videotape, or tape-record. The results of the investigations are then presented to the seminar for discussion and analysis. Some of the teachers choose to write up their studies and will, upon completion, submit them for publication to professional journals.

In one research project stimulated by this seminar, a second-grade teacher with a long-term interest in developmental issues, particularly moral development, looked more closely at examples of students taking the perspective of others. Her interest in the question was stimulated by her desire to know whether the standards and expectations she has for students were reasonable and fair. For the first phase of her investigation, she arranged to have students interviewed individually to determine their views of class meetings. It was clear to her that each year between September and June her students became better listeners in class meetings. She hoped to understand better the reasons for that change, considering the possibilities that: they are interested in what other people say; they know they're not allowed to interrupt; they want a chance to talk and they understand that other people do too. Later, she invited another teacher in the seminar to observe in her classroom and designated a time each week for writing notes on her classroom to record instances of student behavior that exemplify perspective taking or lack of it. In all her thinking about this issue, she has wanted to understand students' behavior and capabilities in "natural" settings—in situations that normally arise in school or on the playground. By contrast, much of the research she has read has been based on interviews about hypothetical situations. That research was interesting and informative as background for her questions but did not answer the question she posed for herself.

While this teacher used both interview and observation techniques, others relied exclusively on observation. For example, a third-grade teacher in a suburban school, who previously had successful and enjoyable teaching experiences, found herself this fall bewildered by the lack of cooperation among the students in her room. She identified five or six students who appeared to be the primary sources of conflict and began to document their behavior by keeping a journal. Later she invited an observer to the room on several occasions and observed her own class as it was taught by a substitute for a day. Though the documentation and the participation in the seminar provided the teacher with the possibility of clarifying her thinking and gaining support for the efforts she was making, the situation in her classroom did not improve substantially. Then quite abruptly, in late winter, one particularly difficult student left her room. The teacher continued her efforts to develop cooperative behavior among the students in her class and found that she was more successful. She kept extensive notes throughout the year and is now writing a description of her experience.

The questions that teachers in the seminars have selected represent a wide range of topics. A suburban art teacher investigated teachers' attitudes toward asking young children to draw from observation. A junior-high-school art teacher conducted a survey of student and parent attitudes toward the school. A fourth-grade teacher investigated the use of computers in her classroom.

This seminar could serve as an example for school systems that wish to expand the range of staff-development opportunities for teachers and to establish closer relations with the world of research. Such seminars could be organized by public school systems in cooperation with university research departments with little or no outside funding. The school system could provide some released time for teachers, video recorders and tapes, and meeting space. The university could provide, through a research course oriented to the needs of schools, technical support and data collection by graduate students. Teachers would benefit from an opportunity to look more closely at their own practice, and interested researchers would benefit from a deeper understanding of the concerns of individual teachers.

Teachers joined the TERC seminar as individuals; their investigations were therefore limited to questions that could be addressed within the context of their individual classrooms. There are other questions that teachers or administrators might choose to investigate which would require the cooperation of the system as a whole. Those questions are now usually unasked, unrefined, and, of course, unanswered except implicitly by people's actions. I propose a research committee for a public school system or a consortium of small systems that would solicit research questions from teachers and administrators, clarify and refine the questions, determine which questions could not be addressed within the school system, and inform local research institutions of the results. The committee might communicate with researchers by distributing a periodic newsletter ("requests for proposals"), by inviting local institutions to send representatives to the committee meetings, or by hosting a conference of researchers and practitioners with presentations of questions by school staff. Researchers could respond to requests that closely matched their research interests and could also relay the needs to graduate students in search of research opportunities. Such a committee would not require extensive funds and would, again, be of benefit to both practitioners and interested researchers.

SUMMARY

Schools in the United States are in need of support, improvement, and more careful thought about the ways in which good practice occurs. Partly because educational research has had fewer positive effects on schools than might have been expected, researchers are increasingly interested in finding ways to make their results applicable to school settings and are establishing more collaborative relationships with practitioners.

Practitioners, however, have not yet taken a sufficiently active role in these efforts. We need, for our own benefit as well as for the benefit of students, to exert more influence on educational research. There are, undoubtedly, many ways to do that. Two that seem well within the range of possibilities at the current time are to make public, professional evaluations of research publications and to initiate and carry out classroom-based investigations. We need not see "research" as beyond our ability or level of skill. There is a place within the broad range of needed research for more carefully articulated statements of current practitioner knowledge.

REFERENCES

Brickell, H. M. *Needed: instruments as good as our eyes.* Kalamazoo: Evaluation Center of the College of Education of Western Michigan University, July 1976.

Carini, P. *Observation and description: An alternative methodology for the investigation of human phenomena.* Grand Forks, N.D.: North Dakota Study Group on Evaluation, February 1975.

Carini, P. *The art of seeing and the visibility of the person.* Grand Forks, N.D.: North Dakota Study Group on Evaluation, September 1979.

Denny, T. *Story telling and educational understanding.* Kalamazoo: Evaluation Center of the College of Education of Western Michigan University, November 1978.

Duckworth, E. *A comparison study for evaluating primary school science in Africa.* Newton, Mass.: Education Development Center, October 1971.

Duckworth, E. *The African primary science program: An evaluation and extended thoughts.* Grand Forks, N.D.: North Dakota Study Group on Evaluation, February 1978.

Elliott, J. *Developing hypotheses about classrooms from teachers' practical constructs.* Grand Forks, N.D.: North Dakota Study Group on Evaluation, September 1976.

Elliott, J. & Adelman C. *Teachers' accounts and the control of classroom research.* Mimeographed manuscript, Centre for Applied Research in Education at the University of East Anglia, England, February 1975.

Florio, S. & Walsh, M. *The teacher as colleague in classroom research.* East Lansing: Institute for Research on Teaching of Michigan State University, February 1978.

Hull, B. *Teachers' seminars on children's thinking: a progress report.* Grand Forks, N.D.: North Dakota Study Group on Evaluation, April 1978.

Jervis, K. *Children's thinking in the classroom.* Grand Forks, N.D.: North Dakota Study Group on Evaluation, September 1978.

Peterson, S. M. & Emrick, J. A. *Research and reflection: School practitioner involvement in knowledge production as a strategy for professional development.* Unpublished manuscript, January 1981. (Available from John A. Emrick and Associates, 745 Distel Drive, Los Altos, Calif., 94022.)

Tikunoff, W. J., Ward, B. A., & Griffin, G. A. *Interactive research and development on teaching study: Final report.* San Francisco: Far West Laboratory for Educational Research and Development, November 1979.

Watt, M. *Thinking about thinking: A description of a seminar for supporting teacher growth.* Brookline, Mass.: Teacher Center Publication, February 1979.

Chapter 12

How Educators Make Decisions about Research: Research in the Brookline Public Schools

Roland A. Dwinell and Janet H. Berman

If properly managed, research activity can serve a valuable function in the public schools. Many educators want to encourage research activity because the perspective of the researcher can act as a valuable counterpoint to the preconceptions and pragmatic concerns of the educational practitioner. Faced with pressures both to maintain a fundamental curriculum and to adapt classroom practice to constant demands for change, teachers can find in research activity a much-needed intellectual stimulus to explore questions that often go unanswered in the day-to-day practice of education. Indeed, both educators and researchers can find opportunities for intellectual growth as they adapt to each other's needs. The presence of the researcher in the public schools, however, presents a set of problems that need to be addressed before the obvious opportunities are exploited.

Having both served terms as chairpersons of the Testing, Research, and Evaluation Committee of the public schools of Brookline, Massachusetts, we present this chapter as a case study of research decisions in this large suburban school system. Our presentation has been designed to be useful to both educators and researchers. The model suggested by this case study will have features transferable to other school settings although, certainly, educators will need to adapt the features of the Brookline model to their own setting. We hope that researchers will also benefit from this case study by learning of the concerns and the procedures that they will encounter when they approach public school systems with research proposals.

Because Brookline is a suburb of Boston, the Brookline public schools receive many requests to conduct research. There are a large number of universities in the Boston area and, in general, the professional staff of the Brookline schools fits well within this academic environment. Indeed, in many cases, a collaborative tie between academic researchers and particular teachers already exists, since many of our staff members are pursuing advanced degrees at these institutions and, in fact, some of them teach at the college level as well as in the Brookline schools. This close connection results, we believe, in quite a sophisticated attitude toward research among most of our teachers. Not only do they, in general, welcome good research, but several members of the professional staff have actually originated research projects of their own. This extraordinarily heavy volume of research requests created the need for systematic review of all proposals; thus, the Testing, Research, and Evaluation Committee was formed in 1975. Although testing and evaluation are important committee functions, this chapter will be limited to the committee's research function.

The committee was formed to ensure that research is done in an orderly fashion and that researchers are cognizant of the needs of the school system, its students, parents, teachers, and administrators. The committee attempts to maintain a spirit of intellectual curiosity combined with careful attention to the privacy needs of children and staff and the dangers of overburdening an already crowded curriculum. We will present guidelines for prospective researchers in the public schools and a description of our organizational structures and procedures as an example that might be helpful to other communities with similar needs. To begin, we will explore the types of research most acceptable to our committee and suggest cautions against certain kinds of research topics. Our remarks are more pragmatic than theoretical, because the committee's role is oriented toward the educational process rather than the research process.

THE RESEARCH TOPIC

The research proposals that we consider can roughly be divided into three categories: straightforward curriculum research (projects that examine aspects of the existent curriculum or that propose new items for the regular curriculum); curriculum-relevant research (projects that could have direct implications for the regular curriculum or its implementation); and theoretical research (research that might be relevant to education, but is designed to answer particular theoretical questions). Although there is a preference for research that can be directly applied within our school system, all three categories have been represented in projects approved in the past.

An excellent example of curriculum research is work on the Holocaust Unit of the eighth-grade social studies curriculum (Strom & Parsons, 1977). This unit relates issues of the Holocaust to a broader understanding of human behavior and concepts of justice and conflict resolution. The original research in developing this unit began in Brookline but is now an independent project funded by several private and government sources. Since the unit is considered an important part of the Brookline curriculum, the committee welcomes sound research designs that will examine aspects of the unit that have not yet been studied. In a case such as this, however, it is important for researchers to remember that we are careful to avoid duplicating any aspect of previous research projects.

Curriculum-relevant research can be quite diverse. For example, in 1978, Harriet Sutfin, a Brookline kindergarten teacher working toward a degree at the Harvard Graduate School of Education, conducted a study on the physical environment in her classroom and its effects on a wide variety of behaviors (Sutfin, 1978). Using a time-series design, she changed several features of the classroom environment and found that these changes led, among other things, to less noise and more cooperative play. Although this project could not be considered a study of part of the curriculum, its findings were directly relevant to day-to-day teaching practice in that classroom and others like it.

A curriculum-relevant proposal that was enthusiastically approved by our committee was the work of Frances Maher (Maher, 1980). Maher reasoned that teaching materials can do one of three things: they can convey knowledge, they can ask students to reason deductively, or they can ask students to reason inductively. Maher suggests that teachers must convey knowledge by referring to each individual student's level of knowledge, background, and experience. Using an inquiry method, teachers can transmit knowledge at the appropriate cognitive level for each student and can then move on to ask all students, whatever their level, to reason with this knowledge. Maher's study investigated ways in which this might occur. Since this teaching methodology might provide effective strategies for dealing with heterogeneous ability groupings of students and for improving basic competency skills, it is not surprising that the committee, composed mainly of teachers, would enthusiastically support this research.

Much of the research represented by the proposals we see, however, can be considered theoretical research. Although the committee does not place as high a priority on this type of work, we have approved several excellent projects that fall into this category. We will give a number of examples here in an effort to give researchers some insight into the kind of work that we consider most worthwhile.

Project Zero, based at Harvard University (Gardner, 1979), conducted a language-arts study in Brookline that was met with considerable enthusiasm by the committee and the staff of teachers. Investigating the development of the understanding of figurative language, this study examined the relationships between abilities to understand five different types of figurative language: sarcasm, irony, hyperbole, understatement, and metaphor. For each of the five types, the researchers were interested in discovering whether having children attend to the humorous content of the statement would facilitate their comprehension of the figurative language. Although this study was based on a particular theoretical conception, many Brookline teachers felt that it uncovered several methods they could use in their classrooms to sensitize children to nonliteral language—for example, by introducing the nonliteral statement within a humorous context.

A different type of psychological research is represented by a study of the relationship between brain dysfunction, poor school adjustment, and lack of reciprocity within the mother-child dyad (Lorman, 1978). One of several hypotheses of this study was that the child's problem-solving style will be freer and more flexible if the mother has empathic accuracy—an understanding and communication of the child's feelings to the child. The study included boys from the Brookline schools as the comparison sample; boys who were being treated at a local psychiatric hospital made up the sample of interest. Although the time commitment for each Brookline participant was considerable (45 minutes for the teacher of each boy, two hours for the mother, and over three hours for the child himself), the study was deemed sufficiently important for the understanding of normal and abnormal development that it was approved. The committee did stipulate, however, that all Brookline subjects be tested after school hours.

Like the Gardner (1979) and Lorman (1978) studies, our final example comes from developmental psychology. Here, however, the concerns were more strictly social-psychological. In this last part of a longitudinal study of adolescent world views and their development, children in grades four, five, six, and eight were asked to complete a rather detailed questionnaire on their perceptions of current events. In this study (Broughton, 1978), these students constituted the control group; the group of interest comprised a number of young adults who had been tested in a similar manner when they were in early adolescence. The study was designed to determine whether the change in world views in the experimental group was due to the rapid rate of change in our social environment or due more to inherent development change. Given the concern among teachers with the effects of social turmoil on their students' development, this project generated considerable interest.

As a general rule, then, the prospective researcher would do well to determine the educational goals and objectives in the specific school system to which his request is made and to ask himself how his research relates to the needs of the particular school under consideration. Teachers are reluctant to allow their students to be researched for a purpose that does not fit the stated or implied goals of their grade, school, or curriculum. Principals need to justify any student time not spent on direct instruction. It is difficult for them to justify research projects, however impressive, if these projects fail to relate to the functions of the school, curriculum, or teaching process. A researcher may be able to defend his sometimes narrow contribution to knowledge academically, but teachers and principals need to focus on the needs of the children and the reality of the classroom.

There are some kinds of proposals that are fairly consistently rejected. The committee is reluctant to approve any project on certain overly researched topics. For example, it is safe to say that, in our school system, there is now a moratorium on research projects raising new questions on Kohlberg's sequence of moral development (Kohlberg, 1964). Those who know this research suggest that it becomes increasingly difficult to assess stages of moral development as the student becomes more sophisticated and test-wise through familiarity with the standard questions asked. Our students have had so many repeated exposures to these questions that we consider additional work at this time both unnecessary and of doubtful validity.

Finally, both teachers and students need to be protected from being overly researched—regardless of the specific project. If, for example, a particular grade level is involved in some sort of long-term research project, the committee will often declare a moratorium on any additional research for that grade. Even when teachers might be interested in participating in a variety of research projects, the committee feels that it must look out for the best interests of the educational enterprise.

THE RESEARCH DESIGN

Once the committee has decided that a research topic is appropriate, it turns to a consideration of the proposed research design. The central question is, "Does the proposal make sense?" The researcher should ask if the methodology employed will in fact test the hypothesis presented. Certainly, we expect that doctoral and masters degree candidates will have the approval of their thesis committees. We have no bias for or against a master's or doctoral study, but we cannot presume to substitute for the thesis advisors. Basically, our committee wants to be assured that the research is feasible and worthwhile to Brookline, and that the logic of its design can be defended.

There is more to the logic of a research project than just the soundness of its design. Since we are concerned with the plausibility of the arguments made, the researcher should avoid large assumptions or quantum jumps in logic. The committee rejected a proposal recently because the researcher made the assertion that classrooms with chairs in rows were managed by rigid teachers. The use of ordered rows of chairs may sometimes be a symptom of rigidity, but this is certainly not a foregone conclusion. Researchers should be forewarned that if the reader of a proposal spots this type of assumption, she or he adopts a more critical stance.

In addition, the statistical model needs to be considered. Since we are concerned that our teachers and students not be overly researched, the committee sometimes approves a proposal on condition that the researcher use a smaller sample than originally proposed. In such an instance, researchers should be prepared to find an additional source of subjects or to employ sample statistics creatively.

ETHICAL, LEGAL, AND SOCIAL ISSUES

The final and most important issue addressed by the committee is the protection of the rights of individual subjects. Even if a researcher presents us with a well-designed proposal on an interesting topic, we will reject the proposal if it appears that the subjects' rights will be violated by the procedures employed. The most common infringement of subjects' rights that we encounter is the invasion of privacy—the asking of questions that are too personal, the collection of privileged information from students' files, or the use of procedures that might cause embarrassment. In such cases, if the researcher can omit the invasion of privacy from an otherwise acceptable proposal, the committee might rule favorably on it.

It might happen, for example, that a researcher studying some facet of the curriculum such as the Holocaust Unit will want to identify the religion of the student subject, assuring complete anonymity. The law, however, is clear: it is illegal for a public school to require a student to reveal his or her religion except under certain carefully prescribed circumstances (which are not represented in such research proposals). The committee would therefore have no choice but to reject the proposal, or to require that these questions be omitted.

The committee carefully reviews all proposed survey instruments in order to eliminate any illegal questions on race, religion, and so on, and to uncover any blatant or subtle social bias inherent in the instruments. For example, questions aimed at an economically disadvantaged group must not be condescending in tone or implication. Survey items and examples should be free of any sex bias. Researchers should realize that most school systems are racially, economically, and religiously mixed; students, teachers, parents, and administrators are sensitive to any hint of discrimination. Basically, then, in the matter of question to be asked of subjects, the committee is responsible for screening questions that may be illegal or that may violate students' privacy; the objective is to avoid placing anyone in the position of having to refuse to answer a question, or feeling forced to answer an improper question.

In addition, state privacy laws require the school administration to guard student records. Any unnecessary requests for access to these records will be disapproved. If access is critical to the study, the researcher should be careful to spell out precisely what information is needed, who will obtain it, and what legally acceptable processes to guard anonymity will be followed. For example, a researcher might want to examine student responses to some set of stimuli as a function of IQ scores, grade level, place of residence (to determine economic status), and school achievement. With the assurance of anonymity, some of this information would be legally available to the researcher, but in aggregated form only. Even collected in this manner, however, some of this data may not be available. After alerting the appropriate student personnel administrator to the problems it perceived, the committee would probably require the researcher to obtain that administrator's approval. A final decision in such a case would be up to him or her. In any case, the well-being of the student-subjects will always be the paramount consideration.

Ideally, if achievement or IQ scores are critical for a project, the researcher should time the study to coincide with the school system's standardized testing schedule. In this way, scores can be obtained relatively easily without requesting administrative and parental permission to examine a child's file. Of course, if the researcher cannot synchronize with the school's own testing, obtaining permission to go through existing files would be preferable to retesting all the subjects. Whatever method is used for obtaining scores, the research must be organized so that scores can be reported without revealing the identity of individuals.

Occasionally, we receive proposals that include procedures that might be embarrassing to students. For example, a given researcher may find it necessary to determine the onset of puberty as a critical independent variable. Although we welcome projects on adolescent psychology, the committee would reject such a proposal if it required a physical examination. Likewise, a personal interview procedure that invaded the student's privacy would not be acceptable.

Many of these issues are raised not only in the committee's consideration of the proposal itself, but also in its consideration of the required parental consent letter. In that letter it is important, once again, to avoid social bias. In any community, there are parents who are sensitive to real or imagined attitudes toward them. This sensitivity does not need to be bruised by a visiting researcher. Also, this letter should outline the entire procedure that each child will participate in; parents do not want to be surprised after agreeing to allow their child to participate in a study. This letter should assure parents of all the precautions that are being taken to protect the children's feelings and rights, including the rights to privacy, confidentiality of test results, and anonymity of responses. In order to request the informed consent of parents realistically, the letter must be a paragon of clarity at all times, free of jargon, obscure terms, and confusing language.

Finally, it is important that the letter to parents not cause unnecessary controversy. If parents misunderstand the substance or intent of a project, the committee might find itself caught between researcher and parents. The researcher must remember that our primary task as a public school committee is to reflect the needs of the community. We seldom deviate from our perception of these needs. A researcher's objectives are secondary to the community's needs and are difficult to justify when they run counter to the needs of the community.

HOW THE COMMITTEE FUNCTIONS

During the six years of its existence, the Testing, Research, and Evaluation Committee of Brookline has developed a set of operating procedures that have, for the most part, served it well. We will outline these procedures as guidelines for other educators who wish to initiate research evaluation committees, and for researchers who wish to approach a public school system with a research proposal.

A request to conduct research in the Brookline public schools begins at the offices of the Assistant Superintendent for Curriculum and Instruction. At the initial contact, the researcher is given a questionnaire detailing the information that is required. (This document appears in the appendix to this chapter). Researchers are warned at this time that the review process could take up to four months (and it often does). According to present policy, the committee meets bimonthly in September, November, January, March, and May. Generally, proposals receive initial consideration at the first meeting after they are received.

At that first meeting, the proposal may be clearly accepted or clearly rejected, but there is no discussion beyond a motion to accept, a motion to reject, or a motion to ask specific questions of the researcher. When questions are raised, a decision is deferred until the following meeting, and a monitor or shepherd is appointed from among the committee members. It is the shepherd's role to contact the researcher, ask the questions, and report back to the committee at the next regularly scheduled meeting. At that time, both the proposal itself and the shepherd's report are considered; no limit is placed on this discussion. The results of this hearing are communicated to the researcher by both the committee chairperson and the shepherd.

These procedures have proved to be quite effective. Although a large number of proposals are considered at each meeting, we feel that this process helps us give each an honest hearing. It is important to the committee to avoid snap judgments and, in fact, this committee has a reputation (which it intends to retain) of not responding to pressure. In order to ensure fairness and efficiency, these procedures are frequently reviewed by the committee, and appropriate changes are made.

The committee's decisions serve as recommendations to the Assistant Superintendent of Schools for Curriculum and Instruction, who has the prerogative to reverse the action of the committee. This veto power, however, is seldom exercised. Next, the elementary-school principals and the high-school headmaster have veto power over all proposals affecting their schools. The attitude of the committee is that it will do its job conscientiously and stand by its decision. Because a strong committee is an asset to them, school administrators seldom veto a committee decision. A prospective researcher needs to know, however, that this is a possibility.

Approved proposals are followed up by the appointed shepherd since, once it approves a proposal, the committee wants to aid its success. Thus, the shepherd becomes a facilitator when this role appears appropriate; basically, the committee looks to the shepherd to smooth the way for the researcher. The degree of effort required by this role varies. Although researchers must implement their own procedures for recruiting subjects, the shepherd can familiarize the researcher with the specific school setting and can occasionally even help to arrange complex schedules and obtain administrative clearances. In other cases, the shepherd need only introduce the researcher to the appropriate principal or other professional staff member.

The shepherd is also involved in follow-up activity. Researchers are required to submit both an interim and a final report of the study. The interim report provides immediate feedback to the teachers and administrators directly involved in the study. The more complete final report becomes part of a school system file that is used to review research outcomes and generate new ideas for research within the system. These reports are a vital component of the research process. The committee approved the project because it was deemed interesting and useful to the professional staff. Results must be known before they can be implemented. It is the shepherd who receives these reports from the researcher and files them with the appropriate recipients.

All research and evaluation activity is coordinated with a master calendar of all other activities that may usurp instructional time. As mentioned earlier, some grade levels have a very busy schedule, and this calendar can be an important aid in planning. Any approved research proposal or research-related activity must be scheduled around ongoing research and other projects, including the standardized testing program, high-school-level achievement and aptitude testing, basic skills testing, Title I evaluations, any longitudinal research, and any ongoing curriculum-evaluation projects.

The committee itself has representatives from across the school system. The superintendent's office is represented by the Assistant Superintendent of Schools for Curriculum and Instruction and the Director of Grants and Research as permanent committee members. The representative from the psychological testing department is also a permanent member. Two members represent the curriculum areas, and the elementary principals also have a spokesperson. Teacher representatives include a staff member from each elementary school and eight from the high school. Members serve for two years and may serve for two consecutive terms. Officers, including a chairperson, a vice chairperson, and a secretary, serve for one year and may be reelected once.

In closing, we think researchers should appreciate the fact that a public school system is a complex mechanism. Given the many demands placed on staff and students, it would be easy for schools to reject all research requests. But most teachers see the need for research and do want to be involved. At the same time, they do not want to be overwhelmed by extracurricular commitments that might detract from regular classroom instruction or place undue strain on themselves or their students. The role of the research evaluation committee is to allow responsible research to be done, but within a manageable framework. The guidelines and procedures we have described were designed to make this happen.

REFERENCES

Broughton, J. Epistemological self questionnaire. Unpublished research report, Public Schools of Brookline, Mass., and Columbia University, New York, 1978.

Gardner, H. Harvard project zero. Unpublished research report, Harvard University, Cambridge, Mass., May 1979.

Kohlberg, L. Development of moral character and moral ideology. In Hoffman, M. L. & Hoffman, L. W. (Eds.), *Review of child development research.* (Vol. 1.) New York: Russell Sage Foundation, 1964.

Lorman, C. The relationship between assessed brain dysfunction and poor school adjustment. Unpublished research proposal, Public Schools of Brookline, Mass., 1978.

Maher, F. A. Teaching by inquiry—A structural analysis of methods, content, and consequences. Unpublished doctoral dissertation, Boston University, Boston, September 1980.

Strom, M. & Parsons, W. Facing history and ourselves: The Holocaust and human behavior. Unpublished curriculum guide, The Brookline Public Schools, Brookline, Mass., 1977.

Sutfin, H. The behavioral effects of changes in the physical design of a kindergarten. Unpublished research proposal, Public Schools of Brookline, Mass., 1978.

APPENDIX

Testing, Research, and Evaluation Committee Questions

Please number your responses and repeat the questions before answering.

1. What is your institutional affiliation? If you are a student, name your sponsoring professor and degree program.

2. List the questions you plan to be able to answer when you have completed your study. If you have hypotheses, include them.
3. Describe the proposed method of gathering data including:

   a. target population (including N)
   b. instruments to be used (enclose copies)
   c. time requirements
      1. per teacher
      2. per student
      3. per administrator
   d. specific data collection procedures
      (group versus individual, place, assistance of teacher or other personnel, access to Brookline files or records, other relevant information)
   e. names of persons collecting data
   f. time constraints

4. Describe how the data you collect will enable you to answer the questions listed in #2.
5. How will your project differ from previous work in this area? How will your project contribute to the body of knowledge in this area?
6. What orientation, if necessary, would you provide for teachers and students?
7. Do you plan to publish? If your project fulfills requirements for a degree program, please describe your program.
8. Testing of students which is not part of the ongoing regular program of the Brookline public schools can *only* be done with informed parental consent. Therefore, a sample informed consent form must be included with your proposal. Please include the following points in your form:

   a. The purpose of the study.
   b. An explanation of the kinds of activities or tests you plan to administer, with examples whenever possible.
   c. An estimate of the time required for the child to participate in it.
   d. The name of the person(s) administering the tests or interview.
   e. Safeguards you will use to ensure privacy and confidentiality.
   f. Who will have access to the information you will collect.
   g. Who will be conducting the research.
   h. Your name and where you may be reached for further information.

   In writing this form, please be as clear as possible; use as much detail as is necessary to represent your work faithfully, without overwhelming the reader.

9. If you have spoken with any Brookline staff members concerning your proposal, please list their name. (You are neither required nor encouraged to do so.)

10. The Committee requires a written summary of your results and welcomes any additional supporting materials you wish to include. When can the Committee expect to receive a report of your results?
11. Have we missed anything?

Part IV:
Practitioners' Research Needs

Introduction to Part IV

Since many teachers feel that research has little of value to tell them, it would seem to be important for researchers to become informed of teachers' questions, problems, and needs in the classroom. If research can be designed with the goal of fulfilling those needs—or if, at least, the fulfillment of those needs can become one goal of research, the present gap between teachers and researchers might become considerably smaller. Moreover, if practitioners can vividly describe the context in which they work, they might be able to help researchers anticipate the problems that will confront them as they try to work in the world of the teacher. In this section, several educational practitioners present their views of teachers' research needs and the functions researchers might perform in helping to fulfill those needs.

In Chapter 13, Carter proposes that teaching and research are actually very similar activities; both involve long processes of formulating and testing hypotheses, revising procedures, and testing the hypotheses again. It is problematic, however, that teachers do not in any way view themselves as researchers. Carter suggests that both research and classroom practice could be improved if researchers helped teachers to develop a more research-oriented self-image. In addition, he argues that, contrary to many people's belief, teachers are not brimming with questions either for themselves or for researchers. He suggests that teachers need opportunities to develop their own thinking about their work, to "talk" articulately about it, before their insights will become informative for others.

Barth, in Chapter 14, presents another arena in which researchers can be useful to teachers and educational administrators; they can help these educational practitioners to write about their experiences in the classroom. Although this function is often neglected, Barth argues that it is important for educators to write about their practice because of the unique access they have to classroom behaviors and the deep insights they develop into children's behavior over time. Not only are there many potential rewards for writing about practice, but there are also a number of obstacles making it extremely difficult for teachers to do so. Barth outlines several ways in which researchers can offer varying degrees of collaboration and support.

It is probably the detailed, substantive questions about children and about teaching, the questions that arise in some form or other through the daily work of most teachers, that present the richest arena for researchers' collaboration with educators. Often, however, researchers have no idea of what teachers' questions are, or at what stages they might be of most help in answering these questions. In Chapters 15 (Haley) and 16 (McVinney), such questions are framed in the context of specific educational settings. Haley describes an attempt to establish a program for gifted children and the problems encountered at several stages: the definition of giftedness, the literature search, the assessment and identification of gifted children, the development and evaluation of the program. She points out ways in which researchers could have assisted at various stages in the project's growth. McVinney describes the day-to-day practical problem solving involved in establishing a day-care center, and points to the areas in which research expertise could have informed that problem solving (e.g., the grouping of children in the center, the effects of day care on various types of families). She ends with a long list of researchable questions on day care, its impact, and its most effective implementation.

Chapter 13

Teacher Talk as a Tool for Effective Research

Richard C. Carter

The last decade has been a stressful one for public education in the United States. The list of problems faced by public schools has stretched from the failure of school bond issues to teen-age vandalism to battles about racial segregation. But of all the issues, perhaps the most fundamental and disturbing is the belief, expressed by many diverse segments of our society, that our schools are simply not doing an adequate job of educating our children. Today, when faced with a problem, people often turn to science and scientific research to help find a solution. Research is expected to help improve our capacity to deal effectively with the world. Research in education and psychology is expected to improve our understanding of the processes of human learning and education, and one expects that the result of this research should be more effective schools. But along with the current concerns about the effectiveness of our schools, there are also an increasing number of voices that criticize traditional educational and developmental research for its failure to have a significant impact on classrooms (Elliot, 1980; Bassey, 1980; Bussis, Chittenden, & Amarel, 1976).

Although many now claim that neither educational or psychological research is having a productive impact on our schools, I will argue here that this need not be the case, and that instead there is a powerful potential for research to have an important impact on education in this country. I believe that one basis of the failure of academic research to have any significant impact on what goes on in classrooms is a series of assumptions that are held not only by the general public, but also by teachers and researchers themselves. In this chapter I will explore this set of assumptions and suggest that a more productive approach will result from focusing on the similarities between research and teaching. Further, I will argue that one path to educationally relevant research could evolve from a particular kind of "teacher talk" for which there are currently too few opportunities.

The most important erroneous assumption is that teaching and research are two radically different endeavors. This is a misguided assumption and one that stands in the way of our gaining new and useful understandings of teaching and learning. I would claim that good teachers and experimental researchers are both involved in similar processes. In a somewhat simplified view, an experimental researcher can be seen as doing two things: coming up with explanatory hypotheses about some phenomenon, and testing those hypotheses by designing and carrying out experiments: for example, a researcher may begin with a hypothesis that telling a teacher a child is smart will improve the child's performance. Next she must construct and carry out experiments to test the hypothesis.

When people compare the work of academic researchers and teachers, they usually focus on the testing aspect of academic research which involves being an experimenter, using a systematic approach, controlling variables, invoking mathematical models, and so on. Too often the other aspect of research, which requires generating ideas and formulating hypotheses, is neglected. This part of research involves such things as picking out the significant aspects of a given situation, choosing what one is going to look at, and generating specific questions. This part of research is as important as the experimental aspect, but in comparing teaching and research, it is rarely considered.

How does this relate to teaching? We commonly describe a teacher's job as teaching subject matter to students, or as helping them master some set of ideas that the larger community has agreed are important. From this perspective the tasks of a teacher and a researcher may look rather different, but if we look more deeply an alternate picture may emerge. At a very simple level one can ask, how is a teacher to help children effectively master ideas that are new to them? One might describe this task by saying that good teachers start out by gathering data about their students from which they hypothesize about children's levels of understanding and how they learn. These, of course, are testable hypotheses and good teachers do test them.

A teacher's hypothesis making also extends beyond the original assessment of individual students. Research often involves taking some set of complex and often seemingly contradictory phenomena and trying to make a new kind of sense out of them. Similarly, for a teacher, each new class presents a new set of complex conditions. The interactions of the class are unique, as is each child. Teachers are continually confronted with having to make sense out of new phenomena. Children's behavior often presents data that are surprising or even seem contradictory. As any teacher knows, an activity that went wonderfully one year may be a complete flop the next year with a different class. Good teachers take these ongoing puzzles and try to make sense out of them. They get hunches that are derived from their past experience and their view of learning and then proceed to test them through their ongoing interactions with their students.

Here is the strongest parallel between the "intuitive" work of a teacher and the "scientific" work of a researcher. A teacher's view of learning, though often unarticulated, is like a researcher's theory. It is developed from the teacher's past experience (analogous to the researcher's review of previous research). Based on this theory the teacher develops hunches (hypotheses, for a researcher) that she tests in her daily work with her children (this parallels the researcher's formal experiments). Both teaching and research involve taking a complex set of phenomena and attempting to make sense out of them. Given this perspective, the central tasks of teaching and research are not so different.

Yet, this view is in stark contrast to a much more common interpretation of the teacher's role (Lightfoot, 1981). For many, the teacher is seen merely as a technician who administers a curriculum. The job is reduced to monitoring children's movement through 101 behavioral objectives in one of a variety of skill sequences. The teacher is seen mainly as a manager or record keeper. This perspective misses completely the complex and evolving nature of a teacher's task: the process of coming to understand a child more and more deeply, the challenge of finding the right combination of factors (whether social, emotional, perceptual, or curricular) that will help support the individual child's learning, and the necessary integration of this information with that from all the other children.

Thus, at a deep level, the central tasks of research and teaching have strong similarities; in fact, in comparing the creative work done by teachers and researchers one can find significant parallels. Yet the styles and the general approach of the two groups are often quite different. Researchers tend to work in a highly analytical, rationalized, and explicit framework, whereas teachers tend to function on an intuitive and day-by-day basis. Researchers also depend on the ideas and criticisms of an interconnected research community, whereas teachers are often relatively isolated from the ideas and critiques of their peers. When dealing with the complexities of human learning in the context of a classroom, each approach has its strengths and weaknesses.

In the classical model of scientific research, that of the "hard" sciences such as physics, the most important aspect of research is the experimental one of isolating and controlling variables. The problem with transferring this model to the study of human behavior, especially human behavior in groups as one finds in classrooms, is that it is extremely difficult, perhaps impossible, to control all the variables. Faced with this problem, educational and psychological researchers often limit what they explore to things they can control, and design their research around the demand that they isolate variables rather than the question of what seems most significant.[1] The result is often a study that cuts out a lot of the complex reality of a functioning classroom. Typically, small groups of children are often isolated, briefly subjected to some kind of experience, and then tested. Their performance in these artificial situations may be quite different from what they do anywhere else.[2] It has been suggested that it is almost impossible for anyone but a practicing teacher to understand the complexity of a smoothly running classroom, and that it is not surprising that researchers who are not teachers themselves are unable to provide much relevant insight into the nature of effective teaching and learning in a classroom of children (Bassey, 1980). It is no wonder that studies that try to isolate only one aspect of a classroom's reality often end up indicating that the variable studied made "no significant difference," and that teachers consider many of the things that researchers study to be irrelevant (Coker, Medley, & Soar, 1980; Doyle, 1977).

But those who claim that teachers have a privileged access to the significant issues of effective learning in a classroom often participate in a second misdirected assumption—that in the minds of many teachers there are—just below the surface—a host of researchable questions.[3] Though good teaching includes many of the same elements as good research, it is not the case that most teachers are brimming with questions that they are ready to articulate. The belief that they are reflects a naive view of the nature of teaching in present-day American schools.

In most schools it is hard for teachers to move much beyond working on a day-by-day, intuitive level. The multiple demands of teaching and the lack of professional support for reflection make it hard for most teachers to be very articulate about what they do, much less to be articulate about problems and unresolved issues in children's learning that they must deal with every day. Teachers are immersed in an environment rich in data and are constantly confronted with having to make sense out of that data, and, I suggest, many good teachers have well-developed "hunching" or intuitive hypothesizing capacities about individual children and they potentially have a lot to say about many aspects of children's learning. But, because teachers are almost never given the chance to explore, develop, and articulate their thoughts about their experiences, neither researchers nor teachers themselves are given access to the rich resource of intuitive understandings many teachers have. I am suggesting that while many teachers have an intuitive understanding of important aspects of children's learning, they have neither the experience nor the support necessary to use those understandings to the best advantage. I am also suggesting that while researchers have many skills necessary for productive inquiry, it may be that a good classroom is simply too complex to be dealt with in a traditional research mode. If we are to move forward in our quest to understand effective learning, academic researchers may have to accept the limitations of their current methodologies and search out new and more appropriate techniques. As I shall argue, a special kind of collaboration between researchers and teachers is particularly suited for just such a search.

In order to achieve a productive collaboration between teachers and researchers, we must first move beyond these unproductive assumptions about a teacher's job and the nature of teaching. Overcoming these assumptions will necessitate a number of changes on the part of both teachers and researchers. Not only will researchers have to change their view of teachers, and teachers their view of researchers, but possibly traditional researchers will have to change their view of research and teachers—their view of themselves.

The puzzles and problems that teachers run into as they work with children have the potential, if they can be brought out in the open, to provide both teachers and researchers with rich and useful sources of information and insight. But, in order for these potential insights to become more available, in order for the problems and puzzles that teachers must deal with in their everyday work to be brought to the surface, some kind of support mechanism will be necessary. Only through a process of reflection upon the rich data base of their experiences over time in the classroom can teachers begin to articulate the intricate complexities of learning in an effectively run classroom.

If researchers were able to perceive teachers as useful sources of data, and eventually, of researchable questions, they could take an important part in helping teachers articulate their insights. Given the chance to reflect on their experiences in a supportive environment, teachers, if they were able to perceive researchers as helpful allies, might also provide them with new questions and insights into learning. Supporting teachers in their work of making and testing their hunches about children has the potential not only for improving teaching, but at the same time for allowing interesting and significant issues for research to emerge.

One way to effect these changes is to encourage researchers to participate in the development of opportunities for teachers to explore and reflect on the learning that goes on in their classrooms. Happily, the idea of helping teachers reflect on what is going on in their classrooms is not an entirely new one. There have been a number of teacher development projects over the past ten years that have focused on providing teachers with time and support for reflection. In the rest of this chapter, I will describe how the "teacher talk" that occurs in such programs can not only help teachers see themselves in new ways, but can also provide a new tool for effective educational research.

THE TEACHER DEVELOPMENT PROJECT

One project that supported such teacher talk was initiated by Jeanne Bamberger at The Massachusetts Institute of Technology (Bamberger, Duckworth, & Cawley, 1980). After several years of trying to help college students understand the nature of their learning, she wondered whether helping class-room teachers to reflect on their own learning might help them think more deeply about children and teaching. In 1978 she received a National Institute of Education grant to initiate a series of weekly seminars for teachers in which they explored their own understanding in a variety of areas such as music, the movements of the moon, and mathematics. The teachers' work combined experiences with materials such as bells or dice with discussions of their own learning. As described in her project report, Bamberger wanted to give "the teachers the opportunity to stand away from their everyday class-room responsibilities and look upon them from a research perspective, con-sidering both their own learning process and that of the children" (p. 2).

This project yielded several benefits that are relevant to a concern about productive collaboration between researchers and teachers. Providing these teachers with a "research perspective" set in motion a series of changes. As the teachers began to reflect, they began not only to explore issues of their learning, but to see themselves in a new light—as investigators of their children's learning. This in turn led them to begin to articulate issues that they felt affected successful learning in their classrooms.

For one teacher, an important aspect of seeing herself differently was paying attention to her subjective knowledge. The leaders of the seminar described her experience as follows:

> For one member of the group reflection has meant gaining the courage to pay attention to what she calls her "subjective knowledge" about the children in her classroom. While she trusts and acts on these "subjective assumptions," con-cerning what her kids know and can do ("Timmy understands subtraction, I know that, even though he gets wrong answers") others, she believes, only trust "objective facts." As the seminar progressed, she was pressed to reflect on how she gains this "subjective knowledge," and what its content might be. At first she said, shrugging her shoulders, "I don't know, I just know." But with en-couragement, she made herself a program to try and capture how and what it is she trusts and acts on. The overwhelming impression is that she recognized for the first time that it was all right for her to take her "subjective knowledge" seriously. A progression began for this teacher that moved from trusting her own "subjective knowledge" to a realization that "other people don't always have the right answers," and this in turn has led to her development of new knowledge. [Bamberger, et al., 1980, p. 12]

Later on in the seminar, this teacher commented: "What I am thinking about the children and what I feel I need to do in the classroom in order to meet curriculum goals, in order to meet behavioral objectives set by myself or by the curriculum, is going against what I am beginning to discover about humans that are six years old" (Bamberger et al., 1980, p. 13). In doing so this teacher is not only taking on the role of an investigator of children's learning, but she may also be posing a set of new research questions that researchers might find it valuable to elicit, support, and explore further. Children's thinking has often been measured by success on a standard curriculum. What this teacher was "discovering" about her six-year-old students seemed to be at odds with the "curriculum," and suggests that perhaps we have been using the wrong measuring tool. Her comment suggests that we might profit from exploring new questions about children's learning in classrooms that have not previously been examined.

In this seminar, as they watched their own learning in a variety of situations, the teachers began to articulate a variety of questions about the learning their children were doing. Early in the seminar they identified a kind of learning that seemed important, but problematic for all of them. One teacher called it "intellectual interaction," another "really pursuing a problem," and a third said that it involved "question asking and an intellectual curiosity." They all reported that while they felt that this kind of learning was very important, it seemed to occur only "by chance." One teacher wondered what it was that got in the way of "that kind of learning" and how the obstacles might be removed.

This is just the kind of situation where I believe there is potential for productive collaboration between teachers and researchers. Few research studies that I know of have considered the issue of how one can support a child's interest in or capacity for pursuing a problem in a classroom setting, yet here these teachers are identifying this as an important issue in their children's learning.[4] Too often classroom research focuses on things like amount of time "on task" without considering the nature of that "on-task" experience (Berliner, 1978), or the focus is on small artificial tasks. What these teachers are looking for is a deeper understanding of what actually goes on or might go on in their classrooms. Perhaps the nature of a child's involvement in classroom activities should itself become a subject of inquiry.

To date some research has been done on so-called "intrinsic motivation." This might seem to be related to what these teachers are concerned with, but the data for this kind of work have typically been derived primarily from paper-and-pencil self-report questionnaires and not from the study of actual instances of learning in classrooms. The result is that teachers viewing research of this kind often question its relevance. But here is a place where I believe a dialogue between researchers and teachers might help both clarify their thinking and consider new avenues for collaborative investigation. For example, a researcher might help these teachers collect more classroom data on this kind of thinking and compare it to ideas developed through paper-and-pencil data collection. Having clarified the ideas, researchers and teachers might combine their differing observational skills to explore if in fact this kind of learning does occur "by chance," or whether there might not be patterns of interaction within the classroom that do support the kind of intellectual engagement they describe. While doing this a researcher might find new and useful sources of data, as well as new questions and issues for investigation. In addition, teachers might gain useful insights while being exposed to new techniques for collecting data.

Another interesting issue arose when one teacher made a comparison between adults' and children's learning. She had a hunch that "when thrown into completely new and different situations children and adults go about things in pretty much the same way," that "their hunches are similar" (Bamberger et al., 1980, p. 4). She went on to suggest some experiments she wanted to try out in her classroom to compare the adult reactions with those of her children. In the succeeding discussion, the teachers, through giving examples from their classroom experiences, explored the question of when adults' and children's approaches to a situation might be the same or different. They suggested situations where the differences were basically informational, where they were social or emotional, and where simply the amount of experience would have an effect. They speculated about learning situations in which adult responses might be similar to children's and some in which one might find meaningful differences.

The issue of how children are and are not like adult thinkers is currently a lively one in cognitive development research (Carey, in press; Flavell, 1981). Teachers in this project deal with the young children on a daily basis in contexts that are quite different from the short experimental sessions that characterize most cognitive research. They have a lot of information about how individual children behave in familiar settings, and thus have a lot to bring to bear on situations where children they know well encounter something new or unfamiliar. A researcher might find it useful to help these teachers explore how their students respond to new situations, to articulate more clearly what differences they see in the children's responses, and to help them sharpen their comparisons with adult learning. Perhaps some patterns would emerge that are different from ones found in experimental studies, or their findings might confirm and add significant alternative evidence to some currently held ideas.

These examples detail two important results of the seminars. The first is that participation in the seminar helped teachers become articulate about what they may have known previously only on an intuitive, unconscious level. Second, as the teachers began to see themselves differently they began, through the shared dialogue of the seminar, to explore and extend their knowledge about their children's thinking and learning. The teacher who commented on what she was learning about six-year-olds did not view herself as simply administering content to static children, but as an active explorer of children's learning. In these seminars, the two processes are self-reinforcing. Seeing oneself differently leads in turn to looking more carefully and deeply at children, which again contributes to a change in one's professional image.

An important aspect of this kind of teacher talk is that researchers having access to it could possibly find new topics for investigation, as well as new insights into the areas of children's learning they are already investigating. But, if this teacher talk is to be a useful tool in the development of effective educational research, changes will need to take place on all sides. It is not enough that teachers might come to see themselves as active investigators, and that this process has the potential for engendering useful new perspectives on issues of children's learning. Productive cooperation will also depend on the willingness of researchers to explore actively with teachers alternative approaches to research that might better speak to the full complexity of living classrooms. The seminars themselves are one way to gather significant new ideas and relevant data on children's learning, but to explore alternative methodologies we must look more closely at the way teachers in such seminars raise and pursue questions from their own classrooms.

CHILDREN'S THINKING SEMINARS

Examples from another series of seminars reveal a method of investigation that is very different from traditional academic research. The Children's Thinking Seminars, initiated by Bill Hull in 1972, also focus on teachers exploring the thinking of children in their classrooms (see Chapter 9). These seminars involve weekly meetings where teachers discuss interesting or perplexing instances of children's thinking from their own classrooms. Ideas in these meetings develop in cyclical ways and themes tend to evolve out of a growing collection of incidents reported by the participants. This provides a stark contrast to the rigid operational definitions often demanded by traditional research. It can be argued that the greatest strength of the seminars is their flexibility in allowing ideas to evolve and reveal new meanings.

An example is the theme of persistence. The label "persistence" first appeared when one teacher described an instance in which a child of hers, who was stuck on problem, announced, "I *never* give up!" Several of the group members felt that this was important and one responded by wondering if there weren't some activities in school that they could identify as being especially good for training in persistence.

After the reporting of this instance, examples of "persistence" came up repeatedly and the teachers began to connect it to a range of other experiences. In one session persistence was linked with reading problems by a teacher who described two children in her classroom who were trying to decipher a crossword-type code sheet:

The six year old, working vertically, discovered "Alf" which pleased him greatly. Even after the older child helped him realize that the message was written
horizontally he kept checking in his vertical theory. 'Look it says yroder!', he
cried. When I asked him what that meant, he said, 'You know, your smell.'!
After sharing the instance the teacher commented: "I was struck by the persistence of the 6-year-old in trying to make sense out of nonsense." Another teacher
responded: "I wonder if there is a correlation between good readers and those
children who are able to tolerate nonsense. The children who are having trouble
with reading are often those who need everything to be precise. They are not
willing to plunge into these odd looking signs on the page. [Hull, 1981, p. 122]

The concern with persistence connected with another common theme that
is not as easy to articulate. It involves the importance of having problems
that are not immediately solved. "Wondering" might be one name for it.
One teacher phrased the question as, "Could one's readiness to consider
problems be related to whether or not you have had success in pursuing
problems which at first seemed beyond you?" (Hull, 1981, p. 122). Later in
this same meeting another teacher described an instance of children coming
up with explanations of where sea shells came from. He commented, "I had a
sense that my questioning forced the child to quickly come up with a solution. It makes me think of the child who invented the M&M mousetrap [an
earlier instance] who *could* say 'I haven't thought about that'," (p. 122).
Another participant added, "Might it be useful at times not to push for an
answer right away, to allow answers to emerge after weeks or months?" (p.
122). The teachers seemed to agree that the chance to pursue a problem, not
to find an immediate "right" answer, had, in their experience, been an important element in many instances of effective learning.

The discussion of persistence led to still other important insights on rather
different issues. At a meeting following a discussion about persistence one
teacher identified a child who often continued on projects for long periods of
time. One day she heard him say that he didn't care if he finished what he
was making, it was the making that he enjoyed. She explained that for her,
this didn't quite fit for this child: "Clearly the finished project is important to
M and often he becomes very helpless and frustrated when making something that isn't going well and the process becomes no joy at all" (Hull, 1981,
p. 134). She feared his sense of persistence was based on his sense of duty and
desire to please a teacher who was obviously interested in persistence, rather
than his own interests and involvement. This seemed to hit a common chord
for many of the teachers and one asked, "Is there anything one can do to help
a child who seems to be saying one thing while feeling something else?" (p.
134). It was also suggested that a related kind of persistence could be seen in
the "blind repeating" of an activity. As one member summed it up: "When a
child is blindly repeating something it has a different value than when a child
is also innovating as he is doing something which he has done before. In such

a situation it might be important to ask whether the satisfaction is coming from the hoped-for approval as opposed to delight in the process, the aesthetic experience, or an interest in mastery?" (p. 134).

One could describe this series of discussions as a research process involving the identification of a significant issue in children's learning (persistence) and the development of several broadly stated hypotheses (e.g., "wondering" has important intellectual value). The hypotheses have been developed out of widespread observation of children. They have gone through some preliminary "testing" as teachers relate them to a broad range of their own experiences, and they have provided a way of looking at learning—something to continue to "test" and develop as a useful and powerful way to understand, explore, and support effective learning.

One power of this approach is its lack of closure. As the teachers built up instances around the topic, they became sensitive to layers of possibility that surrounded their generalized descriptions. For example, not only did they explore the potential of persistence as a tool of a powerful thinker, but also the possibility that it could get in the way of a child's thought through things like "blind repeating" or an inappropriate sense of duty.

Here, as in any research project, we have an evolving set of problems, questions, speculations, and hypotheses, yet the seminars use a very different mode of developing understanding from that of traditional academic research. Rather than using formal experiments, these teachers are drawing on their past and present experiences to develop, explore, and test out their ideas. They are examining the questions over an extended period of time, in a cyclical way. They are clarifying meanings by repeatedly considering specific contexts in great detail, and they are refining their central themes from a variety of perspectives. The questions they raise, such as those about persistence, are in no sense resolved or proven, nor do the teachers expect that they will be. The seminars are a place of ever-broadening and deepening exploration and reflection. Admittedly, this work lacks all of the trappings that are supposed to make traditional research "valid"; yet, in responding to this, we must bear in mind that the impetus for this seminar grew out of the frustration with the seeming inability of traditional modes of investigation to deepen our understanding and improve our practice meaningfully.

CONCLUSION

I believe that the path to relevant and applicable educational research can best be found through a collaboration between researchers and teachers. From the seminars I have described here, it is clear that many teachers will need support to experience what they do as hypothesis development and testing, and encouragement to articulate the issues and problems in children's learning that can be culled from their daily work with their students.[5] Because of this I think that collaboration with researchers must begin with finding ways to support teacher's reflection about their own classrooms. The approach of these seminars differs from most attempts at staff development in that those who initiated them were committed to allowing the teachers actually to reflect on *their* experiences of *their* classrooms rather than putting them in a situation where "experts" told them how they should understand or look at something that happened. Unless teachers receive help in developing their own insights, I am afraid that we will never get a meaningful perspective on the contextual complexity of effective learning.

Another strength of the seminars is that they are made up of groups of teachers. The group provides a kind of self-checking mechanism. Common themes that emerge are ones that many teachers feel are significant. This is a process that is too often neglected in academic research. How does the educational researcher know that the issues he is addressing have relevance? How often do educational researchers use practicing teachers to check the relevance and validity of what they are doing? Expanding the realm of academic research to include teachers as well as expanding the seminars to include researchers might help both achieve greater clarity. I believe that seminars such as these provide the ideal vehicle through which researchers can support teachers in exploring the learning of their children and through which teachers can make their fund of knowledge and experience available to each other and to researchers. It is only through efforts such as these that we will be able to create an effective way for researchers and practitioners to work together and make significant progress in improving classrooms where our children learn.

NOTES

1. It should be noted that not all educational and cognitive research falls into this trap. Lately there has been a growing interest in so-called qualitative (as opposed to quantitative) research (Hein, 1979). These researchers use observational and ethnographic description as the basis for their work, but, in the words of Sarah Lawrence Lightfoot of Harvard, these new methodologies "represent [only] a drop in the bucket in a vast ocean of educational research" (Lightfoot, 1981, p. 9).

2. The psychological researcher Urie Bronfenbrenner characterizes much of cognitive-development research as "the science of strange behavior of children in strange situations with strange adults for the briefest possible periods of time" (Bronfenbrenner, 1977, p. 513).

3. A good example of research that tries to involve the teacher as a researcher is the Michigan Institute for Research on Teaching. The difficulty with this project is that they took teachers out of their classrooms and put them in a heavily academic setting, and from my perspective the results have been disappointing. The power of the seminars described here is that they supported teachers who were actually involved in teaching on a daily basis. Being attuned to the complexities of classrooms is a fragile thing, and in my experience it only thrives within daily

practice. Finally, in order for teachers to turn that attunement into relevant and growing ideas, much time for mulling and exploration is needed.

4. An exception is Lepper (1980). In addition, both Carl Rogers and Herbert Thalan have developed models of teaching that are supposed to affect children's involvement with problems, but no research has been done on whether these methods actually stimulate the kind of thinking for which they were designed (Joyce, 1980).

5. Another important teacher-development project that uses this seminar approach, but with a focus on children's classroom conversations, has been carried out by Edith Churchill in Cambridge, Mass. (Churchill & Petner, 1977).

REFERENCES

Bamberger, J., Duckworth, E. & Cawley, M. *An experiment in teacher development—Quarterly Report (Oct. 1978 to Dec. 1978)—Interim Report (June 1980)*. Unpublished manuscript, 1980. (Available from Division for Study and Research in Education, Massachusetts Institute of Technology, Cambridge, Mass.)

Bassey, M. Crocodiles eat children. In *The theory and practice of educational action research*. Classroom Action Research Network. Bulletin #4 Summer 1980. Cambridge Institute of Education, Shaftsbury Rd., Cambridge, England.

Berliner, D. Changing academic learning time: Clinical intervention in four classrooms. In Fisher, C., Cohen, L.; Filby, N.; Matliave, R; & Berliner, D. (Eds.), *Beginning teacher evaluation study (BTES) supplement: Selected findings from phase III-B*. San Francisco: Far West Laboratory, May 1978.

Bussis, A., Chittenden, E., & Amarel, M. *Beyond surface curriculum: An interview study of teachers' understandings*. Boulder: Westview Press, 1976.

Bronfenbrenner, U. Toward an experimental ecology of human development. *American Psychologist*, July 1977.

Carey, S. Are children fundamentally different thinkers and learners from adults?" In Glazer, R. (Ed.), *Teaching thinking*. New York: Academic Press, in press.

Churchill, E., & Petner, J. *Children's language and thinking: A report on work-in-progress*. Grand Forks, N.D.: University of North Dakota Press, 1977.

Coker, H., Medley, D., & Soar, R. How valid are expert opinions about effective teaching? *Phi Delta Kappan,* 1980, **62**, (2).

Doyle, W. Paradigms for research on teacher effectiveness. In Shulman, I. (Ed.) *Review of research in education*. Itasca, Ill.: Peacock, 1977.

Elliot, J. Paradigms for research and staff development. In Hoyle, E. & McGarry, J. (Eds.), *World book of education*. London: Kogan Page, 1980.

Flavell, J. *On cognitive development*. Paper presented at the meeting of the Society of Research in Child Development, Boston, April 1981.

Hein, G. E. Evaluation in open education: Emergence of qualitative methodology. In Meisels, S. (Ed.), *Special education and development*. Baltimore: University Park Press, 1979.

Hull, W. "Notes and commentary." Unpublished manuscript, Cambridge, Mass., 1981.

Joyce, B. & Weil, M. *Models of teaching*. Englewood Cliffs, N.J.: Prentice-Hall, 1980.

Lepper, M. Intrinsic and extrinsic motivation in children: Differential effects of superfluous social controls. In *Minnesota symposium on child psychology*. (Vol. 14.) Hillsdale, N.J.: Erlbaum, 1980.

Lightfoot, S. L. "A question of perspective: Toward a more complex view of classrooms." Address given at Lesley College, Cambridge Mass., March 31, 1981.

Chapter 14

Writing about Practice

Roland S. Barth

Those who systematically examine and write about schools come, for the most part, not from the school community itself but from higher education. For scholars and researchers, schools can be frustrating social institutions. Attempts by university people to find meaning in school life run up against a host of well-known impediments. Gaining physical access to classrooms and schools that reject foreign bodies with defiance is one such problem. Getting inside "the culture" of a school or classroom presents an equally perplexing obstacle. Often researchers find themselves on the outside looking in, drawing inferences about school behavior but seldom permeating teachers' and students' innermost thoughts and motives or getting at complexities that might help interpret a complicated world.

A recurring problem for researchers is corroborating observations with school people. The scholar who checks out findings with teachers, principals, and parents risks offending those teachers, principals, and parents whose perceptions of reality are invariably violated by the researcher's account—any account. The researcher who does *not* convey findings to the adults in the school risks joining the tainted cadre of outsiders who take advantage of schools for their own professional purposes and run, leaving behind little benefit to the school in return for the precious energies that practitioners have invested in the study. In short, schools can present university researchers with a perilous quagmire. Few scholars have managed to serve both the academic community and school practitioners well.

If those who are foreign to the school culture have difficulty gaining access to its innermost secrets, if this information is important to so many, then why don't practitioners themselves study and write about their school worlds? It would seem that writing about schools as an "insider looking in" offers unusual opportunity for insight into formal education. Obviously, teachers have constant access to a classroom and school setting, not to mention their own ideas, motives, satisfactions, and methods. And the teacher acquainted as colleague or trusted friend with parents, administrators, and other teachers would be assured of an understanding, sympathetic, even grateful audience. In short, one might suppose that practitioners who write about schools would encounter few of the constraints so familiar to university researchers. So it would seem.

I have just completed a book about my experience as principal of a public elementary school. In the preparation of the manuscript I became all too familiar with some formidable obstacles facing a school practitioner who attempts to write about schools from the vantage point of "inside looking in." Some of the difficulties are familiar to university researchers. Others may be peculiar to school practitioners. Taken collectively they suggest why so few school people write about their work. And taken collectively they constitute a large agenda for university faculty who would assist school practitioners in reflecting and writing about their practice. I will attempt here to set out some of the sources of resistance to writing which practitioners encounter and then consider how the university community might address or alleviate these constraints.

First there is the obvious constraint of *time*. Writing takes time, lots of it. The university researcher, of course, works under time limitations but within the university culture one is paid, allotted time, and rewarded for scholarly reflections and writing. This is hardly the case for teachers and principals who labor these days under conditions where more is expected to be achieved with less—more student achievement with fewer resources. For any "free" or unaccounted time in the instruction of students, there are a thousand things related to the job a teacher should be doing. A principal can take notes, organize information, make outlines, write drafts, edit, and revise drafts only when the "desk is cleared" of other obligations, which, of course, never happens.

My own vivid recollection of writing while running a school suggests that time for writing comes, if at all, out of *my* time, not company time. When I did find time it was on a Saturday morning. But even then I found, as doctoral students writing theses in education find, that wallowing in, reflecting upon, and trying to untangle school issues, school problems, and the inscrutable behavior of colleagues is taxing. One can only take so much. On weekends and holidays most adults (and probably children) who work in schools badly need detachment, separation, and relief from their intense work, not further engagement with it. It is no more reasonable to expect a teacher or principal to spend the weekend writing about schools than to expect an air-traffic controller to spend the weekend on a simulator analyzing airport traffic patterns.

So the problem for the practitioner-writer is not only finding enough time, given the intense and demanding nature of schoolwork. The problem is to identify for oneself and supply the conditions under which it becomes likely one *will* write. I have found conditions that support my writing both exacting and difficult to provide. I needed a year's leave of absence, a foundation grant, and a secluded farm in Maine to say what I wanted to say and put my book together. I needed another year to revise, edit, and say it the way I wanted to say it. Seven hundred days to write three hundred pages! And I needed the greater part of a third year to solicit criticism and shepherd the manuscript through the stages of publication. Few practitioners enjoy conditions that would permit, let alone encourage, them to write.

A second obstacle I encountered as I attempted to write about my work in schools was the *complexity* of the subject. What happens in schools—even very good schools—is often illogical, unsystematic, irrational, and unplanned. Effective written language, on the other hand, is essentially logical, systematic, rational, linear, sequential, and deliberately planned. How do you transform the former into the latter? How do you convert into organized language the massive, simultaneous onslaught of complex individual and institutional behavior that bombards school practitioners each day? While it is true that school people have ready access to an extraordinary source of rich data, few have at hand organizing principles and lenses that allow them to collect, select, organize, and find meaning in an overabundance of apparently random information.

My own strategy emerged pragmatically. As a principal for ten years, I collected. Whenever something especially noteworthy or satisfying or problematic occurred—a particularly successful meeting, a remarkable change in a child, a heated letter from a parent, a sudden insight from a teacher—I jotted it down and added it to the sediment forming in the bottom drawer of a desk. I set out for the Maine farm with three bushel baskets of these anecdotes and incidents. For two months I played card-sorting games: I placed each item in a variety of shifting categories until some piles persisted and each piece of paper came to rest in an accommodating category, or in the wastebasket. Each of the enduring piles then became the basis for a chapter in the book.

Within each pile I shuffled, arranged, and rearranged until I was able to find, or impose, some meaning and organization. I have a dreadful memory that seldom allows me to recall names and events, let alone details. But I found that each item I had squirreled away gave rise to a train of associations and rich reminiscences with which I was able to recall the details of long-forgotten incidents. This inadvertent strategy enabled me to convert the random raw data of school life into a more or less ordered language. Other practitioners discover other means. But many remain baffled, overwhelmed, and discouraged by the distance between the rough, disordered school experience and the polished written word.

A third difficulty for practitioners who attempt to write about their school experiences is one shared by those who attempt to write about almost anything—*fear*, often terror, of writing itself. Far more critical than insufficient time in discouraging, if not thwarting, practitioners' writing is the underlying fear that "I have nothing to say," that "others will criticize or ridicule what I write," that "my writing will neither be accepted nor used by anyone." These fears of rejection are well grounded. They are the fears of second-graders, seventh-graders, and college and graduate students—fears of being demeaned by papers returned so marked up by corrections and criticisms that it appears a bowl of spaghetti sauce has been spilled on them. The criticism, the red pencil, the ridicule of having a paper read before the class, the low grades all leave permanent scars that inhibit adults' writing.

Effective writing requires both competence and confidence, which our formal education system often does more to extinguish than cultivate. For many practitioners then, the fear of being judged an inadequate writer (and therefore an inadequate person) is realistic. Consequently, although there are many distinguished teachers and principals, few are distinguished writers. Many are dreadful writers. Almost all experience a gap between the great deal they know about educational practice and a limited capacity to express this knowledge in writing.

The terror of writing presents a particular burden for school people charged with responsibility for *teaching* precise, effective writing to others. Teachers and principals are expected to be accomplished writers themselves, else how could they teach students to write? Publicly revealed incompetence in writing is therefore not only a personal admission of failure but a devastating professional indictment as well. No wonder teachers resist pupil-evaluation systems that require written comments or reports. No wonder principals say as little as possible in PTA newsletters!

A fourth difficulty practitioner-writers encounter is the problem of *generalizability*. Writing about what happens in schools is an attempt to assemble and organize information, find meaning and depict reality as one person sees and experiences it. The university researcher may study one classroom or school setting at a time but usually bases conclusions upon larger samples, thereby gaining credibility and perhaps generalizability. But many school practitioners have never worked in more than one school. What a teacher or principal writes about is often based upon a restricted and nonrandom sample—one teacher, one classroom, one school.

There is seldom agreement about what constitutes "reality" in a school, whether it be the effect of a new language program or a description of how the faculty meeting went. School people, like others, reconstruct experiences and their own places in them as they *wish* they had been. We need to emerge from the school drama as heroes and our accounts tend, therefore, to glorify us. If we acknowledge our limited sample, our bias, and qualify our observations as "one person's view," we can counter the objections and alternative interpretations of others. But if this disclaimer is employed, then both the usefulness and generalizability of the account is brought into question and frequently diminished. Who wants to read (or publish) a precious case study by one teacher about one classroom that perhaps has little or no bearing upon any other? If there is to be an audience for a practitioner's written account, the writing must have some generalizable elements.

In fact I suspect most practitioners, like university researchers, hope that what they write *will* have meaning and value beyond the particular situation. For the university member this aspiration is acceptable and respectable enough. But the desire to generalize, to "stick out" and be recognized, leads the school practitioner up against another obstacle—the taboo within the school culture against distinguishing oneself, or even appearing to distinguish oneself, from colleagues.

The practitioner who writes is haunted by the questions, "Am I good enough? Are my experiences, ideas, and accounts sufficiently noteworthy to be of interest and value to colleagues?" If the answer is "no," then, at best, one encounters mental blocks before the typewriter and, at worst, ends up spending Saturday mornings taking the kids skating. If the answer is "Yes, I know something others don't or can do something others have not thought of," then one has indeed attempted to distinguish oneself from colleagues and is therefore subject to the penalty for violating the taboo. "Who does he think he is anyway? What's so great about that? It's pretentious. I do that all the time!" This response of colleagues is further aggravated by charges of exploitation. "I could write, too, but I am too busy doing what I am *supposed* to be doing . . . working with children or helping teachers."

The school practitioner who writes, then, can expect little support and recognition from those around him. The culture of schools places little positive value—and often, in fact, places negative value—upon teachers and principals using their positions as participant-observers to reflect and write about practice. Writing is revealing yourself and many school people don't write for the same reason they construct walls in open spaces—in order to conceal themselves from those around them.

There is another issue concerning the generalizability of practitioners' writing. American education, like social-science research, seems preoccupied with a search for "the one best system." Examples of good practice are often scrutinized less for their particularistic merit than for the answer they may provide to generic problems. I can write about how we reduced discipline problems in one school; readers want to know how to reduce discipline problems in all schools. But whether a practitioner intends to generalize or not, it is unclear whether one individual's observations, interpretations, and conclusions can or should be more widely applied. Suburban to urban schools? Elementary to secondary? Public to private? In my book I sidestepped this question by suggesting that *problems* of education are generic, generalizable from one setting to another, while solutions to these problems are particular and unique to each context. Furthermore, I placed the burden upon the reader to determine which, if any, parts of my account of one public elementary school might be generalizable to other settings. I had my hopes but I made no claims.

The practitioner-writer faces a variety of *interpersonal and political problems*. Writing about practice invariably means writing about other people—parents, teachers, students, and administrators. Like the university researcher, the practitioner must be prepared to share findings and manuscripts with school people. But in addition, the practitioner must *live* each day with the consequences of what is written. Teachers and administrators who write about their work must assume that everyone in the school will read what they write. And indeed, many practitioner-writers observe that most of the responses to what they write come from within their own school community.

Usually the worst fate that befalls the university researcher whose classroom-based findings offend his subjects is to become *persona non grata* in that school. But these difficulties are eased by time, distance, and the availability of subjects in other schools. School principals or teachers, on the other hand, preside over a fragile house of cards. For them there *are* no other schools. To write anything at all is likely to offend someone. Most already have plenty of unmanageable problems. Why generate additional problems unnecessarily? In short, for school people the consequences of writing about practice are immediate and lasting, impinging on those upon whom they must depend for effectiveness and satisfaction. Thus, the teacher or principal who writes about a school setting must decide whether to "tell it like it is" and risk offending others, or edit, launder, and disguise the account so it will be unlikely to offend others—and probably unlikely to interest others as well. It's no wonder that Henry Kissinger, Jimmy Carter, and others write about their professional experience only *after* they have removed themselves to a detached and sheltered place!

Finally, there are the mechanical and legal problems of the practitioner who writes for publication. One might expect, for instance, that teachers and principals would encounter little difficulty gaining permission to use the information so freely available to them. It came as an unpleasant surprise for me to receive this letter from an editor at Harvard University Press:

Dear Mr. Barth:

I hope that your summer's been a good one so far. I also hope that I don't ruin it with the news this letter brings. Your manuscript has some serious problems in terms of quoted material. Let me try to give you a sense of the whole picture:

Only a few excerpts in the text belong in the category of "fair use": those passages that come directly from previously published sources. They are fair use because they are under 250 words in length (which is the approximate criterion for any work of substantial length) and you have given them proper citations. No permission is needed to include these passages in your book.

However, if you want to quote works like letters or poems (or any very short works) either in whole or in part, whether or not a citation is given, permission is required. This applies to all of the letters which were written by parents, numbering around 70 to 80. You hold no claim to these letters, even though they were addressed to you—and disguising the names of the authors is irrelevant.

In dealing with these letters, you have three options: (1) You can quote directly from the letters and get a signed form from each author (a sample of which is enclosed), giving permission for use in your book. In this case, you should probably keep the names disguised anyway. (2) You can paraphrase the letters in the text, being very careful not to quote directly. (3) Or you can create fictional parents who express similar viewpoints in language that is distinctly different from the language in the actual letters. In this case, you should include a very clear statement in the preface that all of the people represented in your book are fictional.

In any case, please be aware that you are solely responsible for making the manuscript legally suitable for publication—which means picking out the problem passages, and either deleting, revising, or doing the paperwork necessary to let them stand. Should you decide to obtain permission for any or all of the cases involved, the necessary forms and explanatory sheets are enclosed.

So much for the parents' letters. Now we come to all the works written by employees of school systems: superintendents, principals, teachers, etc. Permission to quote from a letter by a Newton teacher, for example, does *not* come from that teacher *if the letter was written in an official capacity*. Such works are termed "works for hire," which means that all rights to an official work belong to that organization for which the work is created. I'm sorry to say that even all of *your own* Greensheets, memos, letters to parents or school personnel, minutes from meetings, personal notes taken at meetings, etc., are works made for hire. You must obtain permission from the *school boards* involved before we can publish any of these documents.

Well, that's the situation. The sooner the better in terms of clearing these obstacles out of the way. Editing can't begin until all the revisions have been made, and publication can't happen until the entire manuscript is legally sound. Please let me know what you've decided as soon as you've mulled all this over.

The fact that all of the information that school practitioners gather or generate as part of their regular working day belongs to the school committee of the district, while understandable, is sobering. If I have to run a gauntlet of central office administrators and school committee members before I may use for publication even my own memos to faculty, it clearly becomes less likely that I shall write for publication. It certainly becomes less likely that what I do write will contain the seamier (and more interesting) anecdotes and insights, for who would give permission for me to use information that might reflect unfavorably upon them or their system?

These, then, are some of the constraints I encountered while writing *Run School Run*. I suspect these are also among the reasons other teachers and principals find it difficult both to practice and to write about practice. While "I don't have time" may be the most commonly verbalized impediment to writing, I find lack of time hardly the most discouraging element—as many other practitioners who *do* have time could attest. Taken individually, these many sources of resistance might not curtail writing; taken collectively they have the effect of discouraging writing and reducing the likelihood that the rich information and insights of the school practitioner will ever appear on the printed page.

Given this rather discouraging picture, why do any school practitioners write? What satisfactions can be sufficient to compensate for these hurdles? Teachers and principals find many. A primary motivation is the satisfaction and recognition that comes from seeing one's ideas in print and knowing that others also see them. Writing about practice lends legitimacy to both writer and practice. Most school people feel that education is an important, worthwhile endeavor, but can't help but be influenced by society's low regard for their profession. In the view of many educators, education is important but not quite important enough. Being a teacher or principal *and* a writer is more prestigious than being "just" a teacher or principal.

Writing about practice can help the profession as well as the author. Practitioners can communicate to cynical taxpayers as well as to interested colleagues, the complexities, the difficulties, and the successes that characterize life in schools. Statements by school people are curiously, and unfortunately, lacking from the ongoing debate about American education. Yet who has more to say on the subject?

Sharing and validating educational ideas with other practitioners has other benefits. The teacher who reads what another has written finds an extended universe of alternative ideas, materials, and methods from which to choose in responding to daily instructional challenges. A principal reading what a colleague writes finds it easier to order his own school world. In short, a writer's description of practice can dignify all practice, while at the same time confirming for each reader that, "God, I'm *not* crazy, nor am I in this alone."

Another satisfaction for the practitioner-writer comes from the very tangible quality of writing itself. Those who work in schools can never be certain whether teachers, students, parents, curriculum, or "school climate" are different in June from the way they were in September *because of* their efforts. This is frustrating, to say the least. There is something very concrete, on the other hand, about a published manuscript. You can see it, touch it, feel it. What was a blank page is now an article. Certainty of accomplishment stands in welcome contrast to the uncertainty and diffusion of school life. I find myself enjoying many of the same satisfactions from writing as from shingling a barn. At the beginning of the week the roof was unshingled; at the end of the week it was shingled. It's better than it was, and I did it.

A third positive outcome I find in writing about practice is the power it affords to clarify practice. In order to translate the disordered, irrational world of schools into the logic and precision of language, one has to reflect upon and organize what one does and sees in schools. Bringing a higher level of meaning and clarity to frenetic days is a luxury few school people enjoy (and few can do without) in these days characterized by sheer survival. By helping to translate one's experiences into a form that can be represented in words, the act of writing frequently makes both our thoughts and our experiences more accessible and comprehensible to us. A reflective capacity is a condition for personal and professional growth. Thus, by helping to order the disordered, writing supplies a powerful catalyst for professional change and personal growth.

For many practitioners, writing about their work enables them to *stand* and to *withstand* practice. Without periodic opportunities to look with detachment and perspective at the consuming world of school life, teachers and principals find themselves consumed by it. Writing helps to objectify practice and to distance practitioners from it as well as offering a personal nourishment that can energize school people through the many bleak moments and hours of school life.

Thus, many practitioners find writing about their work a kind of job-relevant moonlighting, the fruits of which can be channeled right back into the job, making it more considered, perhaps more tolerable, certainly more effective, and maybe even easier. The labors of the weekend at the typewriter frequently pay off on Monday morning in a variety of unpredictable ways.

There is some indication that when teachers and principals write about their work, *students* may benefit as well. Seymour Sarason (1979) puts it this way. "The more a teacher can make his own thinking public and subject for discussion . . . the more interesting and stimulating does the classroom become for students" (pp. 185–186). Students benefit from the power of adult modeling of desired behavior. Don Graves (1980) points out that there is no better way for adults to impart the importance and the skills of writing than to be writers themselves. Put more strongly, Graves argues that "we can't expect a teacher to practice the craft of teaching writing who doesn't practice the craft of writing itself."

The principal who is preoccupied with control over supplies, reluctant to give teachers magic markers and masking tape, begets teachers preoccupied with control over supplies, reluctant to give students magic markers and masking tape, and students who go without magic markers and masking tape. In the same way, through this mysterious process of modeling, the principal who writes often and with ease may find teachers who write more often with ease, and students who do the same. I always thought that the hours I spent writing a single paragraph each week for the school newsletter conveyed some unstated messages to the school community: "We value precise, effective, entertaining written language here and we are working hard to develop it." There were many ripple effects. Teachers struggled over their written pupil evaluations and I made the struggles no easier by brooding over their drafts as I would term papers. But teachers' communications with parents became more precise, effective, and entertaining as well. Although this is difficult to prove, I am convinced that adults who write often and effectively in school teach students as much about writing as those who deliberately set out to teach writing.

And I have found that writing about practice is immensely helpful in *speaking* about practice. The skills and ideas exercised in writing are easily, if not automatically, transferred to speaking. Most teachers and principals are regularly called upon to display the latter skills even though they may not appear to need the former. I find that prior experience writing about a topic contributes to command over the spoken word.

Finally, for the practitioner-writers, like all writers, the psychic energy to stay up all night crafting a manuscript comes from the simple yet mysterious desire for immortality. We all, I'm sure, have the desire to "leave our mark" which will persist long after we're gone. For many parents this comes through the children they bear and rear; for architects, through the buildings that endure. For teachers the "mark" might be the scores of children who have been touched by and who will always carry a bit of their instructors with them. For a principal, perhaps the "mark" is a school, a collection of teachers, a community that have all somehow been shaped by the administrator. And for some, promise of immortality lies with articles in journals, books on shelves, and entries in bibliographies that will also persist long after author and typewriter have ceased to function. We entertain the fantasy that somehow, somewhere we may touch and profoundly influence another practitioner in the way a particular article or book has influenced us.

Writing about practice offers something of immense value to readers as well as to writers. I believe the writing many practitioners do represents a legitimate kind of research. It may be questionable whether anecdotal experiences of school practitioners are generalizable to other settings in the way that traditional research findings may be. And it may be that practitioners' writing is more an exercise in the personal and professional development of the author than a creation of new knowledge. Yet large-scale, aggregate, social-science research, preoccupied with transferability, is often dependent upon huge sample sizes that tend to ignore or obscure the rich meaning of individual cases. A need exists for investigation of individual cases as well as the aggregate of cases. As Vito Perrone (1981) puts it, "The individual case informs; collections of cases enlighten."

Recording examples of successful practice and documenting the process of education as it occurs is data collecting, desperately needed to fill out—and sometimes correct—the picture that more elaborate and systematic research only begins to paint. A discussion of standardized tests as they are used and abused in a particular school can shed as much light on the decline of test scores as an elaborate study conducted by the Educational Testing Service which documents a ten-point national decline in SATs. In short, good writing by practitioners about practice is not only personally satisfying and professionally rewarding, but offers a rich contribution to the literature of educational research. Policy makers and school practitioners need access to both.

If writing about school practice offers considerable potential rewards for practitioner, author, and reader alike, and if so few of the nation's teachers and principals write about what they do, an obvious question is, "What can anyone do to make it more likely that more school people will want to write, be able to write, and actually engage in effective writing about schools?" More specifically, what can university faculty and schools of education do to enable school practitioners to examine, bring meaning to, and share in writing with a wider audience the rich and unusual data about teaching, administration, parents, curriculum, and students to which they have access?

Answers do not jump to mind. To be useful, answers must address and attempt to remedy the kinds of impediments to writing cited above: lack of time, the overwhelming complexity of the subject, the terror of writing, the problem of generalizability, interpersonal and political problems, and the technical problems of publication.

The "Writing Center" at the Harvard Graduate School of Education, under the leadership of Joseph Featherstone and Bruce McPhearson, is one promising means for offering graduate students, teachers, and school administrators opportunities to strengthen their competence and confidence in writing through formal and informal coursework. These kinds of efforts promise to help practitioners develop ways of observing practice, collecting data, and organizing and presenting ideas in writing. Helping practitioners develop confidence in their ability as writers is no small contribution.

What many practitioners lack in order to set pen to paper is the "handle" for a manuscript or an article, something distinct about teaching or administering that can provide the occasion for writing about it. Perhaps a writing center can help provide a practitioner with a conceptual framework. For, given an "organizing principle," many would probably find writing much less overwhelming. If the efforts of other writers about practice—many of them undistinguished—were available to read, practitioners might be less awed. "I can do it, too." Or "I can do it better."

One commodity the university has that school practitioners lack is a "protected setting," and the power over membership in that setting. One reason higher educators write is that they live in an environment that values writing and encourages it. The presence of a library, colleagues who regularly read and criticize one another's papers, a distance from the hurly-burly distractions of the "real world" all represent the positive side of the "ivory tower." Universities may not be able to insulate practitioners from the interpersonal and political problems that accompany writing about their schools, but they may be able to convey to practitioners citizenship in the academic setting. For instance, at Harvard we are planning to appoint each year one or two different practicing school principals as "visiting practitioners." They will leave their schools for a year to help administer an internship program, provide resources to fellow principals, and use the protected setting as an occasion to reflect and write about practice before returning to their schools the following year. In this way the community can convey time and encouragement for writing, neither of which is available in most school communities.

Universities might also commission selected school practitioners through some form of "minigrants" to write case studies or prepare manuscripts on specific topics, such as "ways of encouraging creativity in the classroom," "teachers' uses of reward and punishment," or "a principal looks at the advantages and disadvantages of informal classrooms." Designation of the focus and assurance in advance of "acceptance" of the manuscript, coupled with the dignity and legitimization that comes with an honorarium, would encourage many who might not otherwise consider writing about schools. I suspect a large number of manuscripts could be generated in this way, which could prove valuable in university courses and research projects. We plan, for instance, to commission several practicing principals and teachers to write about an element of their own practice that they consider particularly successful or important—"fund raising," "promoting the professional development of teachers," "building coalitions with parents and teachers"— and then use these little "case studies" as instructional aides in formal courses, possibly calling upon the author to accompany the case in class. Assembling a library of these practitioner accounts may help to diminish the distance between "theory and practice" which so limits both the university and the school culture.

A promising way of assisting and encouraging school people to write might be a simple, deliberate pairing of a university researcher with a school practitioner as co-authors sharing the burdens and responsibilities of writing with the professional rewards and satisfactions. I'm not sure how many university researchers would be willing to engage in this kind of paired investigation, risking "dilution" of their efforts, lack of control, and possible sacrifice of academic rigor. I think the risk is worth taking. I suspect that any school practitioner and any researcher would be able to find certain complementary skills and a common ground for cooperation. For example, I know of a principal now presiding over the closing of her school—an important and current issue these days. She is forming a partnership with a university researcher examining this question. The researcher would gain from principal and teachers access to data and insight that only an "insider" could provide. The teachers and principal of the school would receive assistance from the researcher in the form of familiarity with the literature of other school closings and skills in analysis that might help them deal with this difficult issue. And perhaps with the cooperation and assistance of a university person, principal and teacher will feel more confident about what to write and how to transform raw experience into prose. Once the pump has been primed, the practitioner may continue to write about school closings or other issues without the assistance of the university partner. In short, higher educators, comfortable and capable as researchers and authors, can help convey some of these qualities to lower educators, thereby engaging in some important "independence training." The key here is a relationship not of subordinate to superordinate so typical of "cooperative" school-university efforts but rather one of parity and first-class citizenship for each party.

The idea of school-university collegial investigations is not new, nor is it an idea with an outstanding track record. After six years of court-ordered "pairings" between Boston area universities and particular Boston public schools aimed at improving the quality of education, it is clear that most of these collaborations have been disappointing. Attempts by William Tikunoff and Beatrice Ward at the Far West Laboratory for Educational Research and Development, however, offer a striking example of the promising potential influence on practitioners' professional development and researchers' effectiveness when school people are "worked with" rather than "worked on" in the educational research process. In their words, "Each member of the team has parity and shares equal responsibility for decisions made by the team from identification of the question/problem to the completion of all resultant R and D activities."

One reason school practitioners seldom write for publication is that they are unfamiliar with the sometimes byzantine process of having manuscripts considered and accepted for publication. To whom does one submit a manuscript? At what journal? In what form? What appears to be a mysterious process shrouded with unknown protocol, coupled with a fear of rejection, often curtails tentative exploration. A university might provide a valuable service by helping edit and then broker manuscripts of practitioners to appropriate and promising publications, as many university faculty do for their graduate students. It is important to realize, for instance, that a worthwhile forum for the discussion of educational practice is the host of nonacademic periodicals such as *Learning, Teacher, Instructor, Newsweek, The New York Times* editorial pages, and local magazines and newspapers. Frequently authors are paid for contributions that will reach a broad audience. These kinds of periodicals might offer practitioners more satisfaction and peer recognition than more scholarly journals such as *The Harvard Educational Review*. The latter may be taken seriously and read by university researchers; unfortunately they mean little to most school teachers, administrators, and parents.

These are a few of the ways in which university members might assist school teachers and principals in writing about what they see and do. There is ample room and need for a wider repertoire. I strongly believe that there are a great many teachers and principals out there with an unfulfilled potential for writing about education from the vantage point of practitioner-author. Efforts of the university community are needed to avoid this great loss of rich insight.

I recently had lunch with a colleague who, for a dozen years, had been editor of a national educational journal. I asked him if he could put his finger on the characteristics of authors of the very best pieces he had published over the years. He replied that these were people who clearly knew a great deal about education and schools; in addition, they wrote with great detail. Each had a rich lore of anecdotes and examples to support generalizations. Moreover, these were people who cared passionately about their subjects, and this passion shone through their writing. If these are indeed the important characteristics of good writers about education, they are also the characteristics of scores of school practitioners. Who knows in more detail and cares with greater passion about what goes on in schools than teachers and principals?

The work of teachers and principals is not visible to the public or even to other teachers and principals. One way of making it more so is through writing. Yet few educators speak out for the abundant accomplishments of schools. Many students out there *are* learning and achieving, thanks to many school people who *are* teaching and leading. No one else can tell the story as well. Practitioners who work aggressively to convey their ideas in print have an opportunity to convey to the public the message that schools are complex institutions, teaching is difficult, and that good as well as bad things are happening in classrooms; that good schools do make a difference for students, their parents, and professionals alike.

Perhaps the most substantial contribution the university community can make to encourage school practitioners to write is to legitimize their efforts—to convey in a thousand ways that what goes on in schools is important, that those who work in schools are important, and that systematic observations by school people, organized in some coherent way with personal accounts and insights, are important. The academic community accepts the value and legitimacy of sophisticated, validated, large-scale, discipline-oriented, university-based research. But useful knowledge can come from the identification of good practice, the codification of good practice, and attempts to communicate good practice. When university people come to recognize that the thinking and writing of teachers and principals can also be characterized by integral rigor, even elegance, they will indeed be ready to help.

REFERENCES

Graves, D. Speech to the Symposium on Writing, Harvard Graduate School of Education, October 4, 1980.
Perrone, V. Personal communication. Spring 1981.
Sarason, S. B. *The culture of the school and the problem of change.* Boston: Allyn & Bacon, 1979.
Tikunoff, W. J. & Ward, B. A. "Research and development: A resource in the resolution of conflict." *IR and DT Bulletin* **1**, October 1977. San Francisco: Far West Laboratory for Educational Research and Development.

Chapter 15
Case Study I:
A Program for the Gifted

Mary Ann Haley

educate—1. to give knowledge or training to; train or develop the knowledge, skill, mind, character of, especially by formal schooling or study; teach; instruct; 2. to form and develop (one's taste, etc.) . . .

gifted—having a natural ability or aptitude; talented

—Webster's New World Dictionary

What are we doing, what could we be doing, what should we be doing in order to ensure that the "gifted" children in our schools are being "educated"? This problem was posed to me and a number of other classroom teachers several summers ago. We were members of a mathematics curriculum committee in a suburban public school system. Each of us had had a minimum of seven years of teaching experience in the system. None of us had had any formal training in education of the "gifted."

That was three years ago. Since that time, members of the committee have attended numerous conferences and courses on the education of the gifted, searched the literature, implemented a small pilot program, and secured federal funds for the purposes of continuing to explore and to implement educational practices that can provide a high-quality education for our more capable students. Currently, we are in the second year of a federally funded project that focuses on practices that can be implemented in a regular classroom, where students of all ability levels will be found.

The purpose of this chapter is to describe the steps that led us to where we are now, to examine the difficulties we have encountered along the way, to discuss questions that have been raised, and to explore the ways in which we could have used research expertise or assistance throughout this time.

GENERAL ISSUES

A four-week summer session marked the beginning of our work on the topic of educating gifted students. Our committee was composed of four fifth-grade teachers and one middle-school teacher. Although we had been assigned the responsibility of examining gifted education for those four weeks, the expected outcome was somewhat unclear to us. We concluded that we were primarily expected to explore the issue of educating the gifted, to see where it led us, and, ultimately, to come up with some recommendations.

Anxious to get started, we looked at the most readily available resources—our own experiences as classroom teachers—and began by discussing issues we had been personally concerned with in trying to provide for our most capable students. Within the group, a variety of strategies had been used. These included: homogeneous ability grouping for math and reading instruction; accelerating "top" groups of students by providing materials and instruction designed for one or two grade levels above; introducing topics that would not ordinarily be covered in the regular curriculum; and providing options for independent study. Less frequently, we had secured tutors for individual students, skipped them over a grade, or made arrangements for them to spend some part of the week in classes at the middle school or high school. We were in agreement that these students are exciting and stimulating to work with, but, at the same time, that they present a real challenge to us as teachers. We felt that they often require and deserve a greater investment of time than we had been able to commit, either for locating resources for them, developing appropriate materials, or guiding their independent work. By the end of this discussion, we had formulated a list of questions that we subsequently tried to explore: (1) What is a "gifted child"; how does one discriminate between those who do well in school and those who might be further distinguished as "gifted"? (2) How should these students be grouped for instruction? (3) What type of instruction should be offered? (4) Whom should we be concerned about most—the students who are already achieving or those who we feel have the potential to achieve but are apparently not exercising their potential?

Again we turned to resources at hand, beginning with an annotated bibliography that summarized 43 research studies that dealt with the issue of ability grouping in schools. Here we encountered our first major difficulty. The studies summarized were so varied in terms of research designs used, length of time for change to be measured, ages of students involved, measurements employed to determine the ability groupings, and so on, and the conclusions reached in seemingly similar studies were so diverse that we couldn't identify a single trend that was convincing. No single study or group of studies seemed to point conclusively to significant short- or long-range positive effects of grouping on either gifted students or average and below-average ability students. Moreover, there were no critiques of the studies in the bibliography to guide us. Ultimately, our analysis of the information contained in the bibliography left us with little certainty regarding a mode of grouping that would be the most advantageous for our most capable students. This was, by no means, an exhaustive exploration of the literature on our part. I believe, however, that we felt both restricted by time, in that we had many other issues to consider before the four weeks ended, and frustrated by the lack of direction provided in what appeared to be a fairly comprehensive study of the available research on this issue. Perhaps, someone with more research expertise could have been helpful to us here either by providing a more accurate or precise scrutiny of these studies or by locating additional bodies of research that might provide the conclusiveness for which we were looking.

The more we investigated the issues of ability grouping and instructional tactics, the more we hungered to learn and realized how fascinated we were by these students. Yet, we began to wonder whether other teachers in the system shared our enthusiasm as well as our concern. We decided to develop a questionnaire to survey teachers' attitudes and perceptions of how well we were serving gifted students and what our needs as a school system were regarding the improvement of educational services to these students. This led us to the question, "What is a gifted child?" as we felt that some definition had to be provided for teachers if they were to respond to the questionnaire in a meaningful way.

A DEFINITION OF GIFTEDNESS

A consultant, who had both university training and many years of classroom experience in this field, had been hired to work with us for two of the four weeks. We turned to the consultant for advice and assistance, given that we were unable to develop our own precise definition of giftedness. She cited for us the definition adopted by the United States Office of Education in 1972. This definition stated, in part, that:

> Gifted and talented children and youth are those identified by professionally qualified persons, who, by virtue of outstanding abilities, are capable of outstanding performance. . . . Children capable of high performance include those with demonstrated achievement and/or potential ability in any of [several] areas. [Marland, 1972, p. 10]

Although this definition was intended by the United States Office of Education to be a guideline for educators across the country for determining the population that should be served by special programs, it raised several additional questions for us: (1) What makes a person professionally qualified to identify these students? (2) How does one define "outstanding performance"—relative to what? (3) "Demonstrated achievement" might be easy to identify—what about those who have the "potential ability"—what does one use to identify "potential ability" that has not yet resulted in demonstrated achievement? For want of any better definition, however, we decided to use it as the preface to our questionnaire. We felt that time was running out and we needed to get some input from the staff at large. Furthermore, we may have thought that other staff members might not have the clarification problems with which we were struggling. Finally, we felt that the definition did provide at least some guidelines for them.

We spent the remainder of the four weeks working with the consultant, developing the questionnaire. In addition, we began to study programs for the gifted as they were being implemented locally and around the country, and continued to read literature on the subject.

The "needs-assessment" survey (as we called our questionnaire) was circulated to the staff in September. We interpreted the data gathered through this instrument as indicating considerable agreement among our teachers that: (1) gifted students have special needs; (2) more support services are needed when dealing with gifted students; (3) there had not been equal access in our schools to services available for the gifted; (4) attention should be given to the special needs of gifted students at all grade levels; (5) the schools should provide more services for gifted students; and (6) it is important for gifted students to work within heterogeneous classrooms for at least part of the day. The greatest disparity within responses occurred on an item that asked whether "our schools meet the needs of gifted students." Although 45 respondents answered the question in the affirmative, 36 answered in the negative. Given the points of agreement listed above, I feel that this presents something of a paradox, which more likely indicates a problem with the questionnaire construction. In retrospect, I believe that, in the development and interpretation of the questionnaire, we should have sought the assistance of someone with expertise—someone who could help us to identify our own biases (to avoid "loading" the questionnaire), to devise well-worded questions, to include an appropriate array of response choices, to analyze the results correctly, to interpret overall patterns, and to identify any problems with the information gathered and any additional information that might have been needed in order to determine future directions. Nonetheless, the questionnaire responses indicated to us that there was reason for us as a committee to continue to probe the issue of serving our gifted students.

DEVELOPMENT OF THE PROGRAM

Year 1—Planning and Securing School Committee Support

Teachers indicated, through responses to certain items on the questionnaire, that, in serving the gifted, they favored: acceleration, working within a higher grade-level classroom, enrichment rooms, and itinerant resource teachers (teachers who could travel from building to building). Although these gave us some indication of what would be acceptable to teachers, this list represents a considerable range of financial implications (for example, acceleration and working at a higher grade level can generally be accommodated without adding personnel, whereas enrichment rooms and the use of itinerant teachers require additional staff positions). In coming to some conclusions about the sort of program we should develop, we took into account not only the teachers' responses, but also our synthesis of the research literature, our analysis of existing programs for the gifted, and our own experience as classroom teachers. In the late fall of that first year, we presented a report to the administration and the school committee. This report included the federal definition, a summary of requirements for worthwhile programs for the gifted and talented, and 13 program prototypes.

Our list of requirements included, among other things, a delineation of characteristics that, singly or in combination, might describe target groups of children: students with specific academic aptitude; highly creative students; students with talent in a specific area; students with high ability as determined by IQ scores. We suggested that screening and identification procedures employ multiple criteria. For the learning environment itself, we proposed ways in which the environment should meet both the cognitive and the affective needs of gifted students. Finally, we suggested that the gifted program be integrated into the regular school program, and that ongoing evaluation of outcomes and subsequent modification be an integral component of the program.

Our "ideal" program prototype would have included the establishment of positions for resource teachers, who could support the efforts of regular classroom teachers in a variety of ways. This recommendation was based on our experience as classroom teachers and the intuitive sense that if knowledgeable, capable persons filled these positions, and program development were monitored carefully, services would have to improve. The primary obstacle that prohibited us from recommending this one "ideal" prototype was the cost of adding staff positions. We knew that in order to commit the kind of money involved, the school committee generally requires more conclusive or convincing evidence of the gains that will result. Perhaps the evidence existed somewhere in the literature, as a result of both short- and long-term evaluations of other programs, but we were unaware of it and didn't know where to go to find it within the existing time constraints. Once again, had there been a link between ourselves, as practitioners, and researchers, who make it their business to locate this type of information on an ongoing basis, we may have been able to be more assertive. We feared, however, that the entire effort could come to an abrupt halt unless we could soon entice the school committee to make a committment to something that would keep the exploration moving in some way.

The school committee took no action at that time, except to agree to give our suggested options further consideration. As the year progressed, it became obvious that we, as a committee, had to come up with yet some other program options, which would involve minimal cost, since the school committee did not appear to be ready to make a financial committment. Looking at all of the existing resources available and using our best creative problem-solving skills, we, along with the administrators, proposed a sort of "program on a shoestring" to be piloted.

This program would be set up in a double fifth-grade classroom (2 team teachers, 48 students), in one of the four elementary schools. Reasons for determining this particular setting were: the pupil/teacher ratio at this grade level in this school was lower than others in town; one of the teachers assigned to this classroom was the chairperson of our committee; the classroom could be considered heterogeneous (that is, students from that grade level in that school identified as gifted, using even a very liberal definition, would represent only as much as one-half of the classroom population), yet the teacher could work with the identified students for large portions of time in relatively "homogeneous" ability groups. This latter consideration (need for very able students to work together for periods of time) was mentioned frequently in the literature. The only cost involved was a minimal one— hiring a full-time aide to work in this classroom. The school committee voted to support the establishment of this pilot program for the next school year.

Year 2—A Pilot Program

The goals of the pilot program were defined as follows: (1) to determine who are the gifted—to develop, use, and evaluate screening and identification procedures for selecting students; (2) to learn what can be done in a heterogeneously grouped classroom setting to meet the needs of gifted students; (3) to learn of appropriateness of materials and techniques for working with gifted students; (4) to develop curricular materials that support the needs and interests of the involved students. It is clear that our intention was, in a sense, to conduct our own research through the pilot, by taking the generalized conclusions we had come to and testing them out in the practical setting, with the hopes of reaching more specific conclusions about definitions, grouping patterns, teaching strategies, and curricular materials.

In order to select the students who would be included, we began with group-aptitude and achievement-test data, which were easily available to us. Owing to the repeated warnings in the literature regarding the limitations of using this type of group test data as a singular identification measure, we chose, for this initial step, to look at all students who had consistently (for three years) scored above the mean for their class. We then administered an individual IQ test and a group "creativity" test. The students' classroom teachers completed a behavioral checklist on each student regarding learning, motivation, creativity, and leadership characteristics. Teachers also provided informal input on day-to-day classroom performance. We felt that these measures were diversified enough so that any outstanding intellectual, academic, and/or creative aptitudes would be picked up in at least one of these ways.

A team of staff members, including the school principal, social worker, language-arts consultant, fifth-grade teachers, and members of our committee, studied all of the data on each student and selected 21 students as the pilot group. Individual intelligence test scores (WISC) on 14 of these students were 130 or above. The other 7 ranged from 120 to 129. One student was included because of an outstanding score on the creativity test and her daily performance and motivation, despite the fact that her intelligence and aptitude scores were lower than most other students who were being considered. Many of the students were selected to participate in the total program. Others participated in only a portion of the program (e.g., language arts or math, depending upon their individual strengths).

Students' needs, as outlined in the program requirements we had formulated, were used as a basis for determining curricular and teaching practices with these 21 students in the pilot year. The Enrichment Triad Model (Renzulli, 1977) which details guidelines for types of enrichment practices believed to be important in programs for the gifted, was used as an overall guide. This model suggests that enrichment-program practices should include opportunities for students: (1) to broaden their awareness of topics or fields of study beyond those which they would ordinarily encounter in the regular curriculum; (2) to exercise and polish creative and critical thinking, problem-solving and research skills; and (3) to identify and structure realistic solvable problems that grow out of their interests.

Special activities for the gifted group covered a broad range. Reading activities included the exploration of a variety of children's authors and several different types of literature (mythology, mystery, science fiction, tall tales, poetry, fantasy, and adventure). Multidisciplinary units exploring newspaper journalism, advertising, and broadcasting were designed specifically for this group of students. These included an emphasis on creative and critical thinking skills. Acceleration and enrichment were practiced in the math program, where problem solving was emphasized through daily "brain teasers" and logical thinking exercises. Practical problem solving and word-problem solving were emphasized as well. Much of the science and social-studies material was covered within heterogeneous groups involving all of the students within the double classroom. The students involved within the pilot program moved through some of the units at an accelerated pace or engaged in more in-depth projects than were required by the regular unit activities.

At the conclusion of that year an evaluation was written by the pilot program teacher. The evaluation included attitudinal comments from students in the program and their parents (taken from teacher-developed questionnaires), the principal, and the pilot teacher himself. Student comments indicated that this year had been a very challenging and exciting one for them. Parental attitudes were also very positive. Those units, topics, or activities most frequently cited as favorites were ones that had been specifically designed as extensions, adaptations, or additions to the regular fifth-grade curriculum. The principal's commentary was very complimentary regarding the program. A number of individuals, however, outside of this classroom (teachers and parents) expressed concern about the practice of "skimming" gifted students out of other classrooms to place them together, feeling that crucial role models had been removed from those other classrooms, along with a spark of interest that gives class activities flavor and depth.

Regarding the first program goal (to determine who are the gifted), the teacher felt that the screening and identification procedure had worked well. At no time during the year did any fifth-grade teacher feel that any student had been excluded who would have profited from program participation, yet there was a real blend of students selected for the pilot program (i.e., high potential/high achieving, high potential/low achieving, lower potential/high achieving). He noted that the testing of students and teacher input can help us to gain greater knowledge of the many dimensions of our students and that this can help us to determine which types of enrichment are most appropriate for a particular student or if the regular classroom program is appropriate. In addition, the teacher felt that the day-to-day progress, productivity, and performance of the student group indicated that all of the students selected belonged in the group and needed an enriched, challenging program.

Regarding the second program goal (to determine what can be done in a heterogeneously grouped classroom), it was noted that the double classroom lent itself well to maintaining heterogeneity, while, at the same time, affording one teacher and a large group of very capable students considerable time to focus on enrichment experiences, resulting in considerable intellectual stimulation. The pilot teacher noted that the enrichment group was demanding, exhausting, and required a great deal in human resources from both himself and the hired assistant. The question which he felt remained was, "Can a teacher in a self-contained classroom meet, with qualitative responses, the diverse needs of gifted students, those well-served by the regular curriculum, and those who are not even ready for the grade level curriculum?"

Regarding the third and fourth goals (to develop and learn about appropriateness of materials and techniques for working with gifted students), the teacher felt that those we had developed on the basis of the Triad Model were responded to very favorably by students and that we should continue to use the model for determining and defining enrichment practices.

Finally, the teacher noted that Renzulli (author of the Triad Model) had, in a recent paper, proposed a definition of giftedness or gifted behavior (as demonstrated by creative, productive performance resulting in outstanding contributions made by people to the world) as the result of the interaction among three clusters of human traits—above-average (not necessarily superior) general abilities, creativity, and task commitment (Renzulli, 1978). Renzulli, in proposing these three clusters, underlined the importance of the *task commitment* and *creativity*, as he had witnessed the multitudes of programs for the gifted where students were selected primarily on the basis of IQ scores. The pilot teacher had noted the lack of task commitment in some of the selected students and underlined a concern that we continue to look at this dimension of student behavior, both as a selection criterion and as a measure of program success.

During that year members of our committee submitted a proposal for federal funds that would enable us to continue and expand our efforts to include other schools. The proposal was funded in July.

Year 3—Expansion and Modifications

Funding enabled us to add a full-time staff member who would serve as project director/coordinator. I was selected for this position. I began by addressing myself to the only real criticism of the pilot program that had been expressed by some teachers and parents, as well as by the building principal: the practice of placing all the identified students in one classroom. We had become familiar with this concern not only in our own school system, but through much of our reading about and study of other programs. There are commonly two opposing arguments on this issue: one is that gifted programs create or foster an elitist attitude among the most capable students by selecting them out and placing them all together; the opposing view is that these students need to have opportunities to spend time working together because they stimulate and, more importantly, tend to understand one another, whereas in very heterogeneous settings they are frequently seen as "odd" or "different." There is not sufficient space here to list all of the arguments for each side, nor have we been able to locate respectable research that can substantiate either side of the argument in a definitive way.

At any rate, as we expanded the program to include another school, we decided to attempt a compromise by placing carefully selected clusters of no fewer than five of these students (20 percent of the total classroom) in each fifth-grade classroom. We used the same screening procedure as in the pilot and came up with 70 names (50–60 percent of incoming fifth-grade students).

We administered the same IQ and creativity tests to each of these students, and gathered the same teacher input on day-to-day classroom performance. We ended up with a voluminous amount of data; studying it was fascinating but somewhat overwhelming. Students with the highest IQ scores, with very few exceptions, did not score highest on the creativity tests. Teacher ratings on the creativity checklists were not very consistent with high scores on the creativity test. Students whose group aptitude scores fluctuated markedly over a three-year period in some cases achieved high individual IQ scores. It seemed that the more varied and numerous the sources of data, and the larger the group of students being looked at, the more complex the task became to select a group of "gifted" students. Perhaps this was due to the kinds of data we gathered or the instruments and sources used. At any rate, we were following guidelines that we had gleaned from the literature in the field, using multiple criteria and the types of instruments recommended. Perhaps researchers with more expertise would have found the data easier to study or could have identified inherent problems. It is regrettable that someone who had the time, interest, and expertise was not offered access to all of this data for further study because programs for gifted students are currently receiving a great deal of attention nationally, and identification of students for inclusion in programs is frequently the most controversial and complex issue faced by program developers. We were trying to use "state of the art" measures and guidelines, but this resulted in a very complex and confusing selection process.

What saved us was that because enrichment for these "gifted" students would be delivered primarily within the classroom, we could encourage teachers to study the strengths of students not included in the target group, and to include these students in enrichment activities as deemed appropriate on a day-to-day basis. That is, if particular enrichment activities or curricular extensions seemed to be beneficial to a given student, then he or she should be included on that basis, rather than on the basis of using our identification system alone. On the other hand, we did identify the cluster groups for the teachers, selecting those students who seemed to have the greatest strengths overall.

Classroom teachers were given the names of these students, as well as the profile of information gathered on each student. The target clusters of students were mostly made up of those who were high IQ (130+)-high achievers. In a very few instances, these students had also scored high on particular creativity subtests or creativity behavioral ratings. Beyond this target group, we had what I consider the "scatter" students—some with above-average IQ but high creativity-test scores (higher than most of the students in the target group); some with high IQ but more average achievement scores, and so on. Teachers were also given this information and were encouraged to consider means for tapping into the particular strengths of these students or to include them in enrichment activities with the cluster group when it seemed appropriate.

The Triad model was, once again, used as a general guide to the types of enrichment, and our goal was that teachers would weave this into the regular classroom program for these students. In major subject areas (language, math, science, social studies), this meant that as students demonstrated that they had satisfactorily mastered concepts and skills of the basic fifth-grade curriculum (which many were able to do more quickly than their agemates), enrichment should be in the form of exposure to a variety of topics that represented extensions of that subject area. In math, for example, a teacher might introduce units on economics, the stock market, consumerism, and logic. This type of unit would also be designed to include creative and critical thinking, problem-solving activities, and more advanced research skills, and might become the springboard for independent study for an individual or small group of students. Teachers were encouraged to use resource people from the community at large (those whose vocations or avocations were related to enrichment units or topics) to come in as speakers introducing a particular topic or to serve as contacts and guides for students who selected a particular independent study topic related to their area of expertise. In general, we wanted "enrichment" to encourage students to question as well as to find answers, to sense problems as well as to solve them, and to identify, utilize, and stretch individual strengths, interests, and talents. Teachers were given the flexibility to select particular enrichment units based upon their own interests and talents and the interests and talents of the students in their classrooms. That is, the Triad model provided the formula for enrichment, but particular topics could be very diverse. Many of these units were initially introduced to the "top" math or reading group in classrooms. These groups generally included the target cluster group students as well as some other students. Expectations for students in the cluster group were that, in addition to completing the regular unit activities, they would eventually select a problem for independent study. The units explored during that year included studies of media and advertising, consumerism and economics, writers and authors, astronomy, heroes and heroines, animation and film-making. Eventually most of the students identified independent study topics, and with the support of assisting graduate students or community resource people, engaged in research and completed their projects in order to share their results. The range of projects completed by these students was quite impressive. For example, individuals or small groups wrote an original radio drama, created an animated film, wrote a how-to book on candlemaking, explored dreams and states of sleep, designed their own space shuttle, put together a presentation on constellations and mythology, experimented with structural designs in architecture, learned sign language, produced and directed original or borrowed plays and musicals, traced their genealogy, wrote for the local newspaper, and designed computer programs.

PROGRAM EVALUATION

There is no question in my mind that these students and many others in the fifth-grade classrooms learned a great deal from the enrichment experiences. The most difficult questions to answer, however, are:

1. How can we measure on a qualitative and quantitative basis the impact of what they have learned and how they have grown?
2. How do the factors used to identify these students relate to their ability and willingness to probe, to question, to take risks, to stay with a task, to identify a strong interest, to attend to detail, and so on?
3. What additional factors contribute to the success of independent projects and investigations undertaken by students and how can we document these?
4. Do students transfer what they learn in one independent study experience to other learning situations? What is the nature of the transfer? How can we observe it?
5. Does basing the program in the regular classroom have a significant impact on the "average" or "below-average" students? What is the nature of the impact? How can we examine this question?
6. In what ways *is* the project affecting classrooms?
7. How can we determine whether the cluster students would benefit more from a part- or full-time program outside of the regular classroom?
8. How well does the information which is used to identify these students predict actual classroom performance?
9. Does identification of students in any way affect teacher expectations for these students?
10. How can we ensure objectivity in our evaluation of our program?

Evaluation of the project up to this point has been primarily of a formative nature. That is, based on perceptions and reactions of students, teachers, graduate students, and myself, we have made attempts to modify the program. Information of this nature was gathered formally through questionnaires and informally through discussions. Questionnaires used were "home grown" for the most part. Although much of this feedback has been helpful and important, I am aware that there are many dimensions of the program to consider and frequently feel that I am too close to the project to maintain a perspective on the whole picture. As well, I tend to want to gather volumes of information on every dimension so that I won't "miss anything." Yet, teachers already have tremendous demands on their time and do not need to spend hours filling out forms, questionnaires, and reports. I suspect that a partnership with skilled researchers could have been very useful at the outset, by helping me to define the questions that I wanted to answer by the end of the project and designing realistic, consistent, and efficient methods for gathering the data that would help me to answer these questions.

During this, the final year of federal funding, the state requires a formal, summative evaluation of the project conducted by outside evaluators. The evaluation is intended to enable a project to measure, in particular, the nature and degree of student change, as a result of the program practices and to demonstrate how the project can be replicated in another school system. The use of standardized tests was strongly advocated in the guidelines given to us. I have spent six to eight months working with three other project directors. None of us had any prior experience in evaluating on a formal basis; all of us were former classroom teachers. We labored over how this could be accomplished and wrestled with the following issues: (1) Which goals and objectives should be measured? (2) Which goals and objectives could be measured? (3) How can we measure them? (4) Who is qualified to put together an overall evaluation design for this type of project? (5) Where does one find these people?

We decided to seek assistance from evaluation consultants and to explore evaluation designs with them. Locating and selecting these consultants was our first challenge. We came up with three names, either because they had conducted evaluations of "gifted" programs elsewhere, or because they were advertising as evaluators of "gifted" programs. We met with each of them for one or two days of discussion. We learned a great deal from these meetings but were not satisfied that we had yet located someone whom we were ready to hire. We felt that we needed someone who had expertise in both evaluation and in gifted education so that they could determine the appropriateness of our objectives as well as how to measure them. I believe, in retrospect, that we were looking for someone who was both a researcher and a practitioner. Eventually, we located a team of two people, one whose field of expertise was evaluation, testing, and measurement, the other who had been a teacher of the gifted, but was currently in a university doctoral program. At this point, I think we felt that they would be able to come in with the "magic formula" and sail through an evaluation. Interestingly, we became suspicious and somewhat annoyed when we were able to provide them with suggestions or cautions regarding instruments, objectives, or methods for seeking information in the school setting. We saw them as the "experts" and felt that they should have all the answers, while disregarding our own expertise as a result of our experience as practitioners. In addition to this, my first priority was to provide direct services to teachers and students and, although I intellectually valued and was enthusiastic about the notion of carefully evaluating an educational program, I tended to resent the time it took away from providing "direct" services.

Evaluation is still in process and will not be completed for several months. Our partnership with the evaluators has been riddled with demands, debates, discussions, suspicions, and frustrations on both sides. I feel, however, that we have achieved a sincere respect and appreciation for one another, and quite a bit of mutual understanding regarding the complexities involved for both parties in conducting and substantiating classroom research.

I realize now that there was a time when I thought the evaluation would determine the project to have been a success or a failure. I now realize that it will do neither on an "all-or-nothing" basis. Rather, I hope that we (the evaluators and myself) have gathered sufficient data to be able to derive some correlations and, perhaps, identify some causal relationships so that we can continue to improve our own program as well as offer support, advice, and assistance to others who are attempting a similar venture.

CONCLUSIONS

Investments of money to support research and development of programs for the gifted have historically undergone a pattern of ebb and flow in this country. Currently, I believe we are cresting a resurgent wave of interest and concern nationally coupled with the belief that these gifts and talents of our students represent our nation's greatest natural resource. The field of education is still riddled, however, with questions and controversy over how to identify gifts and talents, what educational practices will foster their development, and why this concern should take precedence over, or be in competition with, other areas of development in education.

Our four years of effort described here represent a microcosm of what is currently happening across the country. Unless the efforts and findings of people like ourselves become part of a much larger and more unified body of information, I feel that we will continue to experiment in isolation, to repeat each other's mistakes, to see funding and programs come and go, and to raise the same questions 10, 20, or 30 years from now.

Respectable researchers might potentially form the links among these microcosms of dedicated and committed practitioners. Unless, however, there is more familiarity and contact between researchers and practitioners, I fear that little progress will be made. Both need to have opportunities to develop an appreciation and understanding of the expertise that they have to offer to each other, as well as the resources they could make available to one another. Throughout this chapter, I have attempted to show that we often had to draw upon our intuitive perceptions because we were unsure of where else to turn or because we were disappointed in the quality of research or because we were baffled by the contents of some of the literature we read. From that basis, I have attempted to describe ways in which we might have used researchers. I suspect that the latter is far from a comprehensive view of where this intervention and interaction might have been helpful. Therein lies the core of the problem—how do practitioners turn to researchers when they are unaware of the kinds of assistance and support that could be offered?

REFERENCES

Marland, S. *Education of the gifted and talented.* Report to the Subcommittee on Education, Committee on Labor and Public Welfare, U.S. Senate, Washington, D.C., 1972.

Renzulli, J.S. *The enrichment triad model: A guide for developing defensible programs for the gifted and talented.* Mansfield Center, Conn.: Creative Learning Press, 1977.

Renzulli, J.S. What makes giftedness? Reexamining a definition. *Phi Delta Kappan,* 1978, **60**, 180–184, 261.

Chapter 16

Case Study II:
A Day Care Center

Christine McVinney

In the Fall of 1975, I started the Concord Children's Center with my partner, Deborah Begner. Having recently moved to Concord from New York City where she had opened the Gingerbread Day Care Center, Deborah began exploring the possibility of establishing day care in Concord. I had been teaching child development at a local independent school and had been exploring the possibility of starting a center for faculty children at the school. Finding space on campus, however, was difficult; the only space available was an old barn that would have needed extensive renovation. I was ready to abandon my project, since I had no money for the renovation, when I met Deborah. The two of us decided to combine our knowledge of early childhood and our energy with our common goal of establishing a high-quality day care center for preschool children.

From the start, we felt that researching the feasibility of day care in Concord could become a project of its own. We thought of ourselves as teachers and mothers, not business people, and as practitioners, not researchers. As parents, we knew there was a need for day care because we had experienced the difficulties of finding full-time day care for our own children. In addition, we were interested in opening the doors of the center as soon as possible, since neither of us could afford to remain unemployed for the length of time it might have taken to do an extensive survey of the Concord community and its child-care needs. Consequently, the research we did to support our initial desire to start a day care center was a kind of marketing research that focused on three immediate practical concerns: finding the space, the children, and the funding to start the center.

We decided not to spend our time trying to convince the town of the importance and the need for day care. We wanted to avoid the danger and futility of attempting to change people's attitudes about the merits of providing child care outside the home. Instead, our strategy was to establish the best program we could so that people could see, through our example, that day care could provide high-quality education for children and support for the family. Thus, we decided against the alternative of reading all the available research on day care, looking for positive results to be used as ammunition in a direct appeal for day care to the people of Concord. Instead, seeking to avoid a controversy about the merits of day care, we chose to present our center as a "nursery school" with extended hours. We decided to present our center as a "school" because, although day care is not a new concept in our society, we learned from many of the people we talked to that they saw day care as a novel and experimental idea. We saw this decision as the least risky and most expedient way to avoid confrontation and ultimately to further our goal.

SPACE

Fortunately, an old school building in town was being closed owing to declining enrollment. A group of residents who had attended the school as children originated the concept of recycling the building as a community center—a place to offer a variety of educational programs to people of all ages. We saw this building as an ideal space for us, and after a town meeting voted in favor of the community-center concept, we applied for space.

CHILDREN

Once our application had been approved, we wanted to assess more carefully the child-care needs in Concord. Our assumption had been that there was a general need for care, but we wondered where the need was greatest: for what age child—infant, toddler, preschooler, after-schooler? Obviously, we could not provide care for all these ages. We composed a questionnaire asking parents of public-school-age children what their child-care needs were. We realized that our sample population was not really a representative group, but we sent the questionnaire out through the public schools because we could not think of any other way to reach parents. Because these parents indicated a great need for after-school care, we decided to offer after-school care as well as preschool care. We quickly decided against starting a program for infants and toddlers because the low teacher/child ratio meant it would be the most costly program.

FUNDING

A few posters advertising our new school, offering care for children ages three through ten, were placed in stores around Concord and soon we had twenty applications. We charged each family an application fee and security deposit to be used as our start-up funds.

PROGRAM

Now that we had found space, children, and funding for our school, we had to decide what was the best way to set up our program. How would we equip our classrooms? How would we group the children? How would we structure the day's activities? How many teachers would we hire? Deborah and I agreed that we wanted our center to offer more than custodial care for children; we wanted to provide a stimulating and nurturing environment and experiences that would foster a positive self-image. We wanted the atmosphere of the center to encourage children's natural curiosity in learning about who they are and what they can do. Our specific decisions about how to accomplish this were based primarily on our practical experience and on guidelines from our education as teachers. Both of us had been influenced in graduate school by the academic research of people who had studied young children. The works of Piaget, Kohlberg, Erikson, Elkind, Pratt, and Fraiberg were especially influential, and undoubtedly served to shape our program, albeit in an indirect way.

SUCCESS

The Concord Children's Center now provides year-round educational and recreational programs for young children. We care for 95 children ranging in age from twenty months to eight years, with a yearly budget of $150,000. We employ 14 teachers. Next year we will be expanding our program to another town building because we can no longer meet the demand for child care in our present facility. This time, when we applied for space, the town manager met with us personally to tell us that he is committed to making day care available in Concord. It has taken six years of practical problem solving to achieve this status. During this period, our concern about establishing the center as a reputable institution expressed itself in attention to day-to-day details. We had little need and no time for delving into the theoretical base on which our endeavor stood.

Certainly, we had carried out some of that background research in graduate school, when time was set aside for studying the theoretical positions of researchers. At the time we were establishing the center, however, we did not take the time to verify the research, and we did not take advantage of opportunities to consult with researchers in the area. Instead, we concentrated our efforts on changing people's attitudes about day care by our example; we feel that we were successful.

During that time, we sensed that we ourselves were becoming experts on day care through our practical experience. Now this stage of our growth is finished and we no longer need to worry about the survival of our center. We finally have a chance to analyze, organize, and reevaluate what we know and what we still need to learn about day care. In the classroom, we observe, ask questions, test our theories, and draw conclusions intuitively and informally on a daily basis. Yet we are not trained in the scientific method and we are often unaware of the research that already exists in the field of day care. A partnership with researchers at this stage could help us become more systematic in our approach by clarifying our questions about how day care, particularly our center, affects the child and the family. Such a partnership would also allow us to act on conclusions we draw from a more solid base of research.

DAY CARE IN THE UNITED STATES

Any questions about the impact of day care and its implementation must be framed within an understanding of the place of day care within our society. At the turn of the century, day care was conceived as part of a larger movement of social reform to acculturate immigrant families into this society. Day nurseries were established as part of the "settlement houses" intended to offer relief and support for the working poor. The dissolution of day nurseries can be traced to a changing attitude toward the poor and to the growing belief that even poor mothers should stay at home to raise their children. This attitude prompted the passage of the Mothers' Pension Act of 1911 and other various assistance programs that paid mothers to stay at home with their children (Fein & Clarke-Stewart, 1973).

The concept of day care became popular again during World War II as the federal government provided money for child-care centers for women working in war-related industries through the Lanham Act. Once again, day care was seen as an emergency social service to help families in a time of crisis. Federal funds for day-care centers were not renewed at the war's end.

During the years following World War II, an unprecedented growth in the economy and in the birth rate occurred. The "baby boom" and a high standard of living due to a stable and growing economy allowed most women to remain at home to care for their children. In 1948, only 13 percent of mothers with preschool-age children worked outside the home. By the year

1976, however, that figure had jumped to 37 percent. In 1950, the majority (56 percent) of two-parent families were supported by the husband as the sole wage earner. By 1975 that figure had dropped to 34 percent (Kenniston, 1977).

This shift of women into the labor market has created a new demand for day care. In the past, day care was seen as a response to a national crisis. Now there is a new kind of crisis created by the dramatic increase in the number of working women. According to a study of child care by Foreman (1980), the impetus of the women's movement combined with economic necessity has propelled many women into paid jobs outside the home. Foreman cites Eli Ginsberg, chairperson of the National Commission for Employment Policy, who describes this development as "the most profound phenomenon of the Century, whose long-term effects will be equal to or greater than the rise of communism or the discovery of nuclear energy because of its impact on the totality of society, including all males and children" (p. 1).

Currently, 68 percent of all three- to five-year-olds attend some form of out-of-home day care (Foreman, 1980). We have altered one of the primary functions of the family—the care of its children. We may conclude that day care is now a reality, a social institution that will have far-reaching effects on our society.

RESEARCH ON DAY CARE

What do we know about the supposedly far-reaching effects of this phenomenon? Have researchers studied these effects? A substantial amount of research has been done on day care, although much of it *has* been rather narrow in scope. Research to date has focused on two issues. Researchers have been interested in the effect of day-care experience, first on the individual child, and second, on the development of a mother-child bond and the subsequent emotional development of that child. Belsky and Steinberg (1978) reviewed the existing research and concluded that the day-care experience "has neither salutary nor deleterious effects upon the intellectual development of the child," and "is not disruptive to the mother-child bond" (p. 929). As Belsky and Steinberg point out, however, a shortcoming of the existing research is that most of it was conducted in university-based, high-quality day-care centers that are not typical. According to them, in 1975 only 3 percent of children in substitute care attended day care centers.

Researchers may have chosen to investigate the impact of day care on the process of mother-child bonding because of the influence of John Bowlby (1951), who suggested that any substitute care arrangement which deprives the child of continuous access to the mother impairs the development of a strong maternal attachment and adversely affects the child's emotional security. Although conducted 30 years ago on institutionalized children, Bowlby's research has influenced both the researcher and the lay person. Parents applying to our center have voiced their concern that child care outside the home might not be "good for our child." In particular, certain mothers each year express their feelings of guilt about leaving their child at a day-care center. While these parents may not have read Bowlby's study, it is likely that these findings have been filtered down to them and have contributed to the formation of a general consensus that separating mother from child is not in the best interest of the child. Though there may be other reasons why parents are concerned about placing their child in day care, Bowlby's study in particular does not help them feel comfortable about day care nor does it encourage practitioners to argue for the value of and the need for high-quality day care.

There have been exceptions to this kind of research. For example, funded by the federal government, Abt Associates of Cambridge, Massachusetts, conducted a national day care study between 1974 and 1978. Results from this study were intended to inform the federal government in its regulation of day care policy. This study is significant because it offers a broader perspective of day care as a special institution and begins to fill in the gaps in our knowledge about the effects of certain characteristics of care on the quality and cost.

Specifically, the Abt researchers were interested in determining the impact on the quality of care of different caregiver/child ratios, group sizes, qualifications of classroom staff, and other regulatable center characteristics, the impact of these factors on the cost of care, and the trade-offs between quality and cost entailed by alternative federal purchasing requirements governing these characteristics of day care centers. They found that high-quality day care programs had smaller classes taught by teachers trained in early childhood education. Unfortunately the people who would benefit the most from the findings of this report, the providers and consumers of day care, will probably never have the opportunity to read the report. Most research is published in research journals and read only by other researchers or presented at conferences attended by other researchers, or published by the government for its own use. If research is to have any influence on changing attitudes or affecting policy, it needs to be made readily available to the practitioner and the consumer. When research is funded, money needs to be appropriated for the dissemination of the findings to those people who will be affected. When researchers hold their yearly conferences, practitioners need to be invited. If only these suggestions were followed, the barrier between researcher and practitioner could begin to be broken to the ultimate benefit of both.

Breaking the barrier that exists between researcher and practitioner could affect the direction of future research. Practitioners are, by the nature of their work, intimately involved with "the subjects" and consequently they are often able to perceive issues that escape the researcher. For example, any practitioner in the field of day care knows how important the influence of the family is on the behavior of the child while she is attending a center. We see, also, our influence on the family as a support for working parents. Parents come to us for advice on a variety of issues—toilet training, sibling rivalry, illness, eating habits, and thumb sucking. Yet there is no research available on the interaction of centers, parents, and their children.

To conclude, previous research has been limited in several ways. It has depended on subjects from university-based day care centers, despite the fact that the most common kind of care is offered by babysitters or family day care providers. It has ignored the long-term impact of day care on children who spend one to five years in day care before entering public school. It has neglected to compare the variety of day-care services offered to parents.

By the end of this decade, it is predicted that two out of three mothers of children under age six will be working (*Day Care and Early Education*, 1980). Day care services will continue to have an even greater impact on the child, the family, and our society in the future. The opportunity presented to the researcher and the practitioner is at once exciting and awesome. There are so many issues for research, it is difficult to know where to start.

UNANSWERED QUESTIONS

One way to begin might be for researchers to ask practitioners what issues they would like to investigate. There are several questions that are important to me as a practitioner. Specifically, how does the service I provide affect the quality of the personal and professional lives of the families who use my center? Some research could investigate the interaction of day-care centers and parents. Does the availability, type, and quality of care affect parents' tardiness, productivity, and absenteeism? Does day care contribute to a sense of guilt in working women? Do parents learn parenting skills from day care providers or do they abdicate this role to the day care center? Do parents trust day care providers? Do single-parent families experience day care differently from two–parent families? Does the availability of day care change a woman's attitude toward child-care responsibilities and job responsibilities? How does day care affect the relationship between parents and children? Are children expected to be more self-reliant? Do these children feel neglected?

As an administrator of a center, I need to know how I can most effectively influence, support, and train caregivers. What is the optimal number of working hours for caregivers to work each day? What kind of evaluation of caregivers can serve to improve the quality of care? How can I combat the inevitable syndrome of teacher "burn-out" in the face of low wages?

As a teacher of young children, I am interested in knowing how I can provide the best possible environment for my students—one that encourages self-esteem and enthusiasm for learning. How is self-esteem affected by the apparent lack of privacy and the length of time children spend as members of a group? Can children in centers suffer from burn-out from spending ten hours a day year-round in a day care setting? How does day care affect their social skills? Are day care children more aggressive or more cooperative than home-reared children? How are their cognitive skills affected? Do they learn skills earlier or faster than home-reared children? Do they engage in fantasy play more often than other children? What are the long-range implications of day care on children as they grow older? Do day care children cause more behavioral problems in public school? Do they require more remedial help? Are they perceived by their teachers any differently from other children? Are they able to establish relationships with adults more easily than home-reared children because of their exposure to many unrelated adults at a young age? Are they more self-reliant than other children?

As a parent, I would like to see comaprative studies of day care arrangements. Are certain arrangements more suitable for infants and toddlers? What kind of care is most appropriate for my needs and the needs of my child? My child is presently in a family day care setting. How does that differ from center care?

CONCLUSION

As an educator, I believe that working with a researcher to investigate these questions would contribute to my own sense of self-esteem and expertise. I have my own answers to all of these questions based on six years of experience and intuition. Research could support my convictions or show where they are mistaken; it could enlighten and broaden my understanding of my role as a professional in a demanding and vitally important service in our society. With concern for professional survival behind me, I am eager to have access to research findings, to think about the applicability of those findings to my own endeavor, and to form a partnership with researchers to facilitate the ongoing study of questions of mutual concern. Such a partnership would allow for the maximum sharing of knowledge and skill to investigate this vitally important field.

REFERENCES

Abt Associates. *Children at the center*. Cambridge, Mass.: March 1979.
Belsky, J. & Steinberg, L. D. The effects of day care: A critical review. *Child Development*, 1978, **49**, 929-949.

Bowlby, J. *Maternal care and mental health*. Geneva: World Health Organization, 1951.
Fein, G. & Clarke-Stewart, A. *Day care in context*. New York: Wiley, 1973.
Foreman, J. U.S. lags far behind in child-care policy for working parents. *Boston Sunday Globe*, November 16, 1980.
Kenniston, K. *All our children*. New York: Harcourt, Brace, Jovanovich, 1977.
Wilson, L. (ed.), *Day care and early education*. New York: Human Sciences Press, Fall 1980.

Part V:
Prospects for Research
in the Classroom

Introduction to Part V

Although concrete suggestions for improving classroom research and the relationship between researchers and educators have appeared throughout this volume, the chapters in this section are devoted primarily to an exploration of the ways in which such improvements might be undertaken. We acknowledge that there is no solution to the problem of designing and conducting effective classroom research that will please everyone. We think the expectation of finding a single solution is, in itself, an unreasonable goal. Instead, we believe that there are a variety of ways for practitioners and researchers to explore working together.

In Chapter 17, Harter begins by taking researchers to task for their widespread lack of attention to the individual child in the classrooms where they work, his abilities, and his motivations. She suggests that this is the information that could be most useful to teachers—regardless of the nature of the information that researchers need for testing their hypotheses. Harter argues that researchers need to view teachers as peers, that they need to explain research procedures more fully, guide teachers in the use of research, do the research that will provide information the teachers need, and—perhaps most importantly—listen to teachers' views on the problems they are studying.

In Chapter 18, Stubbs advises policy makers and practitioners to appreciate the probabilistic nature of research conclusions; at the same time, she advises researchers to appreciate the immediate decision-making needs of teachers. Far from favoring one methodology over another, Stubbs proposes that classroom research use a variety of designs and statistical analyses, and that it try, as a primary goal, to take into account the complexities inherent in the classroom situation.

Finally, Chapter 19 (Amabile and Stubbs) summarizes the prescriptions presented throughout the volume as a set of general principles, a set of specific guidelines for teachers, and a parallel set of specific guidelines for researchers. Although we realize that these guidelines are far from foolproof, we offer them as suggestions for researchers and teachers to keep in mind as they struggle to define effective collaboration.

Chapter 17

Guess Who's Coming to the Classroom

Susan Harter

Like many developmental researchers, several times a year I find myself embarking on one of the more challenging excursions in our profession, a journey to the local elementary school. In this chapter I would like to explore what researchers are doing there, and how they can do it better, based upon some of my own experiences over the years. As a general framework, I submit that if we are merely searching for a pool of subjects amid a sea of faces, strangely perhaps, we will feel very much like fish out of water. How, then, can we make all of the participants of this enterprise, ourselves included, more comfortable?

Several themes will be pursued, including specific suggestions for the developmental researcher in the classroom. How can we best explain the research enterprise to our educational colleagues in a manner that will be genuinely compelling? How should we describe this endeavor to the children themselves? How can teachers contribute in terms of providing valuable input as well as data? In what manner should feedback be given to the school personnel? At what level should parents be involved? How can we assist teachers in answering questions of their own?

CROSS-PURPOSES VERSUS DIFFERENT AGENDAS

Many who have written on this topic have contrasted the goals of the educator with those of the researcher. Thus, one points to the distinction between basic versus applied interests, between theory versus pedagogy, long-range versus short-range goals, normative data versus information about the individual child, and so on. While these distinctions are very real, it would seem that they represent somewhat different agendas for the educator and the researcher rather than serious cross-purposes or impediments.

In our own research program, for example, we are definitely concerned with basic research bearing on theoretical issues with the long-range goal of providing normative data. Simultaneously, we are concerned with application and pedagogy, as well as short-range implications for the individual child. Specifically, we have been interested in such constructs as perceived competence, self-esteem, intrinsic versus extrinsic motivational orientation in the classroom, optimal challenge, perceived control, achievement, and anxiety. From a theoretical perspective, our goal has been to specify how these constructs are related, and to what extent they undergo normative developmental change. For example, we have now determined that (1) perceived control predicts the child's achievement level which in turn predicts his or her perceived scholastic competence; (2) high perceived scholastic competence is associated with an intrinsic motivational orientation to classroom learning (whereas children whose perceived competence is low tend to adopt a more extrinsic orientation); (3) anxiety is negatively related to perceived competence such that the more competent the child feels, the less anxious he or she is about schoolwork; (4) intrinsic motivation for classroom learning decreases across the grades three through nine (see Harter, 1981a, 1981b; Harter & Connell, in press, for a discussion of these and other related findings).

We have learned with experience that teachers are not particularly surprised by such findings. Some are pleased to discover that our results bolster their own informal theories, in terms of the general pattern of relationships. Data generated by the group design, however, offer little else to the teacher who is basically interested in the individual child. Paradoxically, for researchers the villain in the group design is "error variance," whereas this is precisely what is interesting to teachers—namely, individual differences among pupils within a group!

For some time our own group persisted in telling teachers that we were examining such hypotheses as: children with positive feelings of scholastic competence are less anxious; low feelings of competence are associated with an extrinsic orientation; or that children, in general, prefer optimal challenge if given such a choice on problem-solving tasks. Our normative theoretical blinders obscured what every teacher knows, which is that there are many individual children who do not fit these patterns. For example, while many scholastically competent children do show relatively little anxiety over their performance, there are those who are extremely anxious, despite their high level of achievement. To take another example, although many children with low feelings of competence are extrinsically oriented, there are some who are intrinsically motivated, who seem to be "marching to the tune of their own drum." With regard to preference for challenge, while "children in general" may prefer optimal challenge, there are also those who readily seek out the easiest tasks to perform. Thus, although the constructs themselves were of interest to teachers, documentation of the *overall* relationships among them was not very relevant to their day-to-day task of understanding the performance of individual children.

One could scoff at teachers' singular interest in the vicissitudes of the particular pupil, complaining that they simply aren't interested in the broader theoretical context. Alternatively, one could examine one's own enterprise and determine whether there might not be something that one could offer teachers, given their specific goals and objectives. In shifting to the latter strategy, we have been fortunate in that the measures we have constructed provide scores that can be meaningfully interpreted and used by teachers. For example, our Perceived Competence Scale for Children (Harter, in press) provides a profile of a child's feelings of competence across three domains, cognitive or scholastic competence, competence at athletics, social competence in peer relationships, in addition to a separate index of a child's feelings of general self-worth. Teachers have found these profiles very interesting, particularly with regard to how realistic the child's perceptions appear to be. Potential changes in the child's perceptions over a particular time course, such as the school year or participation in a remedial program, can also be documented through the use of such a self-report scale. The normative data pique the teacher's curiosity in this context, in that they provide a backdrop against which they can assess an individual child.

We have also been able to provide teachers with profiles *across* constructs. For example, we can identify the child who perceives him or herself as highly competent (construct #1) and not very anxious (construct #2), in comparison to the child who perceives himself or herself as competent but is extremely anxious over his or her scholastic performance. To add a third construct, intrinsic versus extrinsic motivational orientation, the first child tends to be more intrinsically motivated while the second child tends to be more extrinsically motivated. From a research standpoint, we are attempting to determine what possible typologies exist with regard to profiles across constructs within a given competence domain. We are hypothesizing that these typologies will be better predictors of performance than single variables alone, or linear combinations of variables. With these typologies we hope to capture the major individual difference patterns of interest to teachers. Thus, broader research objectives can be met while at the same time meeting the specific and more immediate needs of educators.

Obviously, many measures cannot serve such a dual purpose, and investigators may well feel that to share individual pupil scores with school personnel would constitute an abuse of ethical principles. In other cases, the researcher may deem that the data simply would not be meaningful or relevant to teachers. Presumably, these situations would result from measures that had not yet been sufficiently tested or indices intended to assess a relatively abstract theoretical proposition that may not have a direct analogue in the day-to-day behavior of children. Invariably, such judgments are quite sound.

Whether or not the researcher can share specific findings with the educator then becomes a matter of the value each of us places on a particular type of research. The individual differences among researchers in this regard are marked, and if my own shifting values are any index, we need to include a life-span component to the analysis. A number of years ago I was too content to conduct studies that primarily satisfied my intellectual curiosity or fed my own theoretical ego. With development (I prefer to think of this as a positive growth gradient!), it has become increasingly important to conduct research on problems that fall within the broad rubric of "applied," and have direct relevance to the daily lives of children.

As developmental researchers, we might do well to examine our motives more clearly at each particular point in our careers, and communicate these intentions to our practitioner-colleagues more honestly. In conducting more "basic research," I'm certain that many of us have experienced pangs of conscience as we tell educators that "This research will eventually lead to . . ."; "If you just extrapolate to the classroom situation . . ."; "Down the road, we'll be able to better understand . . ."; "These basic processes are probably implicated in . . ."; "Further programmatic research will be necessary to flesh out the implications of this study for. . . ." When we are less than genuine in voicing such sound and fury, the audible hollow ring is heard by the educators as well. If we are sincere, we need to appreciate that the educator rightfully has a different agenda, and we need to be particularly compelling in our conviction that such research will ultimately prove meaningful. Our own lack of conviction in a given situation may serve as a prognosticator, or perhaps a signal to reexamine our motives more honestly.

WILL THE REAL EXPERTS PLEASE STAND UP

It frequently seems that when the research cavalry charges into the school there are a few too many high horses, and we might do well to improve our dismounting skills. We tend to set ourselves up as the authorities, we have the degrees, we are the "scientists" with wisdom to impart. It seems difficult for us to acknowledge that teachers who live with their pupils for six to seven hours a day five days a week might have actually learned a considerable amount about children! Thus, we tend to preach in a rather patronizing manner. How often do we ask teachers to share their insights, how often do we listen to what the educator has to say? On one occasion, I recall that my particular patter seemed to be falling on a roomful of deaf ears. When I shifted to encouraging teacher comments and input, I witnessed an entire room of bland facial expressions change into smiling, enthusiastic, warm human beings who obviously know and care a great deal about children. We could do much more to encourage and use this input, toward the goal of better understanding children and the particular phenomena that have captured our interest.

There are also a number of procedural considerations in dealing with teachers that we often overlook, logistics that will facilitate communication. A given study shouldn't be legislated from on high, merely making arrangements with the principal, and other staff personnel such as school psychologists, counselors, social workers, and the like. The teachers' permission should be obtained, and if time or scheduling does not permit you to meet with them as a group, then make yourself available for individual or small group meetings. Invariably, these smaller team conferences are more successful. It is also critical to obtain and learn individual teacher's names as well as the names of key personnel such as the administrative staff in the main office. Spending time in the teachers' lounge, eating lunch in the cafeteria with the kids, are other ways to appreciate the school personnel as human beings functioning within a complex social community. In addition, many of us have learned that sustained contact with one school is the best route to opening and maintaining the lines of communication, and developing mutual trust and respect. In the short run, the flashy researcher who cuts a wide swath leaving a trail of schools behind may churn out a number of publications; in the long run, however, this strategy does little to further the goal of fostering communication and mutual respect between researcher and educator.

WHAT TO TELL THE CHILDREN

Our responsibility to the children extends beyond securing clearance from our institutional ethics committee. We must attempt to make the experience as instructive and interesting as possible for them. The specifics will vary depending upon the requirements of the particular study. Our group, however, has developed a few general rules of thumb that seem to be successful. Regardless of whether the study involves individual or group administration, we talk to the group (typically a class unit) as a whole at the outset. We identify the general theme of the study (how kids solve problems, what they like to do, how they feel about things, etc.) and indicate that we are interested in how kids of different ages might be different. Children have an implicit understanding of a cross-sectional developmental design, given our tendency toward cultural age-stratification. That is, they believe that age makes a difference in how one thinks, feels, and performs.

In most of our own research, we are not interested in testing abilities per se, and thus attempt to break through any set that might liken our procedure to a testing atmosphere. We try to convince them that there really are no right and wrong answers. Thus, we focus on how we are conducting a *survey* and then ask the kids to tell us what they think a survey is. We have them generate examples, and are bombarded by illustrations such as Skippy peanut butter versus Peter Pan, Crest toothpaste versus Colgate, McDonald's hamburgers versus Wendy's.

We've also learned that by the fourth or fifth grade, children can understand the logic of reliability. On our self-report questionnaires, children often ask why they have to answer several questions that seem repetitive, that ask the same thing. We've explained that if we wanted to know how much they know about math (or geography, or baseball), we wouldn't just ask one question, since that wouldn't be a fair way to test what they really knew or felt. By fifth and sixth grades, children also spontaneously talk about how we want to see if they said the same thing on every question, or "see if we were telling the truth." In a follow-up session with the group, we discuss these comments and try to teach them a little about surveys. (These particular suggestions are relatively specific to questionnaire-type procedures, but a similar strategy can be adapted for other types of measures.) Also, if possible, we encourage the teacher to be part of the pretest and posttest group discussions. Often they extend the discussion in ingenious directions, relating it to other topics or activities in which the class is engaged. These discussions turn out to be one of the most gratifying aspects of the classroom experience (particularly if one doesn't feel the need to display one's degree by insisting that he or she be introduced to the children as Dr. X).

THE TEACHER AND THE SCHOOL SETTING AS A SOURCE OF DATA

In many studies, investigators wish to have teachers rate some aspect of the child's behavior. In our own research, for example, teachers' ratings of children's actual cognitive competence have provided fascinating data on the degree to which the children's perceptions of their competence are realistic (see Harter, in press; Harter & Bierer, 1981). The success of this endeavor and the willingness of the teacher to comply with this request are a direct function of how the study has been presented to the teacher. If the study has been presented in an interesting and compelling manner, particularly if there is some benefit for the teacher, then he or she will invariably be quite cooperative. Our task here is to communicate a genuine appreciation for valuable teacher input; if we merely leave a stack of forms in the teacher's mailbox without appropriate explanation, there is much less incentive for the teacher to comply with our request.

The failure of researcher and educator to communicate goals and needs can result in frustration in this bailiwick, as well as in others. We recently experienced a dramatic example in a school where we had been told that teachers wanted to use scores from our Perceived Competence Scale in their regular parent conferences. We agreed to prepare individual pupil profiles for every child in the school. Many of these same teachers, however, seemed unwilling to fill out the accompanying teacher-rating form as we had requested, leading our research team to think that teachers weren't really taking the scores seriously. Thinking that available time might be the reason, we tried to adopt shorter and shorter rating forms, but that didn't ameliorate the situation. Finally, in a meeting where some dialogue was encouraged, the real reason became apparent. Most teachers were taking the child's scores very seriously, planning to incorporate them into the parent conferences. But they did not want us to plot their own evaluations on the pupil-rating form, graphically presented in black and white. Rather, they wanted to discuss their evaluations of a given child with each individual parent in the most appropriate and sensitive manner possible. Once this was clarified, we agreed not to plot teacher ratings, and then most agreed to fill out our forms! While this particular incident had a happy ending, it sensitized us to how much more there is for researchers to understand about teachers' agendas, and vice versa.

Researchers may well choose not to make the effort, opting to bring children directly into their lab settings, bypassing the school system altogether. This is a strategy employed by many, quite successfully, given their needs. On the other hand, the school setting is a yeasty microcosm of many of the processes of interest to developmental psychologists, and functioning in that setting may greatly enhance our understanding of children. My own incidental observations of peer interactions, my casual conversations with children in the halls and the lunchroom, have definitely influenced my thinking in ways that would not have occurred had I only seen children in my laboratory. If one is a keen observer of children's interactions within the school setting, one cannot help but be overwhelmed by the importance of peer interactions, social networks, age segregation, friendship patterns, the role of social comparison, and the degree to which concerns relating to social relationships dominate children's spontaneous conversations.

Moreover, in certain studies, the validity of one's measures may be enhanced by conducting research in the school setting. For example, asking children to rate their feelings of scholastic competence and social acceptance by peers when they are physically situated in that context, may contribute to the validity of those judgments. Validity here should not be equated with objective accuracy per se. Rather, the salience of the school setting may serve to give us the most appropriate rating of how the child perceives himself or herself in that setting, or wishes to be perceived. Teasing apart the wish and reality is an interesting empirical question in and of itself, which may also best be addressed within the milieu in which these experiences naturally occur—the school culture.

FEEDBACK TO SCHOOL PERSONNEL

Providing relatively swift, interesting, and interpretable feedback to the school system is an arena of the three-ring research circus where performance could be upgraded for most of us. We seem to have myriad excuses for why such feedback is not forthcoming: it takes time to analyze one's data, the appropriate computer program isn't available, our new research assistant needs to be trained in the scoring of the protocols, we can't find a time in our busy schedules for a visit that can be coordinated with the school's schedule, and so on. In fact, we don't give this part of the research endeavor a sufficiently high priority generally. Rather, we often seem to take the data and run. We may feel a bit guilty, but the agony isn't sufficient to mobilize us beyond giving reasons for why immediate feedback cannot be provided. We could do better.

The argument with regard to the length of time required to analyze data properly is often somewhat specious. Most school personnel do not want a technical report including every statistical analysis, but some general feel for the strongest effects obtained. Typically, as researchers sensitive to our data, we can provide this level of feedback relatively quickly, if we take the time to make this a priority. It is the responsible researcher who will do so, out of respect for the school system that has been interested and cooperative.

Moreover, the most effective feedback involves more than a memo by mail. While findings should be prepared in readable prose and made available to the school personnel, a personal visit to discuss the results with those most directly involved is far preferable as a means of communication. Such a visit allows for the kind of dialogue in which questions can be answered and implications can be explored. The extent to which we may attempt to avoid such an exchange may be a partial barometer of how much we feel we have to say. We might do well to ponder this from time to time.

Communication via readable English prose seems to be a skill that many researchers never acquire. We do not choose to learn how to communicate our findings to those beyond our immediate discipline. Thus, it is not uncommon in feedback descriptions to school personnel to find sentences such as the following: "A 4 $\times$ 2 analysis of variance revealed a significant interaction ($p < .002$) between grade and magnitude of the discrepancy scores based on the absolute difference between teacher and pupil ratings of cognitive competence. With increasing grade level, the magnitude of these discrepancy scores became attenuated." Often it's not simply a matter of jargon that is inappropriate for the intended audience. In some cases, our own head set primarily involves variables, significance levels, interactions, regression coefficients, standard deviations, and factor structures, to the extent that we seem to throw out the baby with the bath; we tend to lose the very target of our inquiry, presumably children, in our statistical laundering of the data.

Perhaps we need minicourses in "prose for the populace" as part of our research training, so as not to lose touch with reality. Exercise #1: "In the lower grades, children tend not to view their level of competence at school-work the way their teachers do; however, as children move into the upper elementary school grades, their views of their competence become more and more similar to their teacher's judgments." Are we perhaps afraid that if we make it sound that understandable, it will be taken for obvious at best or trivial at worst? This may be something else for us to ponder.

In providing feedback, there's a fine line between talking in English, rather than jargon and psychologese, and talking down to teachers. We need to guard against a posture in which we imply that our designs or measures are somehow beyond the comprehension of the teacher. While teachers may not have had the technical research training, most designs, questions, tasks, and measures can be explained at a comprehensible level. Furthermore, most teachers have had considerable experience with the type of graphical and numerical presentation of standardized achievement test data, and readily grasp findings presented in a similar format. Often they may have suggestions for improving our mode of presentation, such that the findings will be even clearer for other school personnel and perhaps parents.

Parents tend to be the forgotten element when it comes to feedback. They graciously give us their permission to employ their children in our research but rarely hear about it again. There are several possible routes to providing such feedback. In certain cases, a one- or two-page write-up specifically designed for parents may be appropriate. In other cases, the researcher may give feedback in the form of a talk at a parent meeting. If the research has been presented in a compelling fashion to the school personnel, they may invite the researcher to speak at a PTA meeting. We should welcome these opportunities as a further means of communication. It may also be the case that the school wishes to become directly involved in the feedback process. In our own research program, this was the wish of the school where teachers opted to include the pupil-perceived competence profile as part of the material to be discussed during parent conferences. Whatever the vehicle, we should make every effort to go full circle, and give feedback to the primary link in the chain, the parents.

ASSISTING TEACHERS IN ASKING QUESTIONS
OF THEIR OWN

In many instances teachers have ideas of their own that they would like to research at some level; they may not, however, have the resources or expertise to translate such ideas into a researchable formulation. We, as researchers, may be able to offer some assistance and support at such a juncture. But, we have to let it be known that we are genuinely interested in giving their ideas a fair hearing, and devoting at least some time to helping them implement an actual plan of research. This type of assistance may take many forms. If a teacher has had some research background, he or she may need help at the level of suggestions for data analysis. In other instances—for example, where teachers may want to evaluate the effects of a particular program or intervention—input may involve suggestions concerning research design or a particular measure to be employed.

This type of consultation may also involve discouraging educators from using instruments which might not be the most appropriate. Our group has been in the curious position, perhaps, of trying to dissuade certain educators from employing the instruments we ourselves have devised. While we have been pleased that they think highly of our scale-construction efforts, it is all too easy to use an instrument "because it exists," rather than because it is tailored to the research needs of the intended project.

Recently, we have found that one thing our group has to offer in such situations is guidance in modifying a given instrument for the educator's needs. For example, we have assisted a group interested in health education for children, helping them modify our perceived competence and perceived control scales for use in their project, such that the content would be relevant to the health questions they were addressing. In whatever manner we choose to provide such aid and consultation, however, we should listen carefully to the question the *educator* wishes to ask, monitoring our tendency to impose our own egocentric notions of what might be the most interesting issue to address. In my own experiences of the past few years, I have found that educators have any number of fascinating questions to pursue, and this type of interaction has broadened my own horizons considerably. It has also broadened my understanding of children and my appreciation for teachers.

In fact, appreciation seems to be at the heart of most of the issues involving the relationship between the researcher and the educator. Many of the authors in this volume have urged educators and researchers to *speak* to one another. But, we will only resolve some of the problems posed if each of us also *listens*. Through such listening, perhaps we can each develop a greater appreciation for the goals, needs, and talents of the other.

Often it seems that a major stumbling block involves one group feeling unappreciated by the other. Thus, the researcher may feel that the teacher doesn't really appreciate the significance of his or her research. The educator, in turn, may feel that the researcher doesn't genuinely appreciate the demands of the classroom milieu, and the skills required to cope with these demands successfully. Thus, each participant feels unappreciated, and in narcissistically licking his or her wounds, doesn't consider that the other may also feel unappreciated. As a researcher, one generally has other support systems—colleagues and students—who do provide strokes and register their appreciation. My own observation of teachers in the trenches, however, leads me to suspect that they might not always receive the appreciation they deserve even within the school setting. I've rarely heard a pupil say to his teacher at the end of a day, "Thanks for what you taught me today!" Nor are the products of a teacher's effort always observable by peers and colleagues, particularly those intangibles that might really make the difference.

Unfortunately we cannot legislate appreciation. The avenues are more subtle. Nor is there a pat formula we can apply for the genuineness that must accompany true appreciation. This must necessarily arise out of the particular interactions between a given teacher and researcher. In this chapter, references have been made to "the researcher" and "the educator." Obviously, just as we cannot make sweeping statements about "children in general," neither can we make such generalizations about researchers and educators. Thus, each of us must in good conscience decide upon the appropriate path toward cooperation and collaboration. The issue is not merely the priorities we assign to pedagogy compared to science. The value we place on the quality of our human interaction is also part of the equation, whether we label it explicitly or not. Many of our own experiences have suggested that if we are more attentive to these patterns of interactions, a number of interesting outcomes occur: teachers are happier, researchers are happier, the children are happier, and (perhaps not so coincidentally) the quality of both education and science improves.

REFERENCES

Harter, S. A new self-report scale of intrinsic versus extrinsic orientation in the classroom: Motivational and informational components. *Developmental Psychology*, 1981, **17**, 300–312. (a)

Harter, S. A model of intrinsic mastery motivation in children: Individual differences and developmental change. In Collins, A. (Ed.), *Minnesota Symposium on Child Psychology*. (Vol. 14.) Hillsdale, N.J.: Erlbaum, 1981. (b)

Harter, S. The perceived competence scale for children. *Child Development*, 1982, **53**, 87–97.

Harter, S. & Bierer, B. Accuracy of children's perceived competence judgments as a predictor of their preference for challenge. Unpublished manuscript, University of Denver, 1981.

Harter, S. & Connell, J. A comparison of alternative models of the relationships between academic achievement and children's perceptions of competence, control and motivational orientation. In Nicholls, J. (Ed.), *The development of achievement-related cognitions and behaviors*. Greenwich, Conn.: JAI, in press.

Chapter 18

Beyond the Ivory Tower

Margaret L. Stubbs

Social scientists today find themselves considering with renewed interest the nature of their relationship with the public. Contributing to this renewed interest may be the increasing difficulty researchers are having in securing adequate financial support for their work. Because of the difficulty obtaining funding, it is becoming more and more impractical for a researcher to pursue the investigation of a topic in which she is intrinsically interested, but which does not attract the interest or address the needs of a larger audience. In addition, social scientists today are increasingly being asked to provide information on which public policy may be based. Whether reaching out for support or responding to requests for support from others, the social scientist must consider how best to develop a relationship with groups of people who are not researchers and who have their own set of interests to protect and goals to achieve and their own way of working to accomplish those goals.

A relationship of this kind consists of several key elements. First is the social scientist's understanding of the nature and scope of the type of inquiry in which she is involved. A second component consists of the characteristics that define the interests, goals, and ways of working of the group of people with whom the social scientist is to connect. Third is the form of collaboration that results as the various parties proceed to blend their separate skills and concerns. In this chapter I plan to explore the nature of these components. I will argue that the development of an effective relationship between social scientists—specifically psychologists—and a wider audience requires a thorough understanding of these issues by all involved.

Before any social scientists can offer special problem-solving services to others, they must have a clear idea of just what it is that they can and cannot do. Some psychologists have commented on what they consider to be the nature and scope of psychological inquiry. Gergen (1973), a prominent participant in the discussion of this issue, argues that because studies conducted at different times investigating the same social behaviors produce different results, social psychological phenomena are not stable over time. He feels that social psychology may be described more appropriately as historical inquiry since it deals with facts that are largely nonrepeatable. Believing that knowledge about social psychological phenomena cannot accumulate as a result of one's employing traditional techniques of hypothesis testing, Gergen concludes that it is impossible for psychologists to try to discover universals that underlie behavior, and fruitless to generate predictive theories according to the guidelines of the scientific method as it is traditionally interpreted.

Schlenker (1974) disagrees with Gergen about the degree of relativity to be accepted within the framework of social-psychological inquiry. Encouraging us to recognize the essential nonrepeatability of *all* events, Schlenker points out that even within the physical sciences, the search for underlying regularities is difficult and the failure to recognize them often tells us more about our abilities to look than about the phenomena in question. While admitting that there are wide differences between people and cultures, Schlenker nevertheless considers it a legitimate goal for social scientists to concern themselves with a relatively few general propositions that hold good for human behavior and "from which, under a variety of given conditions, . . . a great variety of different forms of concrete behavior follow" (p. 4).

Assuming, then, that this is a legitimate goal, what methods of inquiry does the social scientist use to achieve it? How is the search for generalizations conducted? How do these generalizations emerge and merge into scientific theory? And, in particular, what can the psychological researcher, equipped with special fact-finding and theory-building tools, do for the educational practitioner?

In the broadest sense, one might describe the social scientist as an analyst of human behavior who is first and foremost an observer. As an observer, the social scientist is positioned at a level that is necessarily somewhat removed from actual participation in the event or behavior that is being observed. The social scientist, often through experimentation, collects many observations of the phenomenon under study and generally uses these to formulate more detailed descriptions. Finally, these more detailed descriptions are used as a basis for making predictive statements about future behavior. But, as Lomax (1978) explains in her discussion of how empirical research has influenced beliefs and practices of society throughout history, research results do not necessarily lead to firm conclusions. Instead, they often encourage the formulation of a new set of questions. This is how inquiry deepens, and only gradually does a smooth theoretical model, which can be accepted as the best approximation possible, emerge. Social scientists, then, are engaged in discovering as much as possible about a particular phenomenon. Their view of the phenomenon may change, depending on research results. Previous assumptions about behavior, if not confirmed, will be abandoned.

As a contrast to the framework in which the social scientist works, it is interesting to consider the framework within which policy makers and practitioners function, paying particular attention to the educator's domain.

Field (1979), in writing about stages of development in teachers, suggests that "Every teacher knows that she/he learned more in her/his first year on the job than in all four years of college" (p. 1). Thinking back on my own experiences as a teacher in elementary- and junior-high-school classrooms, I would have to agree that only a certain amount of what is involved in teaching can be anticipated and that teachers really become teachers by teaching, by developing the ability to use many different skills in accomplishing the tasks that present themselves during the course of a normal day in the classroom. And, as Field points out, there is no specific order in which these tasks occur. Rather, the teacher must adjust as different needs arise by shifting roles when necessary and selecting which skills need to be used in particular problem-solving situations.

In reviewing some of the planning that my co-teacher and I did as preparation for our class of 11, 12, and 13-year-olds, I can see clearly that, in order to be successful teachers, we needed to be able to use skills associated with a variety of occupations. In sorting out our own professional goals and in working to achieve the most appropriate fit of our goals with those of our colleagues, the people who started the school, and the parents of the children we were teaching, we needed to function as philosophers, historians, and politicians. In designing the academic requirements, we had to assess students' learning needs and then purchase or otherwise obtain suitable materials for meeting those needs. In designing and building the classroom environment, we worked as inventors, carpenters, painters, and janitors. We anticipated that in working with the students we would need to entertain, lecture, discipline, evaluate, referee, and counsel.

During the process of functioning in all those different ways, my co-teacher and I were not aware that we possessed the skills required by our various jobs. Rather, as Field suggests, I feel that we must have developed the various abilities slowly over time, and like all teachers, we did not have time to be aware of how that development progressed. Teachers have access to a tremendous amount of information about a wide variety of things. Yet if we look at how it is that we as teachers go about doing our jobs, it almost seems as if we collect and process the information on which we base decision making unconsciously, nonsequentially, and with amazing speed.

Victor Atkins, a practicing educator interested in how researchers and practitioners might work together, believes that some of the differences that exist between researchers and teachers stem from the different method each group uses for making observations and collecting information. As Atkins (1978) sees it,

[T]he research scientist hedges himself about with protections against his own tendency to subjectivity. This helps to ensure that at the end of his search he is left with a small piece of truth which is as objective as he can make it. In this process, he ignores whole dimensions of the phenomenon he is observing in order to devote himself to one relationship. . . . The teacher, as teacher, is never able to devote this degree of undeviating attention to one aspect of the teeming life of the classroom. . . . Teachers don't need precise and objective certainty about a tiny aspect of their professional world. They need swift and economical confirmation or disconfirmation of their professional hunches in the context of an environment in which they are called upon to pay attention to a bewildering range of stimuli. This is not to suggest that teachers shouldn't be observers and even researchers. What it does suggest is that theirs will be observation in a different mode from that of the research scientist: the wide-ranging, easily adjustable, portable binoculars of the birdwatcher, rather than the finely tuned, powerful, and narrow-ranged microscope of the biologist. [p. 136]

In sum, then, practitioners who are participants as well as observers collect information for the purposes of informing decision making; these activities occur simultaneously and in a situation in which controlling one variable in order to look at another is impossible. Most social scientists, on the other hand, do not design research with particular policy applications in mind. Researchers in child development, for instance, are primarily interested in understanding the course of development, while policy makers and practitioners in the society at large wish to make decisions about how certain policies or activities can enhance or facilitate certain aspects of development.

Though researchers, policy makers, and practitioners may differ in their orientations and methodologies for studying a phenomenon of interest, such differences do not necessarily rule out collaboration between the various parties. For a successful collaborative relationship to develop, each party must first be cognizant of the broad differences in approach that do exist.

Those who wish to extract policy guidelines from social-science research must keep in mind that most research refers to probabilities; statistical significance indicates only the probability that a particular behavior will occur given a very specific set of circumstances. Particular cases, with which policy makers and practitioners constantly deal, can never be predicted with certainty. In addition, because of the difficulty in recruiting subjects, a select group of people who may not be truly representative of the general population often serve in research experiments. Consequently, generalizations based on the performance of such a group must be made cautiously, by either researchers or practitioners.

Policy makers and practitioners may have to readjust their expectations about the degree of certainty that can be provided by the research findings of social scientists. In spite of the pressure of needing to intervene quickly in order to solve a particular problem, policy makers and practitioners must be prepared to accept the possibility that though research may suggest a possible course of action, subsequent evaluation may prove that such a course of action was a less effective means of solving a problem than had been anticipated. Though disappointed about the lack of effectiveness of a particular course of action, they should nevertheless be comforted by the fact that even negative results may contribute to a growing body of knowledge about a complex situation. Policy makers and practitioners may find it necessary to take a somewhat broader view of the larger context in which a particular problem occurs, even though their concerns about problem solving are inherently more specific and immediate.

Social scientists, on the other hand, who may be comfortable working within the broader context of contributing to "knowledge," need to work hard to prevent themselves from becoming lost in the details involved in studying a particular aspect of a phenomenon. Traditionally, social scientists have espoused the scientific method, which relies on the collection of observable, measureable, "hard" data. These data emerge from the experimental situation as a result of the researcher's incorporating the appropriate control of extraneous variables within the research design. Indeed, for the research scientist to claim that an independent variable contributed to a significant difference in the responses of participants, he must carefully design the experiment so that any additional variables that might also have affected the participant's responses are accounted for. But too often, as Bronfenbrenner (1977) and others have pointed out, "emphasis on rigor has led to experiments that are elegantly designed but often limited in scope. . . . Much of developmental psychology is *the science of the strange behavior of children in strange situations with strange adults for the briefest periods of time*" (p. 513). The application of results from such experiments to new situations and new populations is often unjustified.

Fortunately, social scientists are now working on developing and using methodologies that will help them conduct ecologically valid studies while not violating the principles of the scientific method that guide their inquiry. The use of quasiexperimental designs, path analysis, and other multivariate techniques, which attempt to explain the role of several variables as they occur within a given context, can contribute to the ecological validity of future applied-research work. Such approaches seek to illuminate rather than eliminate the complexity of the phenomenon under study and should yield research that can be expected to speak more directly to policy makers and practitioners who deal directly with the complexity of real-world problems and people.

In addition, teachers are becoming more aware of how much expertise they command, more interested in looking closely and systematically at what they know, and more vocal in expressing their knowledge. Efforts to encourage teachers to document their collections of observations for the purposes of theory building have increased noticeably in the past decade and have been supported by both private and public funding mechanisms.

The data collected by teachers and other practitioners are perhaps more qualitative than quantitative in nature. While traditionally, quantitative data have been regarded as having the most credibility, it now seems appropriate to acknowledge that those building a theory of learning or instruction may be informed by many kinds of data.

Neither social scientists nor policy makers and practitioners can be content with studying a particular phenomenon of interest by using one investigatory paradigm. The best course would seem to be one that involves the selection of several different methodologies, each of which may reveal different aspects of the phenomenon. One can then look at a composite picture of what has been observed and appreciate the whole as a function of looking at both its details and their interconnections. Regardless of the kind of research that one may be using as a basis for theory building, it is important for participants in research to understand that the process of theory building depends first on learning about particular pieces of a phenomenon and second, on redefining one's understanding of the phenomenon as a whole as a result of carefully considering what has been learned about particulars. Reconstruction on the general level often leads to further investigation of other particulars.

If social scientists and policy makers and practitioners are to collaborate successfully, they must, at the outset of their work together, examine each other's interests, needs, and capabilities so that they can reach some understanding of and agreement about which piece of a particular problem is going to receive attention, how that piece is defined by the larger context in which it occurs, and how new information that may result from an investigation of that piece might modify existing theories about our understandings of that larger context.

REFERENCES

Atkins, V. The teacher as observer. *Review of Education*, Spring 1978, 135–138.

Bronfenbrenner, U. Toward an experimental ecology of human development. *American Psychologist*, 1977, **32**, 513–531.

Field, K. *Teacher development: A study of the stages in development of teachers.* Brookline, Mass.: Teacher Center Publication, 1979.

Gergen, K. Social psychology as history. *Journal of Personality and Social Psychology*, 1973, **26**, 309–320.

Lomax, E. *Science and patterns of child care*. San Francisco: W. H. Freeman, 1978.
Schlenker, B. Social psychology and science. *Journal of Personality and Social Psychology*, 1974, **29**, 1–15.

Chapter 19

Some Guidelines for Collaboration between Educators and Researchers

Teresa M. Amabile and Margaret L. Stubbs

With this volume, we have assembled the thoughts of several educators and researchers on the satisfactions and problems of classroom research. We have the insights of teachers who have spent years observing children, reflecting on those observations, and judging the ways in which research can and cannot enrich their professional lives. We have the insights of psychologists who have spent years training in methodology, designing and analyzing studies of human behavior, and attempting to draw conclusions for classroom practice on the basis of their research. Most importantly, perhaps, we have the concerns of both teachers and researchers who have found classroom research to be less than ideal in many instances. In an effort to summarize the diverse experiences, objections, proposals, and insights that have been presented in this volume, we will attempt to glean from these resources a set of general guidelines for successful collaboration between educators and researchers. To this end, we will present some general principles for collaborative psychological research in the classroom, followed by a set of guidelines for teachers and a parallel set of guidelines for researchers.

FIVE GENERAL PRINCIPLES

1. *No one has a beam on the truth.* In many discussions of how children learn and how they behave in the classroom, some teachers appear secure in the conviction that they alone are possessed of the truth. Similarly, in discus-

sions of research designs or implications, researchers often seem to see themselves as the font of wisdom. Certainly, teachers and researchers do have their special areas of expertise. Nonetheless, it is probably safe to expect that more progress will be made if both groups acknowledge that the other has some valuable insights to offer to both understanding children and doing research.

2. *A little perspective taking can do a lot.* Through a better communication with teachers, researchers should try to understand better the complexity of the classroom—the many variables that might interact to affect the phenomena they are interested in and the many ways in which even the most innocuous procedures might affect the classroom climate. At the same time, teachers should try to understand that one useful way of attacking a complex phenomenon is to break it down into its parts; single studies on isolated variables can fulfill a useful function. In general, attempts by both teachers and researchers to take the other's perspective can only have positive effects. If teachers can take the long view of research—try to see the long-term benefits of knowledge gained from a series of small, single projects—and if researchers can take the short view—try to see the importance of immediate practical benefits for an individual classroom—they may begin to see each other more as allies than as adversaries.

3. *The grass is often browner on the other side.* If educators and researchers were to look more closely at the constraints under which the other operates, they might discover that the practical problems that confront each of them in classroom research are matched in intensity, if not in kind, by the problems that confront the other. Both groups should realistically consider the context in which the other works. Researchers should realize that teachers, far from luxuriating in short work days and autonomous classrooms, have tremendous demands on their time and must deal with myriad political pressures. Teachers should realize that, far from fitting the stereotype of lone figures working serenely in their ivory towers, researchers, too, are beset by too much work to be done and too many expectations to be met.

4. *Everybody's an expert.* In considering psychological research in the classroom, a major question is, "Who's the expert?" Certainly, the researcher can be considered the expert because of her training in conceptualization and research. Certainly, the teacher can be considered the expert because of the depth of her knowledge about children and their learning. Both are experts in nonoverlapping but complementary domains, and both should be considered as such. In addition, both should acknowledge that there are many different meanings of the word "research," and they should give thoughtful consideration to all methods, ranging from the teacher's painstaking case study documentation to the researcher's complicated experimental design.

5. *Some mysteries have been solved.* It seems that both teachers and researchers underestimate the knowledge that has been gained in certain areas through research. Both should make an effort to find that knowledge, communicate it to others, and use it effectively.

GUIDELINES FOR TEACHERS

1. *Think of yourself as a researcher.* Teachers should realize that much of what they do in their daily practice bears a great deal of similarity to the scientific research enterprise. Teachers are constantly formulating and testing hypotheses about children's learning, social behavior, affective reactions, and so on. They should take their hypothesis testing seriously, attempting more effectively to isolate, define, and categorize the problems that are most important to them. Perhaps teachers can best achieve this goal if they conscientiously try to articulate what they know about children and about learning, and if they see themselves as potential initiators of investigations.

2. *Educator, teach thyself.* Often, even competent, professional teachers interested in constantly expanding their skills are almost completely unfamiliar with basic principles of scientific research design. If teachers do wish to be involved in research on their own or in collaboration with psychological researchers, they should first learn these principles the better to contribute to and evaluate such endeavors.

3. *If you can't find time, make it.* Before teachers decide to become involved in research, they must realize that the time commitment may be substantial. A participation in all stages of research, or even many stages of research, requires time for studying the issues, formulating hypotheses, planning the design, conducting the procedure, analyzing the results, studying those results for implications, and communicating the findings to others.

4. *Think of the researcher as an ally.* It appears that, with many of the problems they encounter, educators never even consider enlisting the aid of researchers. Clearly, though, there are many areas in which researchers can provide valuable assistance, including problem definition, observation, literature review, program evaluation, design and analysis of experiments, and suggestion of educational implications. If, however, teachers do not keep researchers in mind, it is unlikely that they will call on them to perform any of these functions.

5. *Avoid seeming "holier than thou."* In the interests of eliminating some of the defensiveness that academic researchers might feel when they venture into classrooms, teachers should be careful not to convey the impression that only they are concerned with ethics, that only they have the best interests of the children in mind. Researchers may need help to ensure that their proce-

dures do not violate anyone's rights in a classroom setting, but they, too, are seriously concerned with ethical principles in research.

6. *Don't give up if you don't understand.* When teachers begin to work closely with researchers, there will almost certainly be issues, terms, principles, and procedures that are unfamiliar and even baffling. It's important for teachers to avoid any of several negative responses to such a situation: (a) "If I can't understand it, it's not worth understanding"; (b) "If I can't understand it, it's suspicious"; (c) "If I can't understand it, I never will." Undoubtedly, there are times when the teacher should be suspicious, or when a baffling concept may not be worth the effort required to understand it. But often, with surprisingly little effort, teachers who decide not to let something they don't understand simply slip by them will be rewarded with a new insight or a fuller comprehension of the research process.

7. *Don't expect too much.* Although it is not unreasonable for teachers to hope that every research project conducted in their classrooms will have both immediate benefits for their teaching and long-range benefits for educational practice, they cannot expect that every project will yield meaningful results or even that every project with significant results will provide them with foolproof prescriptions. Teachers should realize that, while research can afford them some valuable insights into teaching and learning, it cannot answer all questions, and it cannot answer any questions with absolute certainty.

GUIDELINES FOR RESEARCHERS

1. *Learn what teachers know.* Whether through haughtiness or through simple ignorance, many researchers do not seriously consider the possibility that they may have much to learn from classroom teachers. As much as researchers might disdain the informality of case studies, anecdotal records, informal observation, or autobiographical accounts, they should realize that teachers' experiences and intuitions can be profoundly valuable, both in themselves and in their ability to stimulate more effective formal research and aid in the interpretation of research results. Indeed, researchers should encourage teachers' efforts to develop and use their own research methods, and should be responsive to teachers' invitations to collaborate in teacher-initiated research.

Beyond an involvement in teachers' own investigative efforts, however, researchers should become involved in *classrooms*. They should spend time in the school setting, observing children and teachers in their "natural habitat," discussing problems and research ideas with teachers, checking their proposed independent and dependent variables against teachers' assessments of their validity.

2. *Don't let them feel "lowlier than thou."* When it comes to research, many teachers have a decidedly negative self-image. They assume that they cannot understand any of the technical aspects of methodology or statistics and, consequently, they decide to avoid opportunities for full collaboration on research. This self-image can be reinforced by the unequal partnership into which researchers may lead teachers: the researcher is often the senior partner who makes the decisions about the hypothesis to be tested, the design to be adopted, and the procedure to be employed; the teacher is the junior partner who helps to implement that procedure. Respect for the teacher's potential contribution to research should lead the researcher to consider the teacher as a fully equal partner.

3. *Start teaching.* Researchers seldom consider teaching as an integral part of a research project, but it can become a vital function in classroom-based research, especially if that research is done in collaboration with a teacher. It should be the researcher's responsibility to aid teachers' learning about principles of design, methodology, and statistics, and to try to acquaint teachers with the relevant research literature—all with the attitude that the researcher has much to learn from the teacher too.

4. *Make the collaboration complete.* Regardless of who initiates a research project, researchers who decide to collaborate with teachers on research should attempt to make that collaboration as complete as possible. If a formal research project is undertaken and teachers are unfamiliar with research methodology, they should be given the tools they need to become equal partners in generating research ideas, formulating hypotheses, planning designs and procedures, supervising the conduct of research, analyzing and interpreting the data, and writing research reports. It is particularly at the first two stages that full collaboration might be most crucial. Researchers should help teachers to articulate their tacit knowledge about children and to use that knowledge for formulating testable hypotheses. In addition, however, it might be both feasible and rewarding for researchers to work with teachers in writing about research findings for other teachers, in several different forms: writing about a teacher's reflections on his own practice; writing about a teacher's own classroom-based investigation; or writing about the results of a collaborative study. Since many teachers have little experience in writing about research and even less confidence in their ability to do so, the assistance and support of an academician could be invaluable.

5. *Be practical.* There are many senses in which researchers, if they want to have successful collaborative relationships with teachers, must become more practical. First, they should be more sensitive to the practical problems that can lead schools to reject a researcher's request: conflicting schedules, possible disruption of classroom routine, lack of availability of space and resources, and so on. Second, well in advance of a planned study, researchers

should learn about the sort of proposal they will have to present to the school they are interested in—ranging from informal personal contact in some private schools to formal written applications in some large public school systems. Third, they should become aware of the importance of establishing personal contact with someone in the school or school system. This can be crucial in situations where political problems need to be overcome, or where the character of the researcher might be an important factor in allaying possible fears about ethical issues. Fourth, researchers should not minimize the importance of trying to design each study so that it will offer some immediate benefits to the classroom or the school.

6. *Be careful.* Academic researchers accustomed to studying college sophomores drawn from introductory psychology courses might, no matter how careful their consideration of ethics in the university setting, fail to consider adequately all the ethical issues that arise in classroom research. The researcher must be cognizant not only of the rights of the student-subjects (including the question of whether children can truly give informed consent), but also of the rights and concerns of teachers, administrators, parents, and the community at large. Procedures and observations should be as natural and unobtrusive as possible.

7. *"Thanks" is not enough.* In an important sense, teachers, administrators, and students give much of themselves when they agree to become involved in a research project. Researchers should consider whether the customary expression of thanks is really enough compensation and should attempt to provide something more tangible—for example, the donation of some of the researcher's time in the classroom, or the placement of university students as teachers' aides, the donation of a piece of equipment the school might need, or a set of books for the school library, or the offer to address a teachers' or parents' group to discuss a particularly interesting area of research.

8. *Realize what you can and can't offer.* Although researchers are often painfully aware of their frequent inability to offer concrete suggestions for practice to teachers, they may be unaware of just what they *can* offer. Even in studies using group analysis, for example, the researcher might be able to provide teachers with valuable information on the abilities, motivations, and interests of individual children—as long as this does not violate the confidence of students or their parents, and as long as the researcher is careful to specify the proper interpretation and use of the information. In some circumstances, such information can be immediately useful to teachers' day-to-day decision making. In other words, researchers should realize that the "error variance" in their studies—the individual differences between children—may be the teacher's "main effect." Such differences might be the only thing the teacher is really interested in or will really find useful. Researchers should realize that there can be great value in confirming teachers' hunches

about children or about teaching, and that challenging those hunches might even be more valuable.

CONCLUSION

It is easy to be glib about "collaboration" in discussing the problems and prospects of psychological research in the classroom. Indeed, "collaboration" is one word that probably appears in every chapter in this volume; most of the educators and researchers contributing their ideas here suggest that successful collaboration between the two groups is an attainable ideal. We believe that, in many cases, they are right. Rather than closing, however, with the cheery promise that classroom research can take great strides if only researchers and teachers collaborate fully, it might be best to end with a warning.

The obstacles to collaboration between researchers and teachers are very real and very difficult, at both a philosophical and a practical level. Teachers firmly believe that their conclusions based on years of thoughtful observation are more trustworthy and more useful than conclusions based on formal research. Researchers believe, just as firmly, that the results of one well-done study can be more valid than dozens of observations and anecdotes. While teachers are more concerned with maintaining the character of their classrooms during a study, researchers are more concerned with eliminating small variations in procedure or environment that might invalidate their results. Perhaps most seriously, teachers and researchers work in different worlds, with different sets of demands and priorities. Certainly, both groups would agree on the importance of both fostering the growth of our children and gaining knowledge about human behavior. In practice, however, teachers must be primarily concerned with the maintenance of a healthy, stimulating learning environment in which measurable gains in performance can be obtained, while researchers must be primarily concerned with the development of research programs that can yield precise, publishable data on human thought and behavior. Intensely pursuing their individual goals, neither teacher nor researcher may have much time for learning what the other knows and developing collaborative relationships.

Full collaboration between researcher and teacher, then, may be an ideal that can only rarely be fully realized. There are, however, many alternatives to the traditional model of the researcher obtaining the teacher's permission to conduct a classroom study into which the teacher has had no input and from which the teacher will reap no direct benefits. For example, a division of labor might be most feasible, with the teacher playing a large role in the development of hypotheses, the approval of procedures, and the writing of reports directed at audiences of teachers. The researcher, on the other hand, might be more solely responsible for the experimental design, statistical analyses, and technical reports for psychological audiences.

Whatever the model adopted, educators and researchers can benefit from determining whether the major obstacles to their particular psychological research in the classroom are attitudinal, political, or practical, and from trying to overcome them together. With an increased awareness of the other's perspective and a willingness to develop some sort of collaborative relationship, teachers and researchers might find classroom research more satisfying and more fruitful. Both psychology and education can prosper in the bargain.

Author Index

255

Subject Index

About the Editors
and Contributors

Teresa M. Amabile is assistant professor of psychology at Brandeis University. Since receiving her Ph.D. from Stanford University, she has conducted research on creativity, social cognition, person perception, and biases in the processing of social information. A former teacher, she is interested in the implications of creativity research for classroom practice. She is author of *The Social Psychology of Creativity* (in press), as well as journal articles on creativity, intrinsic motivation, and social perception, and book chapters on interpersonal attribution and the teaching of social psychology.

Margaret L. Stubbs is a doctoral candidate in social and developmental psychology at Brandeis University. Her research interests include motivation, creativity, fantasy play, female development, and the application of psychological theory in real-world settings. Prior to beginning her degree work, she had extensive experience as a teacher at a wide range of grade levels in public and private schools. She has carried out her own classroom investigations and has served as co-editor of the *Children's Thinking Network Newsletter* (1981).

Roland S. Barth is senior lecturer on education and director of the Principals' Center at the Harvard Graduate School of Education, where he received his doctorate in 1970. A former public elementary-school teacher and principal in Massachusetts, Connecticut, and California, he is author of *Open Education and the American School* and *Run School Run*. His interests include the professional growth of school principals.

Janet H. Berman is a seventh- and eighth-grade social-studies specialist at the Heath School in Brookline, Massachusetts. A participant in the "Holocaust in Human Behavior" project, a value-oriented curriculum project employing Kohlberg's moral education techniques, she has a deep commitment to educational research efforts in this field. She is co-author of *Get Set for Learning: Study Skills for Middle School Students* and holds a master's degree in education from Boston University.

Richard C. Carter has spent the last ten years working with teachers and children as a staff developer. He has participated in a number of research projects that have focused on helping teachers reflect on their teaching. He is currently doing graduate work at the Massachusetts Institute of Technology and teaching at Lesley College.

Roland A. Dwinell is a business teacher at Brookline High School and a visiting lecturer in the economics department of Framingham State College. He holds graduate degrees in business administration and economics from Northeastern University, Boston College, and the University of Illinois. He has developed curriculum projects, funded proposals, and journal articles in the areas of economic education, human relations, career education, and the education of the economically disadvantaged. He is co-author of *Career Education in the Secondary Schools.*

Claryce Evans is the principal of a public elementary school in Melrose, Massachusetts, and the director of the Teacher-initiated Research Project at Technical Education Research Centers. She has taught mathematics, English, and science at the junior-high-school level, and has extensive experience in school change and curriculum-development projects. Her primary professional interests are staff development and the relation of research and theory to practice and educational policy.

Mary Ann Haley is the director of enrichment programs in the Concord public schools. Since receiving her M.A. in educational psychology from the University of Connecticut's "Teaching the Talented" program in 1979, she has served as a consultant and workshop leader for school districts throughout Massachusetts. Formerly an elementary-school teacher for ten years, she is currently responsible for teacher training, curriculum development, and the location of resources for use in the classroom.

Susan Harter is professor of psychology at the University of Denver. She came to Denver after teaching for several years at Yale University, where she had earned her Ph.D. in developmental and child clinical psychology. For the past 15 years, she has done classroom research on intrinsic motivation, self-esteem, mastery and competence, and children's understanding of emotions. She is author of "Developmental Perspectives on the Self" in *Carmichaels' Manual of Child Psychology* (in press).

Bill Hull, a former elementary-school teacher, has had a continuing interest in children's thinking for over 30 years. He initiated the Teachers' Seminars on Children's Thinking in 1972 and continues to participate actively in them. He has served as co-editor of the *Children's Thinking Network Newsletter*

(1981), and is currently studying the learning processes of children and adults.

Christine McVinney, co-founder of the Concord Children's Center in Concord, Massachusetts, is currently directing and teaching at the center's new facility. Before becoming a day-care professional, she taught child development and education at a private secondary school. She holds a master's degree in open education from Lesley College.

Charles H. Rathbone is assistant professor and chair of the education department at Wheaton College. A former classroom teacher at both the elementary and secondary levels, he served as director of a small alternative school in urban St. Louis. Editor of *Open Education: The Informal Classroom*, he has written articles for several professional periodicals, including *Urban Review, Childhood Education, English Journal, School Review*, and *This Magazine Is about Schools*.

Jonathon Saphier is president of Research for Better Teaching in Newton, Massachusetts, and does consulting to public schools on supervision, evaluation, and staff development. Over a 15-year teaching career, he moved from high-school history to first grade, and had positions as an administrator and a staff developer. He holds an Ed.D. from Boston University and is co-author of *The Skillful Teacher* (1980).

Malcolm W. Watson is assistant professor of psychology at Brandeis University. Since receiving his Ph.D. in developmental psychology from the University of Denver in 1977, he has conducted research and published journal articles in three areas of child development: the early development of symbol use in play, the functions of fantasy and imagination in preschool and school-aged children, and the development of children's and adolescents' understanding of social role systems and family role systems.

Daniel H. Watt is a visiting research associate with the Logo Group at the Massachusetts Institute of Technology, Logo project coordinator for the Brookline public schools, and director of the Computer Resource Center at Technical Education Research Centers in Cambridge, Massachusetts. He has been an elementary-school teacher, a curriculum developer with Elementary Science Study, and a teacher, researcher, curriculum developer, teacher trainer, and resource specialist in computer education.

Molly Watt is assistant principal of the Fort River School in Amherst, Massachusetts. She has been an elementary-school teacher, in-service trainer, and writer. She has participated as a researcher in the Children's Thinking

Seminar, The Prospect Archive and Research Center, the Danforth Project on Democratic Education, and the Teacher Development Research Project through the Brookline Teacher Center.

Pergamon General Psychology Series

Editors: Arnold P. Goldstein, Syracuse University
Leonard Krasner, SUNY, Stony Brook